HAWAII'S BEST HIKING TRAILS

by Robert Smith

A Hawaiian Outdoor Adventures Publication

First Edition 1982

SECOND Edition 1985

Second Printing April, 1987

THIRD Edition 1991

Copyright ©1982, 1985, 1991 by Robert Smith

Maps by Kevin G. Chard

Photos by the author and Diane G. Smith

Cover photo by Barbara Heavener

Library of Congress Card Catalog Number 85-040706

International Standard Book Number 0-924308-03-6

Manufactured in the United States

Published by Hawaiian Outdoor Adventures Publications

DEDICATION

This book is dedicated to Diane — my wife, my best friend, my companion. Mahalo for the love and happiness you have brought into my life.

ACKNOWLEDGMENTS

Many people made significant contributions to this book. In Hawaii, I am indebted to Ruth Wryn and Vi Saffery of the Wailuku Public Library and to Gail Bartholomew, librarian at Maui Community College, each of whom cheerfully responded to my numerous requests. A number of Hawaii State officials offered information and expertise. Robert Hobdy, Maui forester; Ralph E. Daehler, Kauai District Forester (retired); and Mac Hori, State Park Supervisor on Kauai (retired) were particularly helpful. A very special "mahalo" to Nobuko Yamada on Maui; Roy, Carol, Shari, Frances and Mac Fujioka on Kauai; and Bonnie Harwick on Oahu for their hospitality. On the mainland, Fred Samia gave his time and professional advice, and he read the manuscript. Mahalo also to Diane, who shared many trails with me and whose patience, support and love inspired me to push on.

— Robert Smith
Huntington Beach, CA
January, 1991

BOOKS BY ROBERT SMITH

Hawaii's Best Hiking Trails

Hiking Maui, the Valley Isle

Hiking Oahu, the Capital Isle

Hiking Hawaii, the Big Island

Hiking Kauai, the Garden Isle

CONTENTS

INTRODUCTION

Hawaii — The 50th State

"I'm not going to Hawaii; it's overcommercialized; it's like Los Angeles with coconut trees." These are statements frequently overheard on the mainland by people who are unknowing. Admittedly, some of the tourist centers on each of the islands have boomed in recent years, and much sand and open space have been replaced with lumber and concrete in the form of shopping centers, condominiums, hotels, bars, souvenir shops, and the like. However, there remains a nearly pristine Hawaii, a wild and free Hawaii, an alluring and enchanting Hawaii, and an exciting and romantic Hawaii. It's still there, only you have to know where to find it! It is the purpose of this book to reveal some of those places in Hawaii which soothe the body and calm the spirit — those special places which for sometimes unexplainable reasons have an impact on our lives. But with each discovery there is the responsibility to protect and preserve — to "Hi'ipoi i ka 'aina aloha" (cherish the beloved land).

In 1990, over 6 million people visited Hawaii. Some were looking for the dance halls and night clubs along Kalakaua Avenue on Waikiki, some for the slower, more relaxed pace found on the neighbor islands, and some for the beautiful and primitive life in Kalalau or Waimanu Valley. Whatever they sought, they probably found it because they keep coming back to what Mark Twain once described as "the loveliest fleet of islands that lies anchored in any ocean." The "fleet" is made up of 132 islands, although only seven are inhabited and only six may be visited (Niihau is privately owned). A little larger than the state of Connecticut in land area, the 50th state joined the Union in 1959 as the only state where no single ethnic group is in the majority, which accounts for a marvelous blend of races and cultures that serves as an example of relatively harmonious living. Recently, Caucasians became the single largest minority group, followed closely by people of Japanese ancestry, with Hawaiian and part-Hawaiian a distant third. Then add the Filipinos, Chinese, Koreans, Blacks, Samoans and a dash of European groups and you have Hawaii — almost. The last ingredient is "aloha" — a word that cannot be defined. Some will say it means "hello" or "goodby" or "love." But "aloha" is a state of mind; it's a feeling of affection and regard that one person has for another be he long-time friend or malihini (newcomer); it's that inner force that causes one person to care for and to share with friends and strangers alike; it's that spiritual quality that binds "brahs" and visitors; in short, it is "aloha." Don't listen to those who say it no longer exists in Hawaii. It's still there. You're likely to find this spirit of brotherhood in meetings with local people in the tourist shops, on the beach, or on the trail. But remember, it has to be reciprocal.

While Hawaiians are justifiably proud of their aloha spirit, there are other unique and distinguishable characteristics in which they take pride. For example, Hawaii is not only the youngest of the 50 states but also the youngest in terms of creation. It is believed that the islands began to be formed about 25 million years ago by eruptions from a 200-mile fault at the bottom of the Pacific. Geologically speaking, Hawaii is still an infant and is still growing, witnessed by Mauna Loa on the "Big Island," the world's largest active volcano, and by Kilauea, also on the "Big Island," the most active volcano in the world. Additionally, the 50th state boasts the wettest place on the earth (Mt. Waialeale, Kauai, average of 460 inches of rain annually). Hawaiians boast that theirs is the longest state, stretching 1523 miles from the eastern tip of Hawaii, the Big Island, to the tiny speck known as Kure Atoll. But the most alluring characteristic of Hawaii is the climate. Tropical Hawaii has a combination of cooling trade winds and equable temperatures in the vicinity of 75 degrees. For example, in Honolulu, the highest recorded temperature is 88 degrees and the lowest 57 degrees. The highest temperature ever recorded in the state was 100 degrees. In such a setting, outdoor experiences attract thousands each year.

SAFE HIKING IN HAWAII

In 1989, the state Department of Health issued a warning to campers and hikers that portable water filters will not protect them from the dangerous bacterium leptospirosis. Health officials say that only boiling or chemical treatment will control this disease that is found in surface water throughout Hawaii. It enters the body through breaks in the skin or through mucous membranes and can cause flu-like symptoms. The disease can also be fatal.

Portable water filters may protect against giardia, salmonella and other bacteria and parasites, but not leptospirosis. The department's release stated that vigorous boiling is the only reliable method of purification. Tablets containing hydroperiodide will work if boiling is not possible, according to health authorities.

Drinking water is available from streams in many areas, but it should be boiled or treated, since cattle, pigs and goats may share the water supply. To avoid the chance of illness, carry one quart of water per person. In many areas, firewood is at a premium. A small, light, reliable backpacking stove is a convenience and a comfort if you plan to cook out.

Hiking and backpacking have increased in popularity in recent years in Hawaii not only, I suspect, because they are inexpensive ways to travel but also because they are different ways to experience a place. In Hawaii, outdoor experiences are outstanding; however, the outdoorsperson should be aware of a number of problems. For one, violent actions against hikers and campers, while remaining low in percentage considering the numbers who are taking to the trail, have increased. As any community grows and urban centers develop, the ills of city life, including violence and crime, follow. Consequently, hikers, particularly females are cautioned never to hike or camp alone. As a general rule, the farther you hike and camp away from populated areas, the safer your experience is likely to be. NEVER leave valuables unprotected. I always carry a daypack containing those items which I cannot afford to lose — wallet, airline ticket, camera — and I carry it everywhere. Yes, even there!

Another problem facing the hiker in Hawaii is the lack of trailhead signs and trail markers. Most of the trails contained in this book are well-defined, but most are not marked. Consequently, I provide detailed directions to the trailhead and a trail narrative that makes the trail easy to follow. I have included a wide selection of trips from short, easy family walks to long, difficult hikes and backpacks. Most of the hikes are on public lands where well-maintained trails await the hiker. Other hikes are on private land — pineapple and sugar-cane holdings — and some are on military reservations. In spite of the time and effort required to secure permission from property owners, I have included these worthy hikes. I have not included areas from which hikers are forbidden by law (protected watershed) or where the terrain is dangerous and unsafe even though local people may boast of their adventures in these places. Each year numerous injuries and some fatalities occur where people have hiked in spite of the prohibition. Good judgment and a regard for the time-tested rules of hiking are good protection.

Hikers and campers are always relieved to learn that there are no poisonous snakes, no poison ivy or poison oak in Hawaii. Poisonous centipedes and scorpions are found at low elevations, however. The two biggest pests in Hawaii are the mosquito and the cockroach. Both are very troublesome and they can make an outdoor experience disagreeable unless precautions are taken. You will have to live with the cockroach, but all of the mosquito lotions and sprays seem to provide effective protection. Due to the wet climate, be prepared to make frequent applications.

In order to ensure a safe and enjoyable experience and to protect the environment, remember:

    1.   Do not hike alone.

2. Many Hawaiian trails are wet and slippery, and the terrain is loose and brittle.

3. Contrary to popular belief, it is not possible to live off the land. Carry your own food.

4. Although some fruits are available, never eat or taste unknown fruits or plants.

5. Carry your own water or purify water from streams.

6. A tent with a rain fly ensures comfortable and dry nights.

7. Carry your trash out.

8. Bury personal wastes away from streams.

9. Firewood in most places is not available or is too wet for use. Carry a stove for cooking.

10. Darkness sets in right after sunset.

USING THIS BOOK

In planning a hike, the reader is advised to consult the Hiking Chart below in order to give due consideration to driving time, hiking time, and the clothing and supplies necessary. I have rated all the hikes and placed them in one of four categories. A "family" rated hike is for those who are looking for short, easy hikes. The "hardy family" classification requires a degree of effort and sound physical condition. Both the "strenuous" and the "difficult" hikes require a measure of endurance, since they are longer and most of them involve a considerable gain in altitude. They also require good footwear and more equipment.

Obviously, hiking time varies from person to person, depending on such things as pace and the extent to which one chooses to linger for lunch and to swim where pools exist. The time noted in the Hiking Chart is based on a leisurely pace. Trail distance is based either on an exact measurement or on an approximation with the aid of a topographic map.

Elevation gain or loss is cited in the Hiking Chart and preceding each trail narrative when the gain or loss is at least 500 feet. The gain or loss in elevation is from the trailhead or starting point cited in the narrative. On the Hiking Chart, preceding the number of feet, "+" means gain and "-" means loss from the trailhead to trail's end. Where the return trip is over the same trail, a like amount of loss or gain will be encountered. Where an alternative return route may be taken from trail's end, you will need to consult the trail narrative to determine the total elevation gain or loss for your entire trip.

Driving time and mileage cited are based on the posted speed limit and are measured from a major point on each island. Specific driving instructions precede each hike description.

Only two islands — Oahu and Hawaii — have good reliable public transportation systems. For each hike on those islands I have included bus directions to the trailhead. Use the bus; it is both inexpensive and reliable. If you plan to rent a car for transportation, I suggest that you do not volunteer the information to the rental agency that you are going to hike or camp. Most agencies will not rent vehicles to campers because they are concerned about breakdowns in the backcountry and break-ins at the trailhead.

The equipment noted on the Hiking Chart is minimal for hiking enjoyment. As a rule, however, I always carry water, food and a first-aid kit. Although the choice between tennis shoes and hiking boots for some hikes is listed as optional, I prefer hiking boots in most cases. Obviously, your feet are an important consideration in hiking since it is common on an island that has experienced extensive volcanic activity to have volcanic ash or rock underfoot. Usually, the choice of shorts or long pants is optional, except where the brush is thick or when the weather requires warmer clothing.

Before each hike description you will find the hike rating, trail features, hiking distance and time, specific driving

instructions, instructions for getting there by bus and introductory notes. On some hikes it is necessary to walk on private property. Information and addresses are provided so that
you can secure permission in advance. Permission is usually
readily granted either over the telephone or in person when
you sign a liability waiver.

In the trail narrative I usually mention the flora and
fauna to be seen along the way, especially the unusual and
the unique, in an effort to add to your hiking enjoyment. But
I don't mention everything, and you may wish to buy one of
several guides to plants and animals of the islands, available
at many stores.

Preceding each trail narrative is a map that will help
you find the trailhead and locate trail highlights. The maps
show many features of the hikes as well as campsites. The
maps are not to scale.

CAMPING AND CABINS

Take a tent to Hawaii and camp out and you will save
half the cost of a vacation in paradise and, if living in the
out-of-doors is pleasurable to you, you will have the time of
your life. What can be better than free campgrounds (only
county campgrounds — except Oahu — charge a fee), beach
camping with an overnight low temperature in the 70's and
sunsets and sunrises that stir the senses? In the following
pages, I have shown all the national-park, state-park, county
and private campgrounds on the maps and I have provided information concerning reservations and permits for camping
on each island. As a general rule, I recommend the national-
park and state-park campgrounds for not only are they the
best maintained, but also they are free. For those who do not
wish to camp but wish to keep expenses as low as possible,
I suggest that you use the national-park and state-park
housekeeping cabins, which are available on all the islands
except Oahu and which cost only a few dollars per person
per night. Detailed camping and cabin information is provided in the introduction section to each island. However,

since the cabins are popular with local people, make reservations early. Avoid camping areas in or near population centers, for in them all the ills of urban living are present such as thievery, vandalism, drunkenness, and the chance of personal injury. DO NOT camp alone and do not leave valuables and equipment unattended or unprotected.

FOOD AND EQUIPMENT

For most hikes your equipment needs are minimal. Although hiking boots are not essential on most hikes, I prefer them because of the rough lava surfaces. Drinking water is available from streams in many areas, but should be boiled because cattle, pigs and goats usually share the water supply. To avoid the chance of illness, I suggest you carry sufficient water. One quart per person for short, 2–3 mile hikes and two quarts for longer hikes is recommended. In many areas, firewood is at a premium; so a small, light, reliable backpacking stove is a convenience and a comfort if you plan to cook out. Most hikers find shorts or cutoffs adequate in areas up to 5,000 feet. Even during the summer, heavy sweaters and jackets are necessary when hiking in higher altitudes. Hats and dark glasses are also necessary for protection from the weather and the glaring sun.

Although food is more expensive in Hawaii than on the mainland, it is readily available in the towns. You may visit a local delicatessen that prepares box lunches for day hiking containing local favorites such as tempura, sweet-and-sour spare ribs and sushi. Visit a local market or roadside stand for mango, papaya, pineapple, passion fruit, and local avocado which comes in the large economy size. Hiking and backpacking stores can be found on Maui, Kauai, Oahu and Hawaii where equipment, fuel, and dehydrated food can be purchased. Some stores also offer rental equipment.

The following equipment is recommended for day hikes.

General Equipment:
Day pack
Hiking boots or tennis shoes

Plastic water bottle, quart size (one per person)
Swiss Army knife
Insect repellent
Shorts
Bathing suit
Sunscreen and tanning lotion
Sun glasses
Whistle for each child
Camera and film
Hat or sun visor
Poncho or raingear
Towel
Waterproof matches
Flashlight
Hawaii's Best Hiking Trails

Planning and preparation are particularly important for the backpacker. The following equipment is recommended for overnight hikes and for campers.

BACKPACK CHECKLIST

General Equipment:
Frame and pack (exterior frame pack recommended)
Lightweight sleeping bag or blanket (heavy bag above 4,000 feet)
Backpack tent with rain fly
Plastic ground cover
Sleep pad
Plastic water bottle, quart size
Swiss Army knife
Flashlight (it helps to explore lava tubes)
40 feet of nylon cord
First-aid kit

Cooking Gear:
Backpack stove
Fuel
Cooking pots
Fork and spoon
Plastic bowl
Sierra cup
Waterproof matches

Clothing:
Poncho or raingear
Pants
Shorts and/or bathing suit

Hat or bandana
Undershorts
T-shirts
Socks
Hiking boots
Sweater/warm jacket above 6,000 feet

Toilet Articles:
Soap (biodegradable)
Toothbrush/powder-paste
Part-roll toilet paper
Chapstick
Comb
Towel
Insect repellent
Sunscreen and tanning lotion
Mirror

Miscellaneous:
Sun glasses
Camera and film
Plastic bags
Fishing gear
Hawaii's Best Hiking Trails

Hawaiian Made Easy

For your interest, throughout the text wherever a Hawaiian place name is used, I have provided a literal translation if possible. In many instances, Hawaiian names have multiple meanings and even the experts sometimes disagree over literal meanings. The meanings given here are based on the best information available and on the context in which a name is used. As students of the environment, the Hawaiians had a flair for finding the most expressive words to describe their physical surroundings.

Most visitors are reluctant to try to pronounce Hawaiian words. But with a little practice and a knowledge of some simple rules, you can develop some language skill and add to your Hawaiian experience. Linguists regard Hawaiian as one of the most fluid and melodious languages of the world. There are only 12 letters in the Hawaiian alphabet: five vowels, a, e, i, o, u, and seven consonants, h, k, l, m, n, p,

w. Hawaiian is spelled phonetically. Correct pronunciation is easy if you do not try to force English pronunciation onto the Hawaiian language. Vowel sounds are simple: a=ah; e=eh; i=ee; o=oh; and u=oo. Consonant sounds are the same as in English with the exception of w. Rules for w are not adhered to with any consistency by local people. Generally, w is pronounced "w" at the beginning of a word and after a. For example, Waimea is pronounced "Wai-may-ah" and walawala is "wah-lah-wah-lah." Hawaiians also usually pronounce w as "w" when it follows o or u: auwaha is "ah-oo-wah-hah," and hoowali is "hoh-oh-wah-lee." When w is next to the final letter of a word, it is variably pronounced "w" or "v"; Wahiawa is "wah-he-ah-wa," but Hawi is "ha-vee." Listen to the locals for their treatment of this letter. Finally, since the Hawaiian language is not strongly accented, the visitor will probably be understood without employing any accent.

Some common Hawaiian words:

'aina	land
ali'i	royality; chief
aloha	welcome; love; farewell
aloha nui loa	much love
hale	house
haole	foreigner; Caucasian
hapa haole	part Caucasian
heiau	pre-Christian temple
hukilau	fish pull
kahili	feather standard
kahuna	priest
kai	sea
kama'aina	native born
kane	male
kapu	keep out
kaukau	food
keiki	child
kokua	help
mahalo	thanks
makai	toward the sea
malihini	newcomer

mele	song
ohana	family
'ono	delicious
'opu	belly
pali	cliff
paniolo	cowboy
pau	finished
puku	hole
pupus	snacks
wahine	female
wikiwiki	hurry

Some common Pidgin words:

brah	brother
da kine	whatchamacallit
hana hou	encore; again
howzit?	what's happening?
pau hana	quit work
shaka!	great!
suck 'em up	drink up
talk stink	use profane words
to da max	all the way

Hiking Chart

		Hike Rating				Trail Time			Equipment					Features				
		Family	Hardy family	Strenuous	Difficult	Distance (miles)	Time (hours)	Gain/loss (feet)	Rain gear	Boots	Tennis shoes	Carry water	Take food	Swimming	Waterfalls	Views	Historical sites	Fruits
	HAWAII																	
1	**Hawaii Volcanoes Nat. Pk.**																	
	Mauna Loa Summit				X	19.6	3-4 days	+7015	X	X		X	X			X	X	
	Crater Rim			X		**11.6**	day		X	X		X	X			X	X	
	Halemaumau		X			3.2	2		X	X		X	X			X	X	
	Byron Ledge			X		2.5	1½		X	X		X	X			X	X	
	Kilauea Iki			X		4.0	2½		X	X		X	X			X	X	
	Thurston Lava Tube	X				**0.3**	¼					X					X	
	Devastation	X				0.6	¼					X				X	X	
	Sandalwood	X				0.7	¼					X				X	X	
	Sulfur Bank	X				0.3	¼					X				X		
	Halape				X	7.2	4	−3000	X	X		X	X	X		X	X	
	Hilina Pali				X	6.4	4	−2000		X		X	X			X		
	Kau Desert				X	18.9	day	−4000		X		X	X			X	X	
	Mauna Iki			X		8.8	5			X		X	X			X	X	
	Kamoamoa	X				**1.0**	1			X	X			X			X	
	Puu Loa Petroglyphs		X			1.0	¾					X				X	X	
	Naulu		X			2.0	1			X		X	X			X		
	Napau			X		7.0	4			X		X	X			X	X	
2	**Akaka Falls**	X				**0.7**	½					X		X	X			
3	**Kalopa State Park**																	
	Nature	X				**0.7**	1		X		X							
	Kalopa Gulch		X			**2.8**	2		X	X		X						X
4	**Waipio/Waimanu Valleys**																	
	Waipio			X		3	2	±900	X	X		X	X	X	X	X	X	X
	Waimanu				X	9	6	±1200	X	X		X	X	X	X	X	X	X
5	**Puako Petroglyphs**		X			1.0	½				X	X					X	
6	**Kaloko-Honokohau**		X			2	1			X		X		X		X		
7	**Captain Cook Monument**			X		2.5	2	−1400	X	X		X	X	X		X	X	
8	**South Point**		X			3	1½					X	X	X				
	KAUAI																	
9	**Kalalau**				X	10.8	day	±2000	X	X		X	X	X	X	X	X	
10	**Hanalei River**																	
	Hanalei River		X			2	1		X		X	X		X	X			X
	Okolehau			X		2.2	2	+1200	X	X		X	X			X		X
11	**Nonou Mountain**																	
	East side		X			2.0	1½	+1250	X	X		X	X			X		X
	West side		X			1.5	1	+1000	X	X		X	X			X		X
12	**Keahua**																	
	Keahua Arboretum	X				**0.5**	½				X			X				X
	Moalepe		X			2.5	1½	+500	X	X		X	X			X		X
	Kuilau Ridge		X			2.1	1½		X	X		X	X	X		X		X
13	**Kokee State Park/ Waimea Canyon**																	

Mileages in boldface are for loops.

Hiking Chart

	Hike Rating				Trail Time			Equipment					Features				
	Family	Hardy family	Strenuous	Difficult	Distance (miles)	Time (hours)	Gain/loss (feet)	Rain gear	Boots	Tennis shoes	Carry water	Take food	Swimming	Waterfalls	Views	Historical sites	Fruits
Berry Flat/Puu Ka Ohelo		X			1.3	1		X		X	X	X					X
Black Pipe		X			0.4	½		X	X		X	X					
Canyon			X		1.7	2	−800	X	X		X	X	X	X	X		
Cliff	X				0.1	1/6		X		X					X		
Halemanu-Kokee		X			1.2	1		X	X		X				X		
Iliau Nature Loop	X				0.3	¼				X				X	X		
Kaluapuhi	X				1.0	1		X		X	X	X					X
Koaie Canyon				X	3.0	2		X	X		X	X	X	X	X	X	X
Kukui			X		2.5	2	−2000	X	X		X	X	X	X	X		X
Kumuwela		X			.08	1		X	X		X	X			X		
Waialae Canyon			X		0.3	½		X	X		X	X	X		X		
Waimea Canyon			X		1.5	2		X	X		X	X	X	X	X		
Wainininua		X			0.6	½		X	X		X	X			X		
Alakai Swamp				X	3.5	4		X	X		X	X			X		
Awaawapuhi			X		3.1	3	−1600	X	X		X	X			X		
Kawaikoi Stream		X			2.5	1½		X	X		X		X				X
Nualolo			X		3.8	3	−1500	X	X		X	X			X		
Nualolo Cliff			X		2.1	1½		X	X		X	X			X		
Pihea			X		3.7	3		X	X		X	X			X		
Poomau Canyon		X			0.3	¼		X	X						X		
LANAI																	
14 Munro				X	18	day	±1400	X	X		X	X			X		X
15 Kaiholena Gulch			X		3.3	2	+1050	X	X		X	X			X		X
16 Shipwreck Beach	X	X	X		0-8	½ per mile				X	X	X	X		X	X	
17 Luahiwa Petroglyphs	X				0					X						X	
MAUI																	
18 Keanae Arboretum		X			2.3	1½		X		X	X	X	X	X			X
19 Waianapanapa State Park		X			4.0	3			X		X	X	X		X	X	
20 Hana Town	X				4.0	3				X			X		X	X	
21 Waimoku Falls		X			2.0	2	+900	X	X		X	X	X	X	X	X	X
22 Haleakala National Park				X		See text		X	X		X	X			X	X	X
23 Skyline			X		8.0	4	−3800	X	X		X	X			X		
24 Polipoli Park																	
Redwood		X			1.7	1	±900	X	X		X	X			X	X	X
Tie		X			0.5	½	±500	X	X		X	X			X		
Plum		X			1.7	1		X	X		X	X			X	X	X
Polipoli	X				0.6	½		X		X	X				X		
Haleakala Ridge	X				1.6	1	±600	X	X		X	X			X		
Boundary			X		4.0	2½		X	X		X	X			X	X	X
Waiohuli		X			1.4	1	±800	X	X		X	X			X		
Kahua Road			X		3.5	3			X		X	X			X		

Mileages in boldface are for loops.

Hiking Chart

	Hike Rating				Trail Time			Equipment					Features				
	Family	Hardy family	Strenuous	Difficult	Distance (miles)	Time (hours)	Gain/loss (feet)	Rain gear	Boots	Tennis shoes	Carry water	Take food	Swimming	Waterfalls	Views	Historical sites	Fruits
25 Iao Valley																	
Tableland		X			2.0	1½	+500	X	X		X	X	X	X	X		X
Iao Stream	X				1.0	½				X					X		X
Poohahoahoa Stream			X		3.0	2		X		X	X	X		X	X		X
Nakalaloa Stream			X		2.5	2		X		X	X	X		X	X		X
26 Waihee Ridge			X		**3**	3	+1500	X	X		X	X			X	X	X
27 Puu Kukui				X	7	6	+3000	X	X		X	X			X		
MOLOKAI																	
28 Halawa Valley	X				2.0	1		X		X	X	X	X	X	X	X	X
29 Kalaupapa			X		3.0	2	−1600		X		X	X	X		X	X	
30 Hanalilolilo			X		1.5	1	+500	X	X		X	X			X	X	X
OAHU																	
31 Diamond Head	X				0.7	1	+550			X	X				X	X	
32 Makiki/Tantalus																	
Kanealole	X				0.7	½	±500		X		X				X		X
Nahuina		X			0.6	½	±600		X		X				X		
Makiki Valley	X				1.1	1			X		X				X		
Maunalaha	X				0.7	½	±555		X		X				X		X
Moleka		X			0.5	½			X		X				X		X
Ualakaa	X				0.6	½			X		X				X		
Manoa Cliffs		X			3.0	2	+500	X	X		X	X			X		X
Puu Ohia		X			2.0	1½	+500	X	X		X	X			X		X
33 Manoa Falls	X				0.8	1	+500		X		X		X	X			X
Aihualama		X			1.4	1½		X	X		X	X			X		X
34 Lanipo				X	3.0	3	+1600		X		X	X			X		
35 Hanauma Bay																	
Koko Head	X				1.0	½				X	X				X		
Blowhole		X			2.0	1½				X	X		X	X			
36 Kahana Valley		X			**4.5**	2½			X		X	X	X			X	X
37 Sacred Falls		X			2.2	1½			X		X	X	X	X			X
38 Hauula Valley																	
Hauula		X			**2.5**	1½	+600		X		X				X		
Maakua Gulch			X		3.0	3	+1100		X		X	X	X	X			
Papali		X			**2.5**	2	+800		X		X	X			X		
39 Aiea Loop		X			**4.8**	3		X	X		X	X			X		X
40 Waimano				X	7.1	4	+1600	X	X		X	X	X		X		X
41 Manana				X	6.0	4	+1700	X	X		X	X	X		X		X
42 Kuaokala			X		**4.5**	3	+500		X		X	X		X	X		X

Mileages in boldface are for loops.

HAWAII

The Island

"Here today, gone tomorrow" is applied or misapplied to a variety of situations. It might well be the motto of the Island of Hawaii. Certainly no other island in the Hawaiian chain and perhaps no other place on earth experience such dramatic and spectacular changes in such short periods of time. The "Big Island" — sometimes the "Orchid Island" or the "Volcano Island" — is the site of Mauna Loa, the world's largest active volcano and the largest single mountain on earth. In addition to Mauna Loa's frequent eruptions, another reason for all the change is the active shield volcano, Kilauea, in whose caldera Pele, the legendary and mischievous goddess of volcanoes, is said to reside. Kilauea, the "drive-in volcano," is a place where volcanic eruptions and lava flows can be viewed safely from an automobile or even more closely on foot. As of January, 1991, Kilauea had been erupting for eight years along its southeast rift. It was emitting an average of 650,000 cubic yards of lava daily.

With every eruption, the spewing lava alters the island in some way. Roads are overcome by the flowing lava, hiking trails are covered by ash or pumice, sometimes homes are destroyed, infrequently lives are lost, and, on occasion, new land is added to the state. For example, during an eruption in 1960, lava flowed into the sea and added 500 acres of land to the east side of the island. Thus, Hawaii was now 500 feet closer to California! And between 1987–89, successive eruptions from Kilauea closed the Chain of Craters Road (March, 1987), destroyed the Wahaula Visitor Center (June, 1989), overran and burned 71 homes, and presently (January, 1991) threatens Wahaula Heiau, a 700-year old Hawaiian temple. Madame Pele is a very busy lady!

The largest (4038 square miles) of the Hawaiian Islands, Hawaii was formed by the building of five volcanoes. In the north, the now-extinct Kohala volcano is the oldest, rising

HAWAII—TRAILHEADS, CAMPING

to 5505 feet. Its peaks have been eroded to deep, precipitous valleys. Hualalai volcano (8271 feet) in the west last erupted in 1801 and is considered dormant. Towering, majestic Mauna Kea volcano dominates central Hawaii and at 13,796 feet is the highest peak on the island. Snow and winter sports are popular on its slopes. The remaining two volcanoes command most of the attention because of frequent volcanic activity. Mauna Loa (13,677 feet) is the world's largest active volcano, and Kilauea, while a mere 4077 feet, has been the site of the most recent eruptions on the island.

Hawaii is about the size of Connecticut, and nearly five times the size of any other island in the chain: 93 miles long, 76 miles wide and 318 miles around. One can drive completely around the island on good surfaced roads, a convenience not found on the other "neighbor" islands — Maui, Kauai, Molokai and Lanai.

Historically, Hawaii is believed to be the first island reached by Polynesian settlers, about A.D. 750. It is the birthplace of Kamehameha the Great, who conquered and unified the islands in the late 18th century. It is also the place where Captain James Cook was killed after he "discovered" (1778) the islands and introduced Western culture. However, perhaps the most notable resident is Pele, the goddess of volcanoes, who is said to reside in Halemaumau, Kilauea's fire pit.

Hiking and backpacking on the Big Island have increased in popularity in recent years. Backpacks are conspicuous at the baggage counters as more and more visitors seek to discover a Hawaii different from the standard tourist fare. Trails here take you to enchanting black sand beaches, across the world's most active volcano, and to the highest peaks — Mauna Loa and Mauna Kea — over 13,000 feet in the 50th state.

Camping and Cabins

Camping out on Hawaii will add a dimension to your visit. Campgrounds on Hawaii range from adequate to good and contain most of the amenities. The price is right: all but county campgrounds are free. The camping map locates county, state, and national campgrounds as well as camping shelters and cabins.

Campgrounds in Hawaii Volcanoes National Park are on a first-come, first-served basis. There are three drive-in campgrounds in the park. The one at Namakani Paio, 3.0

miles from the visitor center, and the one at Kipuka Nene, 11.5 miles from the visitor center, have water, shelters and cooking pits. The third campground, at Kamoamoa, 30 miles from the visitor center, offers spacious campsites with water, tables, shelters and fireplaces but no water. In July 1989, Kamoamoa was threatened by lava from Kilauea. Even in mid-summer, campsites are usually available at all campgrounds. There is a seven-day limit, and campgrounds are free. I recommend Namakani Paio for a convenient and comfortable campground.

All other national park trail cabins and trail shelters are walk-in facilities. The two cabins on the trail to the summit of Mauna Loa — at Red Hill, 10,035 feet, and at the summit, 13,677 feet contain bunk beds and mattresses and, although you might find blankets, white gas stoves, lanterns, and some cooking utensils, you should not expect to. Carry all the necessary equipment to ensure a comfortable and safe trip (See "Food and Equipment" section). Water is available, but should be treated with purifying tablets or boiled. The trail shelters at Ka'aha, Halape and Keauhou are simple overnight wilderness facilities with shelters, fireplaces and drinking water that should be purified or boiled. The cabin at Kipuka Pepeiao has three beds and mattresses and water that should also be treated or boiled. Check at the information desk at the Visitor Center for current water levels when you pick up your wilderness hiking permit.

Volcano House, the national park concessionaire, offers inexpensive housekeeping A-frame cabins at the Namakani Paio campground, 3 miles from the visitor center. Each cabin contains a double bed and a bunk bed accommodating a total of four persons. For $24 per night, each cabin has mattresses, linen, soap, a picnic table, outdoor barbecue grill, water and a hot shower in a central washroom. Since the cabins are located at 4,000 feet, it is a good idea to bring an extra blanket or sleeping bag with you even during the summer months. Each cabin is a comfortable accommodation in a heavily wooded area. (See Appendix for address).

Permits are required when camping at McKenzie State Park on the east coast and at Kalopa State Park on the northeast side, the only state parks where camping is permitted. McKenzie is a beach park whereas Kalopa is in a wet area and it is not as conveniently located. The state parks are free, and they have potable water, shelter and fireplaces. Reservations are accepted and permits may be secured from the Division of State Parks.

The state also operates four comfortable and inexpensive cabin facilities on the island. They are located at Mauna Kea State Park, at Hapuna Beach State Recreation Area, at Kalopa State Recreation Area, and at Volcano (Niaulani Cabin). Mauna Kea State Park (Pohakuloa cabins) is located on the Saddle Road, 33 miles from Hilo at an elevation of 6,500 feet. Seven cabins accommodating six people each are available at $5–10 per person (the more people, the less cost per person). Each cabin contains bedding, towels, cooking and eating utensils, electricity, electric range, refrigerator, showers, and toilets. The facilities at Kalopa State Park, 42 miles from Hilo, contain the same amenities, with a central mess/recreation hall. There are two cabins with two units in each accommodating 1–8 persons in each unit. The cost ranges from $2.75–$8 per person (the more people, the less the cost per person). The six A-frame shelters at Hapuna Beach State Park, 65 miles from Hilo, are situated above Hawaii's best beach. Wow! What a spot! The wood and screened shelters are simple, containing one table, two wooden platforms for sleeping (a sleep pad or inflatable mattress is a MUST!), electricity, and a central mess hall with refrigerator and electric range that is shared with shelter users. You must bring your own cooking and eating utensils. Cold water showers and flush toilets are provided. Each shelter sleeps four and costs $7 per night. Niaulani Cabin, the fourth state cabin, is located in the community of Volcano, 29 miles from Hilo just outside Hawaii Volcanoes National Park. This single cabin accommodates six persons at a cost of $5–10 per person (the more people, the less the cost per person). It is completely furnished with a living room, two bedrooms, bedding, towels, cooking and eating utensils, electricity, hot shower, electric range and refrigerator and a one-car garage. The state and federal cabins are the best values in Hawaii and are very popular with locals and visitors. You are advised to write early for reservations. (All addresses are in the Appendix).

The County of Hawaii has established a system of beach parks which offer amenities from cold-water showers and drinking water to shelters, tables and firepits (see the camping map). Camping is permitted at 13 parks. Samuel Spencer Beach Park on the west side of the island is the most popular of the county campgrounds and is frequently full during the summer months. I like Mahukona and Keokea beach campgrounds (see camping map). Permits are required in these parks and may be secured in person or by writing to the Department of Parks and Recreation. Camping is limited to one week per park during the summer months and two weeks per park at other times. Fees at county parks are $1 per day for adults and 50 cents for persons 13–17. (Addresses for all agencies are in the Appendix.)

Hiking

Hiking on the Big Island is an exciting and sometimes spectacular experience because of periodic volcanic activity. Few will dispute that the best trails and the most memorable experiences are to be found in Hawaii Volcanoes National Park. However, some prefer the North Kohala Mountains, with their verdant and precipitous valleys. For the backpacker who is looking for that "dream" unspoiled place, Waimanu provides an outstanding hiking experience, while the challenge of hiking to the two highest points in Hawaii — Mauna Kea and Mauna Loa — is irresistible. In any case, hiking on Hawaii does not generally require any special equipment or skill. Many places of unique and extraordinary beauty are readily accessible to the novice, to the family, and to the elderly who are looking for short, relatively easy hikes or walks. Although hiking boots are not essential on most hikes, I prefer them. I recommend strong shoes or hiking boots in the Hawaii Volcanoes National Park because of the rough lava surfaces. Most hikers find shorts or cutoffs adequate in areas up to 8000 feet. Even during the summer, however, warm clothing is necessary when hiking to the summit of Mauna Loa or Mauna Kea, both over 13,000 feet. Because snow and ice are not uncommon most of the year on both peaks, heavy sweaters and jackets are recommended. Hats and dark glasses are also necessary for protection from the weather and the glaring sun.

In 1975 the County of Hawaii began daily public transit service from Hilo to Kona and from Hilo to Hawaii Volcanoes National Park. They operate one bus daily from Hilo to Hawaii Volcanoes National Park and one bus daily from Hilo to Kona. Write the Hawaii County Transit System for more information and schedules. Hitchhiking is legal, but rides are hard to get, especially in outlying areas.

Road closed!

HAWAII VOLCANOES NATIONAL PARK

(Hiking Area No. 1)

Rating: See individual hikes.

Features: Most active volcano in the world, lava flows, national park from sea to summit (13,677 feet), wilderness camping, Nene (rare Hawaiian state bird), camping, 17 hiking trails.

Permission: Written permits (free) required for hiking and camping in wilderness areas may be secured at the visitor center in person or by mail (address in Appendix). Camping is limited to 7 days per campground per year.

Hiking Distance and Time: See individual hikes.

Driving Instructions

From Hilo (30 miles, 1 hour) south on Route 11 to Park Entrance. Entry fee.

From Kona (95 miles, 2 1/2 hours) south on Route 11 to Park Entrance. Entry fee.

Introductory Notes: Some visitors to Kilauea are amazed that they can walk to within feet of molten lava. Others are excited by being able to hike within the park from sea level to over 13,000 feet. Still others marvel at the fact that natural forces have added over hundreds of acres of land to the park since 1969. As recently as November 29, 1975, about 13 acres of land were lost as land settled into the sea in the Halape region of the park — the site of a wilderness camping area — as a result of a 7.2-magnitude earthquake and a *tsunami* (seismic sea wave). The once beautiful lagoon at Halape and hundreds of coconut trees were lost. Yet it is typical of Hawaii that simultaneously about 28 acres of land were added as a result of seaward fault movements. The result was a gain of 15 acres!

Change, change, and still more change is the attraction that draws hikers to the black-sand beaches and the lava-strewn slopes of Hawaii. It is the excitement, the anticipation that one can witness the elemental forces of nature at work close up and still survive. Of course, not everyone does survive. The toll of the November 1975 quake was one hiker and another still missing and presumed dead. Still more change has been taking place at the time of this writing (1991). Kilauea has been erupting along its southeast rift for eight years, emitting an average of 650,000 cubic yards of lava daily. The result to date has been the closing of the Chain of Craters Road (March 1987) when lava flowed over it in several places; the destruction of the Wahaula visitor center (June, 1989), the destruction of 71 homes, and the creation of a striking black sand beach at Kamoamoa. Most exciting, visitors have been able to walk as close to the flowing lava as the heat allows — close enough to roast marshmallows!

Hawaii Volcanoes National Park, established in 1916, includes Kilauea, the most active volcano in the world, and Mauna Loa volcano. Kilauea volcano is 4,077 feet in elevation, while the summit caldera of Mauna Loa presides at 13,677. The park's total land area is 344 square miles — at least that is what it was at the time of this writing. It is no exaggeration to note that this is subject to natural change.

For convenience, I have divided the park into four hiking areas. The division is somewhat natural, for each area has some unique characteristics. First, the Mauna Loa Strip Road area has the most difficult hike on the island — the 19.6 mile hike to the summit of Mauna Loa. Second, the Kilauea caldera area is the most popular hiking area. Most of the hikes here are short and easy and perhaps the most exciting, for two trails cross the floors of active volcanoes. Third, the Kau Desert area is a hot, arid, somewhat barren area where hiking is strenuous and yet rewarding, for most of the trails cross recent lava flows, while others lead to the coastal wilderness areas of the park. Fourth, the Kalapana area is the area where, in 1969, Madame Pele erupted along a line of fissures southeast of the Kilauea caldera and buried three miles of the Chain of Craters Road, thus isolating the

Kalapana section of the park. Subsequent eruptions cut off more of the road. In June 1979 a new Chain of Craters Road was opened, thus completing the so-called Golden Triangle, which enabled a visitor to travel from Hilo to Hawaii Volcanoes National Park without doubling back on the same highway. But then in March, 1987, successive eruptions flowed over the road, thus closing it again, and it remains closed to date (January, 1991) — until further notice! Consequently, the only access to the Kalapana area is from the Kilauea Visitor Center. Hiking trails here take you to some of the best examples of petroglyphs on the island and to an abandoned Hawaiian village.

In planning your hiking in the park, consult the Hiking Chart and the maps in this guide. The former will help you select hikes that fit your interests, time schedule, and physical condition. The maps will reveal connecting trails and combinations of trails to return you to your starting point or to a convenient location for transportation.

Camping in the park is enjoyable for a couple of reasons. It's free whether you use the "civilized" campgrounds, the wilderness campgrounds or the cabins on Mauna Loa. These accommodations are also uncrowded and comfortable. Permits are necessary only to use the trail cabins and the wilderness campgrounds. See the area maps for the location of camping areas and the "Camping and Cabins" section in the "Introduction" for information about camping accommodations.

For safety, you MUST register with the park rangers at the visitor center for overnight hiking and for use of wilderness camping areas.

Namakani Paio Campground is 3.0 miles from the visitor center and Kipuka Nene Campground is 11.5 miles. Both are drive-in campgrounds and do not require permission to use. Be prepared for wet ground and rain at Namakani Paio most of the year. Shelters, fireplaces and water are available at both campgrounds. There is no drinking water at

Kamoamoa Campground in the Kalapana area. Inexpensive rental cabins are also available at Namakani Paio.

Because the hiking surface ranges from hard, crusted lava to soft volcanic ash and cinders, sound hiking boots are recommended for protection and comfort. A poncho is suggested in the Kilauea caldera area, which receives 95 inches of rain annually. Sun protection is a good idea in all other areas.

MAUNA LOA STRIP ROAD AREA

The climb to the summit of Mauna Loa is the most difficult and demanding hike on the island due to the elevation gain. The Mauna Loa Strip Road, which begins about two miles west of the visitor center off Route 11, though narrow, is paved and well maintained.

Mauna Loa Summit, 19.6 miles, 3–4 days, 7015–feet gain (trail rating: difficult).

Visitor Center to Trailhead, 14 miles by car.

Trailhead to Red Hill Cabin, 7.5 miles, 3373-feet gain on foot only.

Red Hill Cabin to Summit Cabin, 11.6 miles, 3215-feet gain on foot only.

Red Hill Cabin to Summit, 12.1 miles, 3642-feet gain on foot only.

The ascent of Mauna Loa should be attempted only after considerable planning and preparation. Bear in mind that even if you take 3 or 4 days, there is a considerable altitude change and mountain sickness is a possibility. Another consideration is hypothermia, which sets in when the body is not able to generate enough heat to keep the vital organs warm. Therefore, even during the summer, carry warm clothing and a warm sleeping bag. The cabins at Red Hill and at the summit may contain blankets, white-gas stoves, lanterns, heaters and some cooking and eating utensils, but it's best to carry your own equipment. The water at each cabin, collected from roof runoff, should be boiled or treated

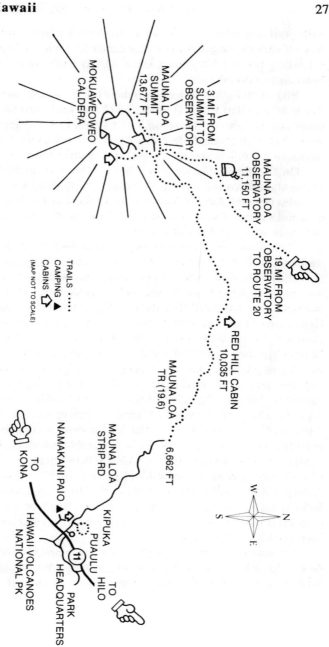

with purifying tablets. Both cabins are free, but you must sign up with the ranger at the visitor center for their use and for hiking permits (they must know who is where in case Pele causes a disturbance).

You should allow at least two days for the ascent: one day to hike to Red Hill (7.5 miles, 3,373 feet gain), and another day to hike to the summit (12.1 miles, 3,642 feet gain). You will probably find that 4 days are necessary for the round trip unless you are a good hiker in good condition.

On the Trail: The trailhead (6,662 feet) is at the end of the Mauna Loa (lit., "Long Mountain") Strip Road some 14 miles from the Kilauea Visitor Center. There is a parking area and a picnic shelter at road's end. You can hitchhike to this trailhead if you don't have a car.

The excitement of this hike begins immediately. At the trailhead look for the nene (*Branta sandvicensis*), the Hawaiian state bird. After disappearing, this native goose was reintroduced to Maui in 1962 and has since increased in numbers. It is estimated that about 1,000 nenes survive on Hawaii and Maui. The Park Service has a program to raise goslings and to return them to the wilds in due course. Natural breeding is difficult owing, in part, to a number of introduced predators, such as mongooses, pigs, and feral dogs and cats, for whom the eggs and the young goslings are easy prey. The nene has adapted to its rugged habitat on the rough lava flows far from any standing or running water, and some people suggest that this water fowl is more accurately regarded as a lava fowl. The most noticeable anatomical change has been the reduction of webbing between the toes, which better suits its terrestrial life. Its size (22–26") and its variety of muted calls, often resembling the "moo" of a cow, make it easy to identify. If you spot a nene, don't be surprised if it walks up to you. It is a very friendly bird and has been known to enjoy a petting!

The trail passes through a gate in a fence designed to protect the park from feral goats, whose voracious eating habits tend to denude the vegetation. Be sure to close the gate. Soon you are above the open ohia (*Metrosideros collina*) forest at the 8,300-foot level. The bright red blossom of the ohia lehua, the flower of the island of Hawaii, is regarded as sacred to Pele. Legend holds that if a person picks this flower on the way to the mountain, it will rain.

The Red Hill cabin at 10,035 feet is a welcome sight in what is now open country with little growth. It is a comfortable overnight facility and offers a panorama of the island. On a clear day you can see Maui to the northwest and its summit Haleakala — the house of the sun. If you are suffering from altitude sickness — headache and nausea — Red Hill is a good place to lie down with your head lower than your trunk and perhaps take an aspirin. Remember to boil or treat the water.

An early start on the second day will enable you to make a few miles before the hottest part of the day. Your hike to the summit follows the northeast rift of Mauna Loa, where you will find some startling cracks and shapes in the strata caused by recent splatter cones and lava flows. The last eruption along this rift, in 1942, extended over a 2.8-mile area. The lava flowed to within 12 miles of the city of Hilo.

About two miles from the summit, you finally arrive at the North Pit of the great Mokuaweoweo (lit., "fish section" — red part of a fish, which suggests volcanic fires) caldera. The giant Mokuaweoweo caldera is an oval depression 3 miles long, 1 1/2 miles wide, and as deep as 600 feet. The trail to the cabin drops into the caldera and crosses the smooth, flat surface, skirting to the right of Lua Poholo, a deep pit crater formed since 1841. If you haven't fallen into Lua Poholo, the cabin is a short hike up to the rim of Mokuaweoweo. You'll find water at the cabin or ice in a lava crack, a short (1/2 mile) walk southwest of the cabin. Remember to boil or treat the water.

To reach the summit you must return to the junction on the north side of the caldera and follow the ahus (rock cairns) to the 13,680-foot summit. At the summit you are standing on the top of the world's largest active shield volcano and the largest single mountain on earth, when you consider that it rises about 30,000 feet above its base on the ocean floor.

Mauna Loa has been surprisingly quiet for over 40 years. The last eruption from Mokuaweoweo caldera was in 1949, when more than half the caldera floor was blanketed with new lava. The eruption of Mauna Loa in 1950, the greatest since 1859, was along the southwest rift, with fissures from 11,000 feet down to 8,000 feet. Lava flowed westward and southeastward, and within a day reached the sea. When lava entered the water, it boiled and steam clouds rose 10,000 feet into the air. An estimated billion tons of lava destroyed two dozen buildings and buried a mile of highway. No lives were lost.

The return trip to the trailhead is easy, but tiring if you do it in one day. An alternative return is to take the Observatory Trail. From the summit, return along the trail for 1.6 miles to a spur trail that goes northwest (left) for 0.3 mile to the emergency four-wheel-drive road and the Observatory Trail. The trail is on the left side of the road, extending for 3 steep and difficult miles to the Mauna Loa weather observatory at 11,150 feet while the road switchbacks to the observatory. Unless you have made arrangements for someone to drive to the observatory to pick you up, it is 19 miles from the observatory to Route 20, and 28 miles on Route 20 to Hilo.

KILAUEA CALDERA AREA

Without question, the Kilauea (lit., "spewing" — referring to eruptions) section of the national park is the most exciting place on the island because dramatic change is so imminent. Like Mauna Loa, Kilauea is a shield volcano with a characteristic broad, gently sloping dome. While the summit is 4,000 feet above sea level, the base of the mountain extends another 16,000 feet to the ocean bottom. The summit caldera, 2 1/2 miles long and 2 miles wide, contains Halemaumau, the "fire pit", which is the legendary home of Pele, the goddess of volcanoes. Halemaumau had an almost

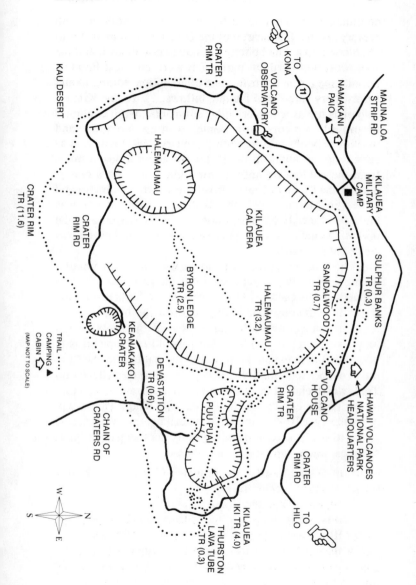

continuously active lake of liquid lava throughout the 19th century and the first quarter of the 20th. One commentator in 1826 noted that "the bottom was covered with lava, and the southwest and northern parts of it were one vast flood of burning matter, in a terrific state of ebullition, rolling to and fro its 'fiery surge' and flaming billows....". Today, Kilauea caldera is not as active or quite as romantic, but it continues to provide visitors with some exciting moments and thrilling experiences. Presently, (January, 1991) Kilauea has been erupting along its southeast rift about a dozen miles from the caldera on and off for eight years. As a consequence, the Chain of Craters Road was overrun with lava and closed in March, 1987, the Wahaula visitor center was burned in June, 1989, and 71 homes were destroyed over the period. On the plus side, a marvelous black sand beach was created at Kamoamoa.

The Kilauea portion of the park is the most popular hiking area on the island because of the presence of active Kilauea and because of easy access to well-marked hiking trails. In planning your hiking, consult the maps and the text for connecting trails, since most of the trails do not loop. For example, one hike that I would recommend is to take the Halemaumau Trail across the caldera to the "fire pit", connect with the Byron Ledge Trail to the Kilauea Iki Trail, which ends at the Thurston Lava Tube, and then return to the visitor center via the Crater Rim Trail. This is approximately a 10-mile loop. No special equipment is necessary. However, I recommend a strong, durable pair of boots or shoes, water, sun protection and food.

Crater Rim Trail, 11.6 mile loop, 5–8 hours (trail rating: strenuous).

Trailhead at Volcano House.

The best introduction to the Kilauea area is to drive the Crater Rim Road or to hike the Crater Rim Trail, which encircles the caldera. It is a strenuous hike with a 500-foot elevation gain. Plan on the better part of a day to complete the hike. You will want to make some side trips to take in some of the sights and to pause frequently to enjoy the striking panoramas of the volcanic landscape.

On the Trail: Pick up the trail in front of the Volcano House and hike counterclockwise (right) in order to pass through the warm Kau Desert in the early morning. The trail initially passes a few steaming vents, which set the mood. At "Steaming Bluff" billowing steam clouds rise from the ground, caused by water getting into the "plumbing" of Kilauea. The steam is accompanied by small amounts of hydrogen sulfide, which smells like rotten eggs. This condition is an eerie introduction to your hike.

The trail continues along the crater rim, passes the Kilauea Military Camp on the opposite side of the road, and climbs slightly up Uwekahuna (lit., "wailing priest") Bluff to the site of the Hawaii Volcano Observatory. From here, scientists have been keeping a watchful eye on Kilauea since 1911, when Dr. Thomas A. Jagger established the observatory. Today, studies continue under the direction of the U.S. Geological Survey. Take time to visit the museum where displays explain the history, culture, and geology of the islands. It is also a good place from which to view Halemaumau and Kilauea and, on a clear day, to admire the striking presence of towering Mauna Loa to the west. This, the highest point on the trail, was once a sacred point for Hawaiians, where offerings were made to the gods.

From the observatory, the trail dips south along the road and then crosses it to the southwest rift of Kilauea and to the trailhead of the Kau Desert region. It was along the southwest rift that an eruption occurred in 1971 which lasted five days and covered an area of 1.3 square miles. A rift is a highly fractured land area on the flank of a volcano along which most of the volcano's eruptions take place.

You might choose to take the Halemaumau Trail to the "fire pit." The fire pit is about a mile off the rim trail across the Crater Rim Road to the east side of the caldera (see the Halemaumau Trail below). If not, you will at least smell the sulfur fumes being emitted by Halemaumau.

The Keanakakoi (lit., "cave of the adzes") Crater marks the beginning of the east rift zone, where in 1974 one of the last major eruptions of Kilauea occurred. During the first part of the year, the Kilauea caldera began to swell, and increased earthquake activity was recorded. Finally in July, rifts opened on the southeastern caldera rim and in the caldera floor, while 200-foot fountains of incandescent lava spurted from fissures. Lava filled Keanakakoi Crater and flowed beyond to cover the Chain of Craters Road.

From here to the fern forest you should find many ohelo (*Vaccinium reticulatum*) shrubs bearing delectable bright red berries. A small native shrub in the cranberry family, it has many branches with small, rounded, toothed leaves. The berries are edible but sacred to Pele. To avoid Pele's wrath, you should throw half your berries into the fire pit saying,

> *E Pele, here are your ohelos.*
> *I offer some to you.*
> *Some I also eat.*

After crossing the Chain of Craters Road, the trail passes through a sparsely wooded area before entering a thick tree-fern forest. Here you will find some outstanding specimens of Hawaiian tree ferns. The hapuu (*Cibotium splendens*) is an endemic fern that can reach 16 feet in height. In old Hawaii, hats were made from the stems. The starchy trunk core was used for cooking and for washing. Another endemic tree fern is the amaumau (*Sadleria splendens*), from which the fire pit Halemaumau (lit., "house of ferns") derives its name. The fronds were used for thatching house frames and for making red dye to color tapa cloth.

Ample rain — about 95 inches annually — sustains this verdant and enchanting forest. The forest is shaded by a canopy of ohia lehua (*Metrosideros collina*) trees with red powder-puff-like blossoms which were regarded as sacred to Pele. Hawaiians believe that it will rain if the flower is picked.

The Thurston Lava Tube is a short spur trail off the Crater Rim Trail; it takes you through a 450-foot lava tunnel (see Thurston Lava Tube Trail description).

Pick up the Crater Rim Trail by crossing the road and the parking lot from the lava tube. The trail follows the edge of Kilauea Iki crater (see the Kilauea Iki Trail description). Kilauea Iki is a pit crater immediately adjacent to the eastern edge of Kilauea caldera. The trail is shaded and cool and offers a number of lookout points with interpretive exhibit cases.

The trail and the road along Waldron Ledge were closed after the November 1975 earthquake when some of the ledge fell into the crater and much of the road was severely fractured. The trail and road have since been repaired or rerouted, and it is safe to proceed and to view the power of nature first hand. A short walk will return you to Volcano House.

Halemaumau Trail, 3.2 miles, 2 hours (trail rating: hardy family).

Trailhead at Volcano House.

As you approach the trail across the lava lake floor of the Kilauea caldera, you may be apprehensive. Knowing that the earth is boiling below your every step can be overwhelming. Consequently, while the hiking is irresistible, you can't wait to finish the hike and to get out of the caldera.

If your starting point is Volcano House, you might plan a loop trip (consult maps) or arrange to be picked up on the opposite side unless you plan to return across the crater.

On the Trail: The trail begins west (to the right) of the Volcano House and descends through a lush tree-fern forest, passing rocks that have fallen and rolled into the crater. The trail drops about 500 feet, intersecting the Crater Rim Trail, the Sandalwood Trail and the Byron Ledge Trail before it crosses the floor of the caldera.

Many of the native and introduced plants are identified by markers in the forest, dominated by the ohia lehua tree with its red powder-puff-like blossoms and kahili ginger with its magnificent foot-high yellow blossoms.

The hike across the floor is hot and dry, so sun protection and water are important. As you approach the rough, brittle, twisted, broken surface, an eerie, somewhat uncomfortable feeling sets in, so that as a piece of lava crumbles underfoot, you swallow hard and breathe a bit more deeply for a moment. The trail is well marked with ahus (rock cairns) and is easy to follow. The shiny black surface of the pahoehoe (smooth and ropy surface) lava sometimes nearly blinds you. The first half mile is fresh lava from a 1974 flow. In fact the trail crosses lava dating from 1885, 1954, 1971 and 1975. See if you can notice the difference.

The caldera has literally had its ups and downs over the years as it has been filled and emptied by successive eruptions. The depth of the caldera changes with almost every eruption as the floor swells and erupts. Some craters fill up and others shrink.

Beyond the junction with the Byron Ledge Trail, the Park Service has constructed a safe viewing overlook into Halemaumau, the "fire pit" and the home of the goddess Pele. Typically, there are steam clouds mixed with hydrogen sulfide, creating an unpleasant "rotten egg" odor. From here you can view the panorama from left to right, beginning with the summit of Mauna Loa, the crater rim with the Volcano Observatory, the Steaming Bluffs, Volcano House and Byron Ledge, dividing Kilauea from Kilauea Iki.

The trail continues across the Crater Rim Road to connect with the Crater Rim Trail. However, you may choose to return via the Byron Ledge Trail or the Rim Road.

Byron Ledge Trail, 2.5 miles, 1 1/2 hours (trail rating: strenuous).

Trailhead off Halemaumau Trail or Kilauea Iki Trail on foot only

This is a convenient trail to connect with other trails or to return to park headquarters after hiking the Halemaumau Trail.

On the Trail: From the fire pit, the trail crosses Kilauea caldera eastward and climbs a few hundred feet to Byron Ledge, which separates Kilauea from Kilauea Iki. From the bluff you have views of both craters and of Puu Puai (lit., "gushing hill"), a 400-foot cone of pumice and ash on the south side of Kilauea Iki formed by an eruption in 1959. After the November 1975 earthquake, the ledge trail was closed due to slides on the west wall of Kilauea Iki. In the summer of 1976 Park Service trail crews re-routed the trail, enabling you to hike once again into Kilauea Iki. The fencing here is a project to control wild pigs.

Kilauea Iki Trail, 4.0 miles, 2 1/2 hours (trail rating: strenuous).

Trailhead off Byron Ledge Trail or from Thurston Lava Tube, 3 miles from Visitor Center by car.

On the Trail: The Kilauea Iki (lit., "little Kilauea") Trail is accessible from Thurston Lava Tube or from Volcano House via the Halemaumau, Byron Ledge, or Crater Rim Trail. From Byron Ledge, the trail descends 400 feet into the crater. This newly constructed trail was built after slides covered the old trail following the earthquake of November 1975. The trail bisects the crater floor, which is covered with fresh lava from a spectacular 1959 eruption. This eruption, which lasted 36 days, had exploding fountains that reached a record-setting 1,900 feet in height. Cinder, pumice and ash piled up on the crater rim over five feet thick. The devastated area (see Devastation Trail description) south of the crater was created at this time, while a pool of lava 380 feet deep remained in the crater.

After the trail snakes about 400 feet up the western wall of the crater through an ohia tree-fern forest, it ends in the parking lot at Thurston Lava Tube.

Thurston Lava Tube Trail, 0.3 mile loop, 15 minutes (trail rating: family).

Visitor Center to Trailhead, 3 miles by car.

This is a short but a "must" trail in the Kilauea section. You can drive to the trailhead via the Crater Rim Road or hike the crater rim clockwise from Volcano House or from the western end of the Kilauea Iki Trail. This prehistoric lava tube was formed when the outer crust of a tongue of flowing lava cooled and solidified while the inner portion continued to flow and eventually emptied the tube, leaving a 450-foot tunnel as high as 20 feet in places.

On the Trail: The trail to the tube entrance descends through a lush tree-fern rain forest. Many of the plants are identified by marker. Native birds are commonly found here. With luck you may see the small (4 1/2") green and yellow amakihi (*Loxops virents*) foraging for food, or the vermillion i'iwi (*Vestiaria coccinea*) with black wings and a long, curved, salmon-colored bill and orange legs.

A metal staircase and bridge allow for an easy entrance and exit from the tube. In addition, electric lights illuminate the tube permitting a safe and comfortable stroll.

Devastation Trail, 0.6 miles, 15 minutes (trail rating: family).

Visitor Center to Trailhead, 4 miles by car.

On the Trail: One of the most photographed and one of the most popular areas in the park, the devastation area was created by a 1959 eruption in Kilauea Iki when 1,900-foot fountains showered the area with ash, pumice and spatter that buried an ohia forest, denuding the trees and leaving their skeletons standing in tribute to the eerie, strangely beautiful effects of Mother Nature. A boardwalk crosses the area to prevent passing feet from creating numerous trails. Today, new growth has altered the landscape so that it is no longer as "devastated" as originally.

Sandalwood Trail, 0.7 miles, 15 minutes (trail rating: family).

Trailhead at Volcano House.

On the Trail: The Sandalwood Trail is one of a number of short, easy trails from the visitor center to scenic overlooks of the Kilauea Caldera. The trail begins west (to the right) of Volcano House and gently descends for a hike along the caldera rim to the steam vents at Steaming Bluff. Several of the plants are identified by pictorial markers. You pass through a rather dense ohia tree-fern forest where many of the plants are identified. A number of steam vents along the trail remind you of the presence of Pele and send off the "rotten egg" smell caused by hydrogen sulfide. You can return to park headquarters via the Crater Rim Trail or loop via the Sulfur Bank Trail.

Sulfur Bank Trail: 0.3 miles, 15 minutes (trail rating: family).
Trailhead at Visitors Center.

On the Trail: An interesting trail from the visitor center will take you to the sulfur banks, where volcanic fumaroles emit gases that deposit colorful minerals. The glory bush with its pretty, deep-purple blossoms and kahili ginger with its foot-high yellow blossoms flourish along the trail. This is an easy walk and an interesting sight, but the presence of the "rotten egg" smell means you won't linger very long.

KAU DESERT AREA

The Kau (lit., "to place") Desert is indeed just that — a hot, arid, dry, relatively barren and bleak area that composes the southern section of Hawaii Volcanoes National Park. There are no precise boundaries, but the desert region is considered to be all the land south of Kilauea caldera and between Route 11 in the west and the Chain of Craters Road in the east. All the trails here are long and hot, without any guarantee of water. It is an area that tests the hikers and his/her equipment, and perhaps appeals most to those who are seeking solitude. Compared to the other areas of the park, there are no sights to speak of — just a lot of lava, a lot of sun, a lot of stillness, and a lot of sweat!

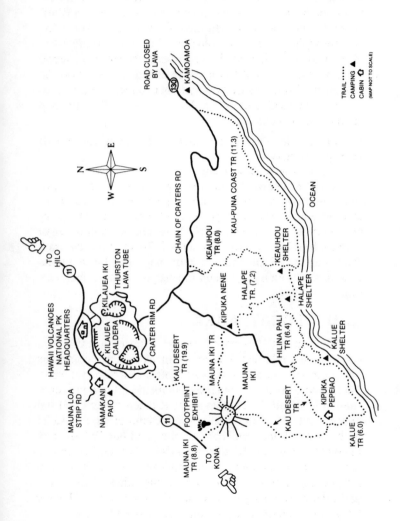

Water is available at the trail shelters and at the Kipuka Pepeiao cabin, but check on availability at the visitor center before hiking. Remember, the most striking characteristic of the park is change. For example, new shelters constructed at Halape were destroyed a few months later by the November 1975 tsunami. Since then, a new shelter has been built and hundreds of coconut trees have been planted.

Halape Trail, 7.2 miles, 4 hours (trail rating: difficult).

Visitor Center to Trailhead, 10.5 miles by car.

On the Trail: The most popular trail in the Kau Desert is the Halape (lit., "crushed missing") Trail from the campground at Kipuka Nene (lit., "goose leap") to the coastal trail shelter at Halape. The well-defined trail descends through the Kau Desert about 3,000 feet to the sea. The trailhead is at Kipuka Nene Campground, a 10 1/2 mile drive over the Chain of Craters Road and the Hilina Pali Road from the visitor center. From the shelter, the trail crisscrosses a jeep road for a couple of miles and passes through low shrub and grass land and then descends over mostly rough lava surfaces. Throughout, it is a hot, humid hike with no shade. From the junction with the Hilina Pali Trail, it is less than two miles to Halape. The allure at Halape was the oasis-like character of hundreds of coconut trees bordering a peaceful lagoon. However, on the morning of November 29, 1975, this was all changed when the island was hit by an earthquake that registered a high 7.2 on the Richter scale at the Hawaii Volcano Observatory. Roads and trails in the park were severely damaged, and at Halape a tsunami (seismic sea wave) battered the shore. This was the largest ever recorded in Hawaii, cresting at 30 feet and traveling at a staggering 187 miles per hour. Simultaneously, the land sank about six feet, an event that experts say reduced the impact of the tsunami. However, to the 32 campers at Halape, it was a nightmare, as successive waves picked up people, horses, boulders, trees and camping equipment and created a swirling mass. One camper found himself floating out to sea on the roof of the trail shelter before he jumped off and luckily swam to safety. Others were thrown into cracks in the earth, while still others clung to trees, shrubs and rocks and, thereby, to life. Miraculously, all but two campers survived. Today, calm has returned to Halape, where a new sandy beach and a cave have been formed. The Park Service worked through the summer of 1976 repairing the trail and the shelter at Halape and planting new coconut trees to replace those that were under 6 feet of water in June 1976. Some of the trunks of the coconut trees remain partly submerged in the new lagoon.

Hilina Pali Trail, 6.4 miles to Halape Junction, 4 hours (trail rating: difficult).

Visitor Center to Trailhead, 17 miles by car.

The Hilina Pali (lit., "struck cliff") Trail begins at the end of the Hilina Pali Road. From the trailhead, the Hilina Pali Trail descends the pali southeast to connect with the Halape Trail some 6.4 miles distant. In 1989, this portion of the trail was overgrown and difficult to follow. Whatever your plan, it is a hot arid hike. The trail's name is derived from the Hilina Pali Fault, a dramatic example of faulting. A fault is created when a fracture occurs in the earth's crust and the block on one side moves with respect to the block on the other. During the earthquake of November 1975, the south flank of Kilauea slumped seaward along the 15-mile Hilina Pali fault to produce major effects.

On the Trail: The trail southeast from the Hilina Pali Road descends about 2,300 feet to the coast and to the trail shelter at Halape via the Halape Trail or to the Ka'aha Shelter via the Kalue Trail. The descent of the pali is a little treacherous, but with some caution it can be negotiated safely. After 2.2 miles the trail reaches a junction with the Kalue Trail, which goes south 1.6 miles to the Ka'aha Shelter on the coast. At another junction 1.2 miles beyond, the Hilina Pali Trail meets a trail that goes southwest 1.6 miles to Ka'aha Shelter. From this junction the trail (overgrown in 1989) goes 3.0 miles to join the Halape

Trail, on which you can head south to Halape or north to Kipuka Nene.

Kau Desert Trail to Pepeiao Cabin, 14.1 miles, 8 hours, or to Hilina Pali Overlook, 18.9 miles, day (trail rating: difficult).

Visitor Center to trailhead, 3 miles by car.

To traverse the entire length of the Kau Desert Trail from the west side of the Kilauea Caldera off the Crater Rim Trail to the trail cabin at Kipuka Pepeiao requires a stout heart, strong legs and water. This is a long, arid trail that descends about 2,000 feet. If you have the time (two days minimum) and are seeking solitude, a vigorous hike can be made by taking the Kau Desert Trail to Kipuka Pepeiao, taking the Kalue Trail to Halape, and returning via the Halape Trail to Kipuka Nene (32.3 miles.)

On the Trail: The trail gradually descends through some low scrub vegetation and then across relatively barren pahoehoe (smooth and ropy surface) lava. Look in the pukas (holes) for Pele's hair, a thin, golden substance consisting of volcanic glass spun into hairlike strands. It is plentiful on this older lava form, as is Hawaiian "snow", a whitish lichen that is the first thing to grow on new lava. From the trail junction with the Mauna Iki Trail, an easy, gradual climb to the summit of Mauna Iki (3,032 feet) provides interesting panoramas of the surrounding area. From the summit you can take the Mauna Iki Trail west to the "footprints" exhibit (see the Mauna Iki Trail for their description). The rest of the trail is an easy descent skirting the Kamakaia (lit., "the fish eye") Hills to Kipuka Pepeiao.

From the cabin, the trail parallels a fault system as it leads to the Hilina Pali Road and Overlook. There are a number of interesting cracks in the earth along the trail which permit you to study a fault system up close. Notice the scars and tears in the pali (cliff) walls where the earth has slipped and has been torn away. From the pali there are dramatic views of the Kau Desert and the coast.

Mauna Iki Trail, 8.8 miles, 5 hours (trail rating: strenuous).

Visitor Center to Trailhead, 9 miles by car.

Crossing the Kau Desert east-west, the Mauna Iki (lit., "little mountain") Trail connects the Hilina Pali Road and Route 11 and bisects the Kau Desert Trail. This convenient trail enables the visitor to cut hiking distance and time to points of interest in the desert.

On the Trial: If you begin your hike off Route 11, you can conveniently visit the footprints exhibit. There is a highway sign noting the trailhead. From here, it is an easy 0.8 mile hike to the footprints over a broad, well-defined trail. Some of the footprints are in protected enclosures to prevent vandalism and to shelter them from the elements. It is here that armies assembled in 1790 to do battle for control of the island. The armies opposing Kamehameha the Great were overcome by the fumes and dust from Halemaumau, and their footprints were left in the hardening ash. Some believe that Pele interceded to assist Kamehameha. If you search the area, you can find other footprints.

The trail continues to the top of Mauna Iki (3,032 feet) and to a junction with the Kau Desert Trail. The trail is well-defined by rock cairns. Some of the lava is from the flows of 1971. Indeed, Mauna Iki is geologically an infant, having been formed in 1920. It is a satellite shield volcano built by lava flows from Halemaumau. There are countless cracks in the area that are part of the southwest rift of Kilauea. It is a fascinating place to investigate, but do so with caution.

From Mauna Iki follow the Kau Desert Trail north 0.7 mile to the Mauna Iki Trail, which traverses the desert to the Hilina Pali Road. Along this trail you can find handfuls of Pele's hair: thin, golden, spun volcanic glass in hairlike strands. It is also a good chance to examine and to photograph outstanding examples of pahoehoe feet and toes where the lava has naturally flowed to form footlike shapes.

Additionally, you will find lava rivers, numerous pit craters and small cinder cones.

As you approach a low scrub area, the trail is not distinguishable, but if you continue due east you can't miss the road and trail's end. From here, it is about 1 mile to the campground at Kipuka Nene, 4 miles to the Chain of Craters Road and 10 1/2 miles to the visitor center.

KALAPANA AREA

The forces of nature isolated the southern section of the Hawaii Volcanoes National Park between 1969 and 1979. Beginning in 1969, a series of eruptions from Kilauea covered miles of the road connecting the Kilauea Visitor Center with the Kalapana area. For 10 years it was a 55-mile drive from the Kilauea center to the Wahaula Visitor Center on Route 13. In 1979, the Chain of Craters road was rebuilt and reopened, enabling visitors to drive from the center of the park to the southern section. It was a scenic and pleasant ride of 32 miles. But then in 1983, Kilauea erupted along its southeast rift causing considerable damage to property and, in 1987, it overran the Chain of Craters Road thus closing it once again. Since 1983, lava has destroyed the Wahaula Visitor Center in Kalapana and destroyed 71 homes. It was still erupting in January, 1991. Most of the hiking trails in the Kalapana area are short and relatively easy.

Kamoamoa Trail, 1 mile loop, 1 hour (trail rating: family).

Visitor Center to Trailhead, 30 miles by car.

Kamoamoa is a quiet, shady campground awaiting the camper looking for solitude. Kamoamoa is the site of an ancient Hawaiian village and a black sand beach created by recent lava flows.

On the Trail: You begin the trail loop at the campground or at the parking lot. Like all Hawaiian shoreline villages, Kamoamoa was built on a bluff overlooking the sea, with a generous supply of beach stones to construct

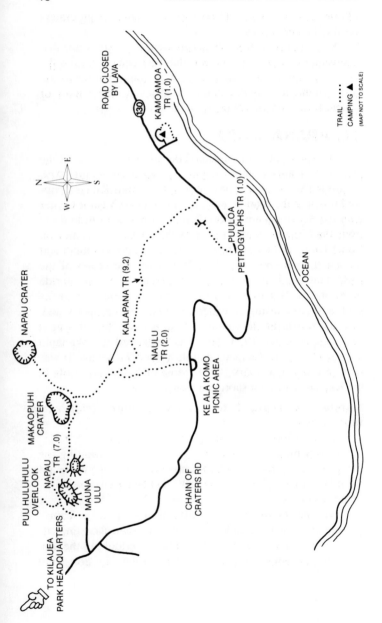

ROAD CLOSED BY LAVA

130

KAMOAMOA TR (1.0)

PUULOA PETROGYLPHS TR (1.0)

KALAPANA TR (9.2)

NAULU TR (2.0)

NAPAU CRATER

MAKAOPUHI CRATER

PUU HULUHULU OVERLOOK

NAPAU TR (7.0)

MAUNA ULU

KE ALA KOMO PICNIC AREA

CHAIN OF CRATERS RD

TO KILAUEA PARK HEADQUARTERS

OCEAN

N E S W

TRAIL ......
CAMPING ▲
(MAP NOT TO SCALE)

dwellings and with a convenient place to launch canoes. Just past the burial grounds, the remains of the long, narrow canoe sheds are apparent. Walk directly to the beach, where you can imagine ancient Hawaiians preparing to launch their outriggers. They had to drag their boats to the beach and then time their move so that the waves would pull the boat and the men out to the open sea.

A sea arch along the coast is what remains of a lava tube that has been eroded by the pounding surf. The many lava tubes found on the islands are unique features of volcanic activity. A lava tube is formed when the *surface* of a lava flow solidifies but the molten lava within continues to flow downslope, evacuating the surrounding crust to leave a tube. Little remains of the dwellings at Kamoamoa because the sides and the roofs were made of wood and grass. The floors and about three feet of the side walls were a mixture of beach stones and lava rocks. The rest of the walls and the roofs were constructed of ohia poles lashed together with hau bark; pili grass was used for thatching. The family mingled and slept in the hale noa (sleeping house), but used other houses for eating and working.

The remains of salt trays can be found near the shoreline. Salt water was poured into these stone pans and allowed to evaporate. As the crystals formed, they were moved to shallower stone pans to dry further, and then put in pans lined with ti leaves to be stored for later use. Nearby is a weather-worn papamu stone, used in a Hawaiian checker game that was extremely popular in every village. The trail passes through the campground and returns to the parking lot. CAUTION: This is an unsafe swimming beach because of strong ocean currents and riptides.

Puu Loa Petroglyphs, 1.0 mile, 3/4 hour (trail rating: hardy family).

Visitor Center to Trailhead, 26 miles.

On the Trail: The trailhead is marked by a road sign 26 miles east of the Kilauea Visitor Center. The trail to the Puu Loa (lit., "long-hill") Petroglyphs is marked and well-worn as it crosses pahoehoe lava, which has a smooth and ropy surface, unlike aa lava, which has a rough, clinkery surface. The view upcountry from the trail offers a panorama of the Kilauea eruptions of 1969 through 1972, which flowed to the sea and covered much of the Chain of Craters Road.

You will find the petroglyphs on mounds. There are hundreds, in varying sizes and shapes. There are dots, dashes, lines and bars as well as some figures that are somewhat indistinguishable. Holes in the lava (pukas) were receptacles in which ancient Hawaiians placed the umbilical cords of their children to insure a long life. Recently, a boardwalk was erected to reduce damage to the petroglyphs. Please protect this interesting and valuable place.

Naulu Trail, 2 miles, 1 hour (trail rating: hardy family).

Visitor Center to Trailhead, 14 miles by car.

The Naulu (lit., "the groves") trailhead is located on the north side of the Chain of Craters Road 14 miles from the Kilauea Visitor Center. Until the lava flows of 1972 Naulu was a popular forest and picnic area. Today, the trail is useful because it provides convenient access to the Kalapana Trail, which in turn provides access to a number of interesting craters.

On the Trail: The trail begins opposite a turnout along the Chain of Craters Road, Ke Ala Komo (lit., "entrance path"), where there was once a populous village. The first 0.2 mile of the trail, over rough aa lava, parallels the road until it emerges on a 1971 pahoehoe lava flow from Mauna Ulu. Since Naulu is a newly established trail, the lava is not worn, so it is necessary to follow the ahus, or stone piles, as you make your way north. There is no shelter or shade from the hot sun, nor any water. On the right and front right, numerous trees and a variety of scrub have survived successive lava flows. After the first mile the summit of Mauna Ulu comes into view on the front left. Near the end of the trail you reach the remains of the old Chain of

Craters Road. Follow the road northwest (left) for a short distance to a junction with the Kalapana Trail. From here you have the option to take the Kalapana Trail east 8 miles to the coastline or northwest 1.2 miles to join to Napau Trail.

Napau Trail, 7 miles, 4 hours (trail rating: strenuous).

Visitor Center to Trailhead, 9 miles by car.

The Napau (lit., "the endings") area provides an opportunity to observe recent lava flows, volcanic craters, and the growth of a shield volcano. To reach the trailhead, drive on the Chain of Craters Road toward the coast and make a left turn at a sign, "Mauna Ulu." Drive a short distance to the end of the road and a trailhead marker.

On the Trail: The first part of the trail traverses the gently sloping flanks of Puu Huluhulu (lit., "shaggy hill"), a prehistoric cinder and spatter cone which stands northwest of a newly built shield volcano, Mauna Ulu (lit., "growing mountain"). Major eruptions broke out along the east rift of Kilauea in 1969, with fountains spewing forth along a fissure that paralleled the Chain of Craters Road. By June 1969 repeated flows and the accumulation of spatter and cinder had built a gently sloping, shield-shaped cone more than a mile across and 400 feet high. Thus was Mauna Ulu born. Subsequent flows filled some nearby craters and covered parts of the road. At a junction one mile from the trailhead, a short trail on the left (north) leads to the Puu Huluhulu overlook.

Some startling shapes formed by the pahoehoe (smooth and ropy surface) lava are found along the entire length of the trail. Search the pukas (holes) in the lava for "Pele's hair," a golden, hairlike substance consisting of volcanic glass spun in gossamer form. The trail passes through a "lava tree" forest. These tree shapes were formed when streams of lava engulfed the ohia trees. The moisture in the trees caused the lava to cool rapidly, leaving tree-shaped shells. Some are 8–10 feet high.

Beyond Mauna Ulu the trail passes north of Alae (lit., "mudhen"), a pit crater created in 1969. In that year, successive eruptions and lava flows from both Alae and Mauna Ulu alternately filled and emptied Alae Crater. It's an exciting and interesting spot.

From near Alae the trail gently descends about 3 miles to a junction with the Kalapana Trail near Makaopuhi (lit., "eye of eel") Crater, which is a crater second in size only to Kilauea. Recent eruptions (1965, 1969) from fissures on the flanks of Makaopuhi (part of the east rift zone of Kilauea) have created havoc and change; the most notable was the destruction of the Chain of Craters Road. From the Napau/Makaopuhi junction, it is two miles to Napau Crater. Not unlike its neighbors, Napau has been active in recent years. Its most dramatic contribution came in 1965 when lava from the crater created a forest of tree molds. This is another interesting place to examine, but after a long, warm hike you may not choose to linger.

On the trail — Kilauea

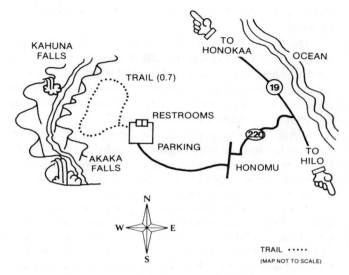

KAHUNA FALLS

TO HONOKAA

OCEAN

TRAIL (0.7)

19

RESTROOMS

220

PARKING

TO HILO

AKAKA FALLS

HONOMU

N
W — E
S

TRAIL ·····
(MAP NOT TO SCALE)

AKAKA FALLS
(Hiking Area No. 2)

Rating: Family.

Features: 420-foot Akaka Falls, Kahuna Falls, native and introduced flora.

Permission: None.

Hiking Distance and Time: 0.7 mile loop, 1/2 hour.

Driving Instructions:

From Hilo (15 miles, 3/4 hour) north on Route 19, left on Route 220 to end.

From Kona (87 miles, 2 1/2 hours) north on Route 190, right on Route 19, right on Route 220 to end.

Introductory Notes: Few dispute that Akaka (lit., "clearness") Falls State Park is everyone's idea of what Hawaii is all about. It is a 66-acre tropical paradise in a canyon park where all of nature's riches seem larger than life. Everything — the ti, the ginger, the bamboo, the tree ferns, the orchids, the azaleas — comes in the large economy size!

On the Trail: A paved trail descends abruptly from the parking lot and thrusts the hiker immediately into the canyon, where a large variety of tropical plants greets one. A guide to Hawaiian flora such as the one by Dorothy and Bob Hargreaves (*Hawaiian Blossoms*) is a handy volume to help you identify the many varieties of plants.

Giant bamboo dominates the first part of the trail. Bamboo has long been an important product on the islands, having been used for fuel, furniture, buildings, musical instruments, utensils and paper. Indeed, bamboo sprouts are commonly eaten as a vegetable on the islands.

Your nose will identify the delicately fragrant yellow ginger (*Zingiber zerumbet*) before you see it. It has a light-yellow blossom that rises at the end of a narrow tube with olive-colored bracts. The leaves are a luxuriant green. You will also find giant torch ginger, red ginger, and shell ginger, with its shell-like flowers. The blossom of the torch ginger (*Phaeomeria magnifica*) is made up of many bracts shaped like a torch which spring up between 15-foot bamboo-like stalks with large, bright-green leaf blades. Ti (*Cordyline terminalis*), which is also quite abundant here, is often seen gracing the hips of hula dancers. Although some girls have switched to a plastic material, purists continue to slit ti leaves and fashion them into a skirt. This green leaf plant grows straight and tall (5–8 feet) with very shiny, thick and strong 2–3 foot blades. And there's more: banana, plumeria, ohia lehua, a variety of hibiscus (the Hawaii state flower), bird of paradise, gardenia, heliconia and azalea, to cite a partial list.

At about midpoint on the trail an overlook offers a spectacular view of Kahuna (lit., "the hidden one") Falls across the canyon on the north side. Farther up the canyon, however, is the showpiece of the park. Towering, 420-foot Akaka Falls slips over the ridge and falls lazily into Kolekole (lit., "raw, scarred") Stream, where it nourishes nature's lush gardens. Seeing it across the verdant canyon is a breathless moment in an exciting forest.

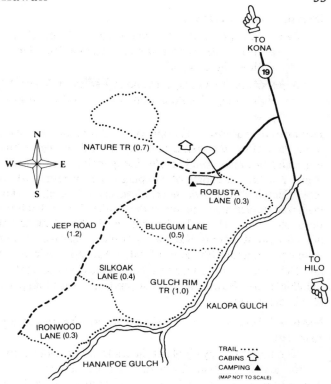

KALOPA STATE PARK

(Hiking Area No. 3)

Rating: Hardy Family.

Features: Native and introduced flora and fauna, camping, rental cabins.

Permission: None. (Camping and rental cabins from Division of State Parks — See Appendix).

Hiking Distance and Time: See individual hikes.

Driving Instructions:

> *From Hilo* (42 miles, 1 hour) north on Route 19, left
> past 39 mile marker at sign "Kalopa State Park".
> Follow signs to park.

> *From Kona* (61 miles, 1 1/2 hours) north on Route 19,
> right at sign "Kalopa State Park". Follow signs to
> park.

Introductory Notes: Kalopa (lit., "the tenant farmer")
State Park offers the visitor not only several enjoyable hiking trails but also comfortable, inexpensive accommodations. You have a choice of camping (free) or rental cabins
(see "Camping" and "Appendix" sections for details). In addition, trail guides are available at the trailheads that detail the
flora and fauna. The only shortcoming is the 90 inches of
annual rainfall making Kalopa a wet place year round. The
state park contains 100 acres of native Hawaiian rain forest
and 515 acres of introduced timber species. About 95% of
the 2500 native Hawaiian plants are endemic (found no place
else in the world).

**Nature Trail, 0.7 mile loop, 1 hour (trail rating:
family).**

The trail guide available at the trailhead provides information and facts about 24 posted stations along the trail.
You'll hear and see several native and introduced birds in the
forest. If you walk slowly and speak in a low voice, you're
more likely to hear them and see them closeup. I recommend
Hawaii's Birds, published by the Audubon Society, as a
companion guide to the park service pamphlet.

Any hike through a true Hawaiian rain forest is a delight. You will find a flat, clear, well-defined trail that is
suited for persons of all ages. Many native trees flourish in
the forest, but the ohia and kopiko dominate. Ohia
(*Metrodideros collina*) — post #15 — can grow to 80 feet
and, when in bloom, its lovely red, pompom-like flowers attract native birds, bees and butterflies. The flowers are a favorite of Madame Pele — the goddess of volcanoes — and it

is believed that if they are picked on the way to the mountains she will envelop the visitor in a cloud of mist. However, according to legend, the flowers may be picked on the way out of the forest without danger. Kopiko (*Psychotria hawaiiensis*) — also found at post #15 — forms a tall shrub or small tree and bears shiny oblong leaves with white flowers and tiny orange fruit. The kolea (*Myrsine lessertiana*) is my favorite tree in the forest — a native whose bright pink leaves in young stages gets your attention.

On my last visit here (1989) I saw numerous kalij (*Lophura leucomelana*) pheasants, hens and chicks, that were introduced to Hawaii from Nepal as a game bird, although they are protected in the park. It is a brown to black bird that has flourished here. You should also see the native elepaio (*Chasiempis sandwichensis*) a tiny (5 1/2 inches) bird with a loud whistle and chirping voice and a tail in right angle to its body. The body is white and brown with a white rump and dark tail. With luck, you may see the io, or Hawaiian hawk, the only large native bird in the forest. This endangered bird — only a few hundred in the world — with a dark body and streaked underparts, has been sighted in the forest.

Kalopa Gulch, 2.8 mile loop, 2 hours (trail rating: hardy family).

Before hiking, be certain to secure a trail guide found at a display in the parking lot near the cabins. It's an easy, delightful, loop hike for the whole family whose length can be shortened by following one of the tie trails — Bluegum Lane or Silkoak Lane — (see map). In 1989, the trail was clear, taped and posted.

You can begin your hike from several places, but I prefer starting where Robusta Lane joins the park road near the entrance, because the trail makes a gradual ascent along the gulch and then descends the jeep road at the end of the trek. The initial part of the trail passes through stately groves of eucalyptus and later silk oak, paperbark, ironwood, and tropical ash. Most of the these trees were planted by the Civilian Conservation Corps for erosion control in the 1930's.

Turn right (south) when Robusta Lane meets the Gulch Trail, which follows Kalopa Gulch for one mile. A short distance from the junction you will cross a small gulch and then meet the junction with Bluegum Lane. Along the trail, look for guava and thimbleberries that make a tasty snack. Guava (*Psidium guajava*) is a yellow, lemon-sized fruit that contains five times the amount of vitamin C than an orange. Thimbleberries (*Rubus rosaefolius*) are red and grow on a low bush with white flowers.

There are a few clearings which provide views into Kalopa Gulch from the trail, but the heavy growth prohibits a clear view. Before reaching Silkoak Lane, Kalopa Gulch swings left and the trail turns right and follows Hanaipoe Gulch until it meets Ironwood Lane just inside the park. The latter trail parallels pasture land until it joins the jeep road, which leads to the campground and the trailhead completing the hiking loop. Be careful walking the jeep road which is very slippery when wet.

Waipio Valley

WAIPIO/WAIMANU VALLEYS

(Hiking Area No. 4)

Rating: See individual hikes.

Features: Ancient Hawaiian settlement, native and introduced flora and fauna, wilderness camping, mountain apple, rose apple, swimming.

Permission: Call Davies Hamakua Sugar Co. for camping permit in Waipio Valley.

Hiking Distance and Time: See individual hikes.

Driving Instructions:

From Hilo (50 miles, 1 1/2 hours) north on Route 19, right on Route 240, to end of road at Waipio Lookout.

From Kona (65 miles, 2 hours) north on Route 190, right on Route 19, left on Route 240 to end of road at Waipio Lookout.

Introductory Notes: When outdoorsmen talk about hiking in Hawaii, they talk about the Kalalau Trail on Kauai, Kipahulu Valley on Maui, and Waipio and Waimanu on Hawaii. These are the ultimate in wilderness experiences in Hawaii.

Historically, Waipio and Waimanu Valleys were important centers of Hawaiian civilization, particularly Waipio (lit., "curved water"), the larger of the two. Fertile soil and ample water reportedly sustained as many as 50,000 people before the white man arrived. In the past, sugar cane, taro and bananas carpeted this six-mile valley.

In 1823 the first white men visited Waipio and found a thriving community. They were told that Waipio was once a favorite place of Hawaiian royalty; indeed, in 1780, Kamehameha is reported to have received there his war god, who singled him out as the future ruler of the islands. Later, Chinese immigrants came to Waipio, where they cultivated rice until the 1930's.

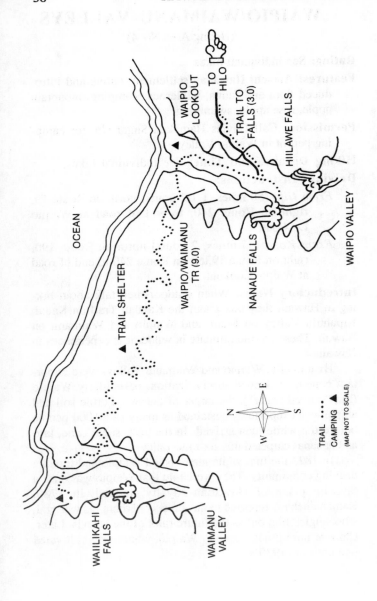

WAIPIO LOOKOUT

TO HILO

TRAIL TO FALLS (3.0)

HIILAWE FALLS

WAIPIO/WAIMANU TR (9.0)

NANAUE FALLS

WAIPIO VALLEY

OCEAN

TRAIL SHELTER

WAIILIKAHI FALLS

WAIMANU VALLEY

N
W — E
S

TRAIL ·····
CAMPING ▲
(MAP NOT TO SCALE)

Today Waipio's population has declined to a few dozen, but taro continues to be an important crop. Most of the farmers now live in towns on the plateau east of the valley, where electricity and other amenities are more readily available. Periodic tsunamis — tidal waves — and seasonal flooding have also discouraged permanent settlement. However, some people are returning to their ancestral homes upon retirement.

Guided tours of the valley are available in four-wheel drive vehicles. (It is impossible for a conventional car to negotiate the 26%-grade jeep road into the valley.) Arrangements can be made at the lookout when you arrive.

Waimanu (lit., "bird water") Valley is not as deep or as wide as Waipio. Nevertheless, this verdant valley once sustained a sizable population, as evidenced by the stone walls and terraces that remain.

Waipio Valley, 3 miles to falls, 2 hours, (trail rating: strenuous).

The trailhead is at the pavilion, a 900-foot high perch providing a striking panorama of Waipio Valley. Your eye can easily follow the trail to Waimanu, which snakes up the northwest bluff and then into the valley, where numerous waterfalls drop into Waipio from the Kohala Mountains.

Carry as much water as you can, since safe drinking water is not available. Water in the valley irrigates farms and serves cattle which graze in the Kohala Mountains. To be on the safe side, use purification tablets or boil your water.

The paved jeep road drops an abrupt mile into the valley to a junction where one road turns toward the beach and another into the valley. As you pause in your descent, look for yellow guava (*Psidium guajava*), some within reach of the road. The yellow, lemon-sized fruit is a tasty treat. The beach trail on the right passes some homesteads along Lalakea (a kind of shark) Fishpond on its way to the gray sand beach. It is common to find locals pushing and dragging their outriggers on Wailoa (lit., "long water") Stream to the open sea for a day of fishing. Note how they use the undulations of the surf to carry them over the rock-laden outlet, and conversely to beach their craft.

The thick, silky, green leaves of beach naupaka (*Scaevola frutescens*) greet the hiker on the beach. A common sight on most of Hawaii's beaches, the naupaka is a native variety that may grow to ten feet. It has a small, fragrant, white, half flower with small white berries following the flowers. There are several legends surrounding the naupaka flower. One claims that lovers were separated leaving half a flower, the young boy, blooming alone in the mountains, and the other half flower, the girl, blossoming alone on the beach. If a whole flower is found on either the beach naupaka or the mountain naupaka, it means the couple has been united. Another legend, recounts the story of the young prince who wished to marry a commoner. The king interviewed the young woman inquiring as to her family background and her virginity. The king was skeptical about the latter, so he charged his son and the girl to search the beach and the mountains for a whole flower on the naupaka, since it was the belief that a virgin could find a whole flower. Legend holds that the pair are still looking! Perhaps you can find one!

Camping in Waipio Valley is allowed on the east side of Waipio Stream by securing permission from the Davies Hamakua Sugar Co. Until 1977 the best and most popular campsites were on the west side of the stream among the trees that front the beach. This property is owned by the Bishop Museum of Honolulu, which closed the area to camping because of overcrowding. The museum has reported that it may allow camping in the future by permit only, limiting the number of campers. Ford Wailoa Stream where it enters the ocean and scout the beach for a picnic spot. The ironwood (*Casuarina equisetifolia*) trees that front the beach provide an umbrella from the hot sun and the rain. Also known as the Australian Pine, the ironwood has long, thin, drooping, dull-green needles whose droppings make a soft mat for a sleeping bag but are a fire danger. Approach ocean swimming with extreme caution: there is a strong surf with riptides.

To explore Waipio, return to the road junction and follow the road into the valley. You will be walking along the stream and toward Hiilawe (lit., "lift-carry") Falls. The falls may not be "turned on" since the stream that feeds it is used for irrigation and the water is frequently taken out above the falls. The road turns to cut across the valley. You pass the ruins of houses, destroyed by a devastating tidal wave and some newly constructed homes. The U.S. Peace Corps once trained near here, but flooding in November 1979 destroyed the abandoned buildings that had served for training recruits destined for Asia. After fording several streams, you approach Nanaue Falls on the north side of the valley.

There is no reliable trail to Nanaue Falls, but with a willingness to get wet, you can find your way to this delightful spot to picnic and to swim. When you are about one-fourth mile from the falls, you will reach a stream, a parking area, and a road that goes left. Follow the road until you reach the stream, cross it and follow the road which soon becomes a path leading to the base of the falls. Remember that annual flooding in Waipio destroys roads and changes the flow of the streams so that my description may not be applicable. But scout around and you're certain to find a way to the falls. Nanaue is really a number of falls, some with generous swimming holes at their bases. You have to climb around a bit to find the larger and deeper pools. Use CAUTION if you climb above the lowest fall. It is extremely wet and slippery.

There are numerous cardinals (*Richmondena cardinalis*) in the valley, which flush from the trees as you make your way. The male, with its all-red body and its pointed crest, and the black-and-red female were introduced from the mainland. Avocado, mountain apple, and yellow guava trees flourish in the valley, but respect the posted "kapu" (No Trespassing) signs. There are some trees as well as passion fruit vines along the road.

Waipio to Waimanu, 9 miles, 6 hours (trail rating: difficult).

The most difficult part of the trek to Waimanu is the ascent up the northwest pali (cliff) of Waipio Valley. The trail is easy to find about 100 yards from the beach in a forest at the base of the cliff. The switchbacks are steep but well-maintained. Obviously, this 1,200-foot climb is best approached in the cool of the morning.

From the ridge, the trail crosses 14 gulches to Waimanu; so it's up and down along the pali overlooking the rugged coastline. There are places where some rock slides make the going a bit difficult and slow, so be cautious. The trail is heavily forested and foliated and in some places overgrown. You're more likely to encounter horses than hikers on the trail since Waimanu is a popular pig hunting destination with locals. The trail shelter is nine gulches from Waipio Valley, or about two-thirds of the way to Waimanu. It is a satisfactory place to lunch or camp, although you may have to share it with other hikers.

As you swing out of Pukoa (lit., "coral head") Gulch, you get your first view of Waimanu Valley. The similarity between Waipio and Waimanu will surprise you. Although Waimanu is about half the size of Waipio, it contains a similar verdant valley and is bounded by precipitous cliffs. It's a sight to behold.

Waimanu Stream greets you on the floor of the valley after a steep descent. The best place to ford Waimanu Stream is about 25 feet above the spot where the stream joins the ocean. For drinking water, hike about 1/2 mile along the west side of the pali to an unnamed waterfall. Once again, either treat the water or boil it before drinking. There are numerous beach-front camping sites, so scout around and find one that suits you. As at Waipio, beware of ocean swimming because of the heavy surf with riptides.

There are no trails, since Waimanu, unlike Waipio, has long been abandoned. You will find stone walls and foundations as well as taro terraces remaining from when it was occupied.

The jewel of Waimanu is Waiilikahi (lit., "water with single surface") Falls, about 1 1/2 miles along the northwest pali of the valley. You must make your own trail to the falls. With luck, you'll arrive when the succulent mountain apples (*Eugenia malaccensis*) are ripe, usually in June. The fruit is a small red and pinkish apple with a thin waxy skin. Its white flesh is crisp and juicy. Interestingly, this was the only fruit on the islands before the Europeans introduced many others. Enjoy your lunch, your apples, and a swim in the large pool below the falls.

Petroglyphs

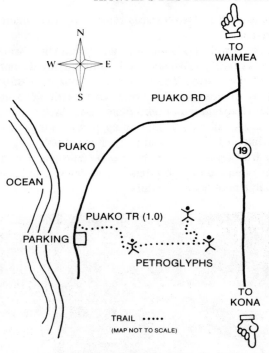

PUAKO PETROGLYPHS
(Hiking Area No. 5)

Rating: Hardy family.

Features: Hawaiian petroglyphs.

Permission: None.

Hiking Distance and Time: 1 mile, 1/2 hour.

Driving Instructions:

> *From Hilo* (75 miles, 2 hours) north on Route 19, right
> at Puako sign. Look for a homemade sign on the
> left near the end of the road, past house #153.

> *From Kona* (31 miles, 1 hour) north on Route 19, left
> at Puako sign. Look for a homemade sign on the
> left near the end of the road, past house #153.

Introductory Notes: Petroglyphs are drawings or carvings on rock made by prehistoric or primitive people. Those at Puako (lit., "sugar cane blossom"), of unknown origin, are some of the finest examples on the islands and probably the most numerous.

On the Trail: Look for a right-of-way passing between two houses and leading to a flat, open area. Arrows, painted on the surface of the lava, lead the way. The trail to the petroglyphs is well-defined, but the painted arrows on the lava detract from the experience. It is a hot and dusty trek through a kiawe forest to the first set of petroglyphs, about 600 feet from the road. All the drawings and carvings are on pahoehoe lava, which has a smooth or ropy surface. The second and third groups are outstanding examples and are a delight to puzzle out. While the meanings of some are obvious, others challenge the imagination. It is almost like browsing in a bookstore or in an antique store. You are irresistibly drawn to look and look and look. To some, petroglyphs are the art of past civilizations and have sophisticated meanings. To others, they are the casual scribbles of an illiterate people — just old graffiti. What do you think?

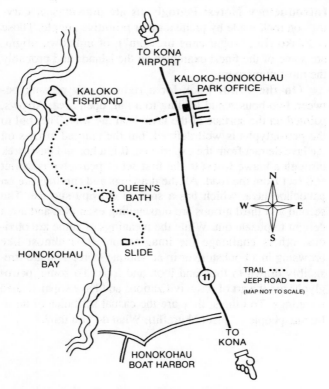

KALOKO-HONOKOHAU
NATIONAL HISTORICAL PARK
(Hiking Area No. 6)

Rating: Hardy Family.

Features: Queen's bath, holua (ancient slide), tidepools, swimming.

Permission: None.

Hiking Distance and Time: 2 miles, 1 hour.

Driving Instructions:

> *From Hilo* (100 miles, 2 1/2 hours) north on Route 19
> (toward Kailua-Kona) right on unpaved jeep road
> opposite Kona Trade Center to end.

> *From Kona* (4 miles, 15 minutes) north on Route 19,
> left on unpaved jeep road opposite Kona Trade
> Center to end.

Introductory Notes: Kaloko-Honokohau (Kaloko, lit.,
"the pond" and Honokohau, lit., "adze bay") National
Historic Park was established by Congress in 1978 to preserve native Hawaiian activities and culture and to demon-
strate historic land use patterns. According to Francis
Kuailani, acting superintendent, the park includes large
Hawaiian fishponds, house sites, a heiau, petroglyphs,
graves, and native and migrant water birds. He told me that
the park is not yet operational and only the northern portion,
Kaloko, is open to the public. He concluded that the government is hoping to purchase the land where Queen's bath
and the holua (slide) are located.

On the Trail: Rangers and park personnel who may
be present at the trailhead are the best source of information
regarding the preserve, and they love to "talk story." Facing
the ocean, Koloko Pond is on the right and the trail (jeep
road) goes left from in front of the ranger's trailer and follows the coastline. Morning glory flowers and beach naupaka (*Scaevola taccada*) dominate the trailside. The latter is a
spreading succulent shrub with white berries and small
white, half-flowers. One version of a Polynesian legend
holds that lovers were separated leaving a half flower of the
girl blossoming alone on the beach and her sweetheart
blooming alone in the mountains on the mountain naupaka,
a relative of the beach variety. If a whole flower is found, it
means that the lovers have been reunited.

After approximately one-fourth mile the trail turns away
from the beach, leaves park land, and requires the hiker to
duck — nearly crawl — under the interlocking branches of
the hau tree where it emerges onto a lava field. The hau

(*Hibiscus tiliaceus*) a true hibiscus, bears bright yellow flowers with a dark center. During the day the flower turns to apricot color and to deep red before it falls.

The trail across the lava field to Queen's Bath is relatively clear to follow as it turns in the direction of the highway and toward ten piles or mounds of lava rock that encircle the bath. It is believed that Queen Kaahumanu, King Kamehameha's favorite wife, bathed here while the king's guards stood atop the lava mounds to ensure her privacy. The bath is quite small, about 30-feet in circumference, is 3-feet deep in the deepest part, and is surprisingly cool. Although it does not appeal to me, you may choose to splash or to sit in the bath.

From Queen's bath the trail goes south, paralleling the beach on the right and the highway on the left and passes between two large lava piles, and turns left in the direction of the main road. The trail becomes obscure as you cross the aa (rough, clinkery type) lava. To reach the holua (sled) loop left around the brush and trees on your right and head for the higher lava flows to the southeast. Don't be discouraged if you cannot find the trail, but be CAUTIOUS walking on the rough underfooting. IT'S HAZARDOUS and razor sharp.

There is no mistaking the holua; it's a large, 15-by-100-foot, long incline that some believe was much longer when first constructed since it probably reached the water or pond enabling fun seekers to end their ride in the water. There are many known slides on the islands since contests were very popular with the royalty and with the people. The surface of the slide was usually covered with mud and pili grass to provide a smooth surface. The papa (sled) was constructed from wood. Some were 8–9 feet long with runners no more than six inches apart. In competition, sledders could reach 30 to 60 miles per hour, and some were known to ride the sled as a surfer rides a board.

Instead of retracing your steps to the trailhead, you could walk south a short distance to a dirt road that leads to the beach where you can find places to cool off, and then return to your transportation by following the coastline north.

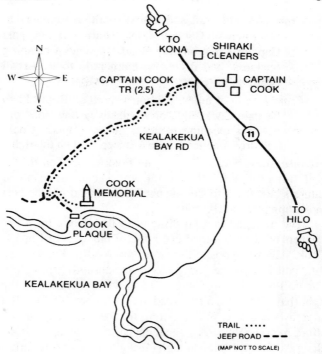

CAPTAIN COOK MONUMENT
(Hiking Area No. 7)

Rating: Strenuous.

Features: Site of Captain Cook's death, mango, papaya, avocado, guava, ancient Hawaiian burial caves, swimming, snorkeling.

Permission: None.

Hiking Distance and Time: 2.5 miles, 2 hours, 1400 foot loss.

Driving Instructions:

From Hilo (113 miles, 3 hours) south on Route 11 to
    the town of Captain Cook, sharp left just past
    Captain Cook on Bay Road, opposite a cleaning
    business, and drive one-tenth mile to jeep road
    (trail) on the right.

From Kona (14 miles, 1/2 hour) south on Route 11 to
    Captain Cook, right on Kealakekua Bay Road op-
    posite a cleaning business before Captain Cook,
    and drive one-tenth mile to a jeep road on the right.

Introductory Notes: This is my favorite hike on the island. It is a delightful 1/2-day trek with a generous supply of
nature's best fruits to suit anyone's palate, and it's the best
snorkeling place in Hawaii!

The trailhead is a bit difficult to find. Look for a dry
cleaners on the main road just north of the town of Captain
Cook. Almost opposite the store, the road to Kealakekua
(lit.,"pathway of the god") Bay drops abruptly to the left.
The trail itself begins about 500 feet down this road on the
right (bay) side. It is a jeep road, on the corner of which is a
large avocado tree. Find the trail, for the hike is worth the
effort. You should carry a small daypack to load up on fruits
along the first 1/2 mile. Mango (*Mangifera indica*) is particularly abundant in the fields and along the roadside. Look
under the trees for those that have fallen and are not too
badly bruised, or find a stick to shake some loose from the
trees. If you find a good long stick, leave it near the trail for
the next hiker.

One of the favorite fruits of visitors and locals is the
papaya (*Carica papaya*). The ripe yellow fruit varies in size,
but can be found growing in clusters at the bases of um-
brella-like leaves. In ancient Hawaii, the leaves were used as
soap and as a meat tenderizer, and the seeds were used medic-
inally. You will find numerous papaya trees along the roadside.

As if this weren't enough, there are also some avocado
(*Persea americana*) trees. Their fruit tends to be too watery
for some people's taste, but perhaps not for yours.

On The Trail: From the trailhead, the trail/jeep road descends about 50 yards to where the road turns right into private property, and your trail goes left into tall — 6 to 8 foot — grass. From here you must push your way through the grass as best you can. In July, 1989, the trail was not marked or posted and the trail was indistinguishable. On the other hand the trail goes straight to the coast, paralleling a stone wall on the left. Go slowly and carefully and don't be discouraged. The trail is heavily overgrown for the first mile, but then opens as you near the coast. Here, the terrain becomes more arid, sustaining only low scrub. You have your first view of the coast, a portion of Kealakekua Bay, and your destination, although the Cook Memorial is not visible. Bear left toward the beach at the first junction in the road. From here, go straight on to the beach. When you reach the beach, follow the coast to the left for a few hundred feet to the memorial. You needn't be concerned about the tourist boats' disturbing your visit, for the passengers do not disembark. The boats simply make a pass by the memorial and anchor in the bay for people who wish to snorkel for a short time. You will find that snorkeling is outstanding here.

There are numerous caves beyond the monument and along the walls of the cliff. If you choose to explore, do not disturb any interesting finds. Local people are seeking to preserve what may be ancient Hawaiian burial grounds.

Captain Cook was killed here at water's edge on February 14, 1779 by the Hawaiians. Cook, an English captain in the employ of the Earl of Sandwich, was in search of a northwest passage when he sighted and landed on the Hawaiian Islands (he named them the Sandwich Islands after his benefactor) in 1778 where he supplied his ships. He was thought to be the god Lono who was revered by the natives, so he and his men were treated well. Cook returned a year later, January, 1779, and anchored in Kealakekua Bay where he was warmly greeted again by thousands (estimates range from 30,000 to 50,000 Hawaiians). For a month the haoles (foreigners) were given a bounty of food and supplies to a point that the native people were deprived. This angered some of the people and Cook wisely left on February 4. He was compelled to return a week later since one of his ships was in need of repair and since storms on the north part of the island forced him to seek calmer waters. He again anchored in Kealakekua Bay on February 11. The Hawaiians, who on Cook's previous visit had "borrowed" or "used" or "stolen" items from the ship, "took" a cutter (small boat) from one of the ships. When the captain learned of the matter, he was enraged and with a number of armed marines when to shore to retrieve the boat. Meanwhile, the natives armed themselves and the opposing forces met on the beach. A fight resulted between a few natives and marines, and as Cook turned his back to the Hawaiians (some believe he tried to stop his men), he was struck in the head and he fell. Daggers were drawn and Cook was repeatedly stabbed by numerous natives. The result was that Cook and four marines were killed as well as an indeterminate number of natives. Some historians believe that the Hawaiians engaged in cannibalism, but there is little evidence of this occurring. It does seem certain that the natives stripped his flesh from the bones (a traditional Hawaiian practice reserved for kings) and hid the bones where they could not be found. An unfortunate end for all.

TO KONA

TO HILO

11

TRAIL (3.0)

OCEAN

N

W E

S

TRAIL • • • •
(MAP NOT TO SCALE)

SOUTH POINT

SOUTH POINT
(Hiking Area No. 8)

Rating: Hardy Family.

Features: Green-sand beach, swimming, beachcombing.

Permission: None.

Hiking Distance and Time: 3 miles, 1 1/2 hour.

Driving Instructions:

From Hilo (80 miles, 2 hours) south on Route 11, left at sign "South Point" to end (bear left at junction near the coast) to small boat harbor.

From Kona (64 miles, 1 1/2 hours) south on Route 11, right at sign "South Point" then as above.

Introductory Notes: Ke Lae or South Point is the southernmost point in the United States, the site of one of the oldest known Hawaiian settlements (about A.D.750) and a place to relax on a green sand beach. You should carry an ice chest with drinks, water, and food in your car since there are no services available.

The 11-mile, narrow, bumpy road off Route 11 to South Point offers noteworthy points of interest. The whirring sound of numerous wind generators — too many to count — intrudes on the solitude about midpoint along the road.

Turn right at the junction, just before reaching the coastline, and you'll reach an automated lighthouse at road's end. Kalalea (lit., "prominent") Heiau, a pre-Christian place of worship, stands here. Even today, some fishermen make offerings of food to the mana (spirit). The heiau is believed to hold the shark god over which prayers are repeated.

Bear left at the junction and you are one mile from a small boat harbor and the trailhead. You will have passed through an abandoned WWII military base and airport before reaching the starting point.

On the Trail: Your trail is a jeep road that follows the rugged coastline for many miles. You'll find numerous jeep roads that crisscross here. Some lead to the shoreline where you're likely to find locals casting for a meal while others lead upcountry to grazing land. Choose the road paralleling the coast that provides the best underfooting although you may opt to follow the beach in hopes of finding "treasure" (junk?) swept ashore from passing or shipwrecked ships. In any event the variety of "stuff" here is a beachcombers delight.

The area is dominated by low grass so that your view upland and along the coast is unobstructed. The only distractions here are the sound of the ocean and the sight of grasshoppers leaping from the ground usually a footstep away. At midpoint, your destination is visible. Look for a black-sand promontory rising above water's edge about one and one-half mile distant. The green sand beach is at the base of the hill.

There is no mistaking the green sand beach. Yes, it is most definitely green. The sand is largely olivine crystals, a semiprecious stone. Use CAUTION when you descend to the beach and if you swim in the water here. It's a choice spot to lunch, swim and relax.

KAUAI

KAUAI—TRAILHEADS, CAMPING

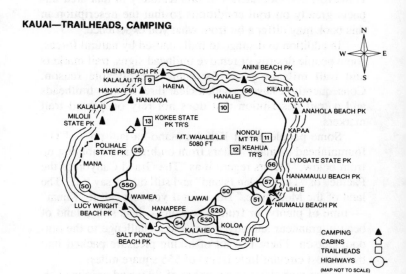

The Island

Kauai offers more natural beauty than most people can absorb. Island trails lead to magnificent waterfalls, to breathtaking vistas into Kauai's canyonlands and to the wilderness area along the Na Pali Coast. No one I have ever known has been disappointed by this enchanted land.

It is important to remember, however, that natural and man-made forces have had and continue to have a dramatic impact on Hawaii's topography. Periodic volcanic eruptions, 400-plus inches of rain in several places, earthquakes, the influx of new residents, and the increasing numbers of visitors affect trail conditions. A trail that was cleared and brushed and in good condition can become overgrown after a few weeks of heavy rain, particularly if it is not heavily traveled. For example, the trails in the Kokee/Waimea area were in very good condition in the summer of 1988. However, 200–500 inches of rain annually in that area impacts greatly on trail conditions so that the description in this book may differ a bit from what you experience.

In addition to damage to trails caused by natural forces, some people destroy or remove trailhead signs, trail markers and trail mileage posts for some inexplicable reason. Consequently, I have provided clear directions to trailheads and a trail description that does not rely on posted trail markers.

Some people call it Kauai-a-mano-ka-lani-po — "The fountainhead of many waters from on high and bubbling up from below." Others regard it as "The Grand Canyon of the Pacific" or "The Garden Island" and still others say it is "The land of the Menehune." But even if you just call it "Kauai" — time of plenty, or fruitful season — it is still a land of beauty, grandeur and adventure, and a challenge to the outdoorsperson. There is a lot of hiking pleasure packed into this almost circular little island of 555 square miles.

Kauai lays claim to a number of firsts and unique characteristics. It is the oldest island in the Hawaiian Islands, it is the northern most inhabited island in the chain, and it was the first island visited by Captain Cook — though that is a rather dubious distinction. Still other things of local pride include Mt. Waialeale, the wettest spot on earth; the only place on earth where the iliau, a rare and unique plant is to be found; and the home of the legendary Menehune, a race of pygmies who were short, industrious, strong, and highly skilled workers in stone.

Not unlike the neighboring islands, tourism on Kauai with its 47,000 inhabitants has grown to the point that over 1,000,000 people annually visit it. Kauai lies 102 air miles northwest of Honolulu — about a 20-minute flight. Most visitors to Kauai are seeking its solitude and slower pace of life, and many find these in the verdant valleys of the remote Na Pali coast and in the lush canyonlands of Waimea.

Conveniently, the State of Hawaii and the County of Kauai have established miles of trails and jeep roads into remote areas which will reveal some of the island's secrets.

Lihue is the county seat (Kauai is a county). There is no public transportation on the island. At present, hitchhiking is allowed, although the county council raises the issue from time to time, and may prohibit it in the future. Check with the information booth at the airport regarding the law. If you hitchhike, be patient, for rides are hard to come by in the outlying areas.

Camping and Cabins

Camping out on Kauai will add another dimension to your visit. Campgrounds on Kauai range from adequate to good, contain most of the amenities, and are either free or inexpensive. The accompanying map locates the state and county campgrounds. A third jurisdiction, the Division of Forestry, also provides a number of campgrounds, camping shelters, and camping areas, which are noted on individual maps throughout the book. (See Appendix for addresses). A word about each kind of campground should be helpful.

First, the Hawaii state parks at Kokee and Polihale offer excellent facilities and are free. Camping is limited to five days per 30-day period for each campground, and is by permit only, obtained through the Department of Land & Natural Resources, Division of State Parks. The Division of State Parks also regulates camping and hiking along the Na Pali Coast: Hanakapiai, Hanakoa and Kalalau — the three major valleys along the wilderness trail. Camping permits are required and may be obtained from the Division of State Parks. Camping is limited to five nights total along the Na Pali Coast in any 30-day period. Hanakapiai and Hanakoa are limited to one night each in that period. Hiking permits are required beyond Hanakapiai Valley, even for day hiking. When writing for reservations for all of the state parks, include the dates desired, the park, the number of persons and their names. The state cabins at Kokee are operated by a concessionaire (see Hiking Area No. 13 for details and reservation information).

Secondly, the County of Kauai has numerous campgrounds and beach parks around the island. County camping costs $3 per adult per day (no cost to Hawaii residents). Persons under 18 are free if accompanied by an adult. Permits are not issued to persons under 18. Camping permits are issued for up to seven days at each campsite. A total of sixty (60) camping days per year is allowed. For reservations, write Department of Parks and Recreation, County of Kauai. Include your name, address, campground desired, dates, and the number of persons in your party, with names and ages. DO NOT forward fees. Payment and permit must be issued in person at the office (M–F, 7:45–4:30) or after hours nearby at the police station.

Last, the Hawaii State Division of Forestry maintains a number of trailside camping areas in the forest reserve, which are identified on the individual maps preceding the text of each hiking area. Camping is limited to three nights within a 30-day period, but this regulation is not regularly enforced. Neither permits nor reservations are necessary. Registration is by sign-in at the trailhead upon entering and leaving a forest-reserve area. All the facilities are primitive and lacking in amenities, but to some people that is their best feature.

Campers are well advised to bring their own equipment because locally it is expensive. For rentals on the island, I recommend Hanalei Camping & Backpacking with a store in Hanalei and Kekaha. Their stores are well-stocked with rentals and a complete line of hiking and backpacking needs, and their staff is well-informed and helpful.

Camping in Hawaii has always been an enjoyable and inexpensive way to experience the Islands. Recently, however, some campers have been beaten and a few have been killed. Most of the beatings have been committed by local men, according to the victims. Most of the assaults have taken place at campgrounds that were close to cities or towns where locals congregate. There has been little or no problem in remote and wilderness areas. The best advice is to avoid camping in areas readily accessible to locals and to avoid contact with groups of people. I recommend Kokee State Park, Haena Beach Park and Salt Pond Beach Park. The latter is one of the best beach camping places in Hawaii.

Addresses for all agencies are in the Appendix.

Hiking

With the exceptions of the Kalalau Trail and some of the trails in the Kokee/Waimea hiking area, hiking on Kauai does not require any special equipment or skill. Many places are readily accessible even to the tenderfoot and to the people not inclined to hike much. Few people dispute that the Kalalau Trail is an outstanding outdoor experience requiring good physical condition and backpacking equipment. However, the first two miles of the trail to Hanakapiai Valley and beach can be made by most people of any age who are willing to sweat a bit. Even so, wear good boots or tennis shoes and carry. water.

If time allows, spend at least three days at Kokee State Park. The housekeeping cabins and the campground are comfortable, and the outstanding hiking experiences include hikes to suit everyone's interest and ability.

Water is available from streams in many areas, but it should be boiled or treated before drinking. Cattle, pigs and goats usually share the stream water with you. I suggest you begin each hike with one quart of water per person. Due to the heavy rainfall on Kauai, dry firewood is rare, so a small, light, reliable backpacking stove is a convenience and a comfort. A hot cup of tea, coffee or soup is invigorating while waiting out a passing storm, and a hot breakfast is desirable after a wet night. Lastly, most hikers find shorts or cutoffs adequate on most trails. However, along the Kalalau Trail some people shed all clothing for either physical or psychological reasons — I have not decided which.

KALALAU TRAIL
(Hiking Area No. 9)

Rating: Difficult.

Features: Wilderness area, camping, coastal views, fruits, waterfalls, swimming, historical sites.

Permission: Camping permits are required for Hanakapiai, Hanakoa and Kalalau valleys. Permits for camping must be obtained from the Division of State Parks (see Camping section in the INTRODUCTION for details and Appendix for addresses).

Hiking Distance and Time: 10.8 miles, day.

Driving Instructions:

From Lihue 38 miles, 1 hour north on Route 56 to road's end.

Introductory Notes: When people talk about hiking on Kauai, they talk about visiting the uninhabited valleys of the Na Pali (the cliffs) Coast as evidenced by the comments registered by hikers on the sign-in at the trailhead. "Fantastic," "Incredible," "Paradise," "The most beautiful place in the world," are just a few of the expressions noted. Kalalau ("the straying") trail to the end of the beach (10.8 miles) is the most exciting hike on the island.

Few who have hiked the Kalalau Trail will deny its grandeur and its captivating allure. Cliffs rise precipitously above the blue-green water and the rugged, rocky north shore of Kauai. The valleys of the Na Pali Coast are accessible only by foot or by boat, and only during the summer when the tides expose a generous sandy beach, which is ripped away each year by winter storms. In the summer of 1990, the trail was in good condition.

Hiking the entire trail to Kalalau requires backpacking equipment for a comfortable, safe trip. Sound hiking boots are essential, since a good deal of your hiking is alternately on soft cinders and ash and rocks along the precipitous coast and on rocky trails in the valleys. A strong, waterproof tent

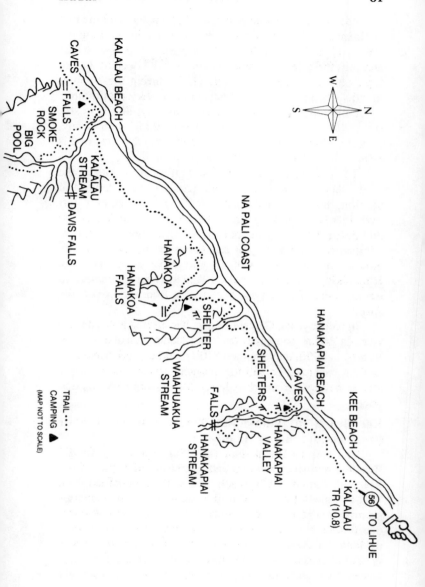

CAVES

≡ FALLS

SMOKE
ROCK
BIG
POOL

KALAU BEACH

KALAU
STREAM

≠ DAVIS FALLS

NA PALI COAST

HANAKOA

HANAKOA
FALLS

≡

⛺ SHELTER

WAIAHUAKUA
STREAM

HANAKAPIAI BEACH

SHELTERS

CAVES

⛺ FALLS ≠

HANAKAPIAI
VALLEY

HANAKAPIAI
STREAM

KEE BEACH

56 TO LIHUE

KALAU
TR (10.8)

TRAIL ·····
CAMPING ▲
(MAP NOT TO SCALE)

is needed to stand up under the wind at Kalalau and the rain at Hanakoa. Although fresh water is available all along the trail, you should boil the water or purify it; people, goats and pigs are using the same stream. A light sleeping bag or light blanket is adequate, particularly during the summer months when the nighttime temperature is very comfortable. Little clothing is necessary during the day, and it is still somewhat common to find both sexes hiking without any. A backpacking stove is recommended since dry firewood is difficult to find and tree cutting is not permitted.

The trailhead for the Kalalau Trail is at the end of the road, where you will find several parking areas. A word of caution, however, may save some grief: vehicles left overnight in the parking places are frequently vandalized, so do not leave anything in your car. Furthermore, if rental car companies learn that you are backpacking they usually won't rent to you even if you have a reservation. Hitchhiking, which is legal on Kauai, is an alternative to renting a car. Taxi service is available from the Princeville Airport.

In recent years, Captain Zodiac has offered a shuttle service via Zodiac boats between the Hanalei area and Kalalau Valley. In 1990, they charged $100 round trip per person including backpack or $55 for one-way service. Look in the tourist newspaper and brochures for current services and prices.

Kee Beach to Hanakapiai Beach, 2 miles, 1 hour (trail rating: hardy family).

The trek to Hanakapiai (lit., "bay sprinkling food") Beach is one steep mile up and one steep mile down from Kee (lit., "avoidance") Beach on a wide, maintained trail. This is a much frequented trail because tourist publications promise a verdant valley resplendent with native and introduced flora. No one is disappointed. Particularly abundant is the hala (*Pandanus tectorius*), an indigenous tree that grows in coastal areas. It is sometimes called "tourist pineapple," since the fruit resembles a pineapple and is jokingly identified as such by locals for tourists. Humor aside, the hala has been a valuable resource, the hollow trunk of the female tree being used as a pipe for drainage between taro patches. The leaves have commercial value being used for weaving many items such as baskets, mats and hats — hats being particularly popular with tourists. In the past, the fruit was eaten in times of famine and was used to make colorful necklaces. When the sections of the fruit were dried, they were used as brushes.

The first half mile up the cliff provides views at a couple of points back to Kee Beach and Haena ("wilderness") reefs. This part of the trail is usually shady because of the large trees and cool because of the trade winds and periodic rain showers. One source of shade is the large kukui (*Aleurites moluccana*) tree from which a beautiful and popular lei is made. To make a lei, each nut must be sanded, filed and polished to a brilliant luster that is acquired from its own oil. Until the advent of electricity, kukui-nut oil was burned for light. Nicknamed the "candlenut tree" its trunk was shaped into canoes by early Hawaiians.

The trail leads up and down from the 1/2 to the 1 1/4-mile marker. With any luck you may find some sweet guava (*Psidium guajava*), a small yellow, lemon-sized fruit that contains five times more vitamin C than an orange. Before eating one, break it open and check for worms. They are tiny and are a little hard to see but are common in wild guava.

Near the 1-mile marker, look for a small springlet that flows year round and provides a welcomed face-splashing. At the 1 1/2-mile marker, you'll have your first view of Hanakapiai Beach below, with its generous beach (during the summer months) and its crashing surf. Look for wild orchids with their delicate purplish flowers, thriving along the banks of the trail.

As you descend to the beach, several warning signs caution visitors not to swim in the ocean because of the heavy surf and the presence of riptides and strong currents. Several drownings occur here in spite of the posted admonition.

From across the stream, you can hike the trail into the valley and to the falls. I suggest a hike to the falls in the afternoon when it is more likely to be warm and sunny in the valley.

If you want to stay overnight at Hanakapiai Beach, you have a choice of campsites. There are numerous campsites on the west side of the stream beginning on the bluff overlooking the beach and extending into the valley. Some daring campers sleep in the cave located in the cliff that drops to the beach. It's too close to the ocean for me.

Hanakapiai Valley Trail, 2 miles, 1 1/2 hours (trail rating: strenuous).

The Hanakapiai Valley Trail follows the stream and passes through a rain forest resplendent with native flora. The beginning of the trail on the west side of the valley contains some of the largest mango (*Mangifera indica*) trees anywhere. One grove surrounding the remains of a coffee mill contains a tree trunk that is 23 feet in circumference. Obviously, it makes a shady sheltered campsite. The mango tree is not native to Hawaii, but its many varieties have done well there, and are popular with locals and tourists. However, the trees in this valley do not bear as well as those in drier areas because of a fungus that kills the blossoms in wet areas. Many people regard the mango fruit as second to none in taste and appearance.

The hike to the falls is a must not only because the falls are spectacular, but also because much serenity and enchantment are to be found in the valley. The first 1/4-mile is an easy trail that snakes along the stream. "Okolehau" ("okole" is translated "anus" or "buttocks"; and "hau" can mean "cool.") is the name of a Division of Forestry trail-crew shelter near the coffee mill which you may use when it is not occupied by a trail crew.

You will make at least three stream crossings. The trail is always easy to find because the valley is so narrow. However, be alert for unstable places caused by yearly heavy rains and flooding. The last 1/2-mile is the most difficult part, but perhaps the most enchanting, with inviting pools and verdant growth. The trail is cut along the walls of the canyon in a number of places. Caution is well-advised.

Although the pool at the base of the falls is inviting, caution is again advised for there is danger from falling rocks from the cliffs and the ledge above the falls. Hanakapiai Falls cascades and falls about 300 feet in the back of a natural amphitheater. You don't need to be told to swim and enjoy the pools and the surrounding area. You will find safe pools away from falling rocks.

Hanakapiai to Hanakoa, 4 miles, 2 1/2 hours (trail rating: strenuous).

Serious hiking on the trail to Kalalau begins at this point as the trail climbs out of Hanakapiai Valley on a series of switchbacks for one mile. This is the most difficult section of the entire 11-mile trek. Hiking here in the morning means that the sun will be at your back and, with the trade wind, it should be relatively cool. The trail does not drop to sea level again until Kalalau Beach, some nine miles along the cliffs.

There are two small valleys before Hanakoa. The first is Hoolulu (lit., "to lie in sheltered waters"), which is first viewed from a cut in the mountain at the 3 1/4-mile marker. From here you descend to cross the valley and climb the opposite side. Hoolulu is thickly foliated with native and introduced plants that are typical of most valleys on the island. Ti, guava, morning glory, mountain orchids, and different kinds of ferns can be identified along with the larger kukui, koa and hala trees. Be careful at points where the trail narrows along a precipitous slope.

Waiahuakua Valley, at the 4 1/4-mile marker, is broader than Hoolulu. In June–August, you are likely to find delicious ohia ai (*Eugenia malaccensis*), or mountain apples, growing along the trail. Abundant in Waiahuakua, these trees have smooth, dark green leaves and some attain a height of 50 feet. The fruit is a small red or pinkish apple with a thin, waxen skin, while the meat is flesh-white, crisp and juicy, with a large brown seed in the center — a very tasty repast for those lucky enough to find some. Additionally, the valley abounds in coffee, ti, guava, kukui, and mango.

At the 5 3/4-mile marker, you will get your first view of Hanakoa (lit., "bay of koa trees or of warriors") Valley which is a broad-terraced valley that was once cultivated by Hawaiians. Many of the terraced areas provide relatively sheltered camping sites. In addition, "Mango Shelter" has a roof-and-table and "Hanakoa Shack," a short distance away, is a Division of Forestry trail-crew shelter that is open to hikers when not in use by crews. In 1990, the "shack" was so dilapidated that it was of little value as a shelter. Both are located along the trail a short distance into the valley. Camping in Hanakoa is quite an experience since it receives frequent rains, and as soon as you dry off, it rains again. However, the afternoon can be warm and sunny, just perfect for a swim in one of the many pools in the stream and a sun bath on the large, warm rocks along the bank. These are a favorite of nude sun worshippers.

To Hanakoa Falls, 0.4 mile, 1/4 hour.

The trail (posted in 1990) begins between the stream crossing and the 6 1/2-mile marker and passes a wilderness campsite and terraced areas once used by the Hawaiians for growing taro from which the staple food poi is produced. The falls cascade down the pali in a breathtaking setting. If you plan to camp in Hanakoa, you should be prepared for a lot of rain and humidity. To compensate, you will have solitude and a private swimming pool if you camp away from where the trail crosses the stream.

Hanakoa to Kalalau Beach, 4.8 miles, 3 hours (trail rating: strenuous).

Your physical condition and your hiking skill will be tested on this portion of the hike. Not only is most of the hiking on switchbacks that alternate up and down along a very precipitous cliff, but also the danger is increased by a number of slides along the trail. Another hazard is the hot afternoon sun unless you begin hiking early. However, the views of the northwest coastline are absolutely breathtaking and staggeringly beautiful. It is difficult to think of another view in the world that compares.

At the 6 1/2-mile marker, you enter land that until 1975 was part of the Makaweli (lit., "fearful features") cattle ranch owned by the Robinson Family who also own the island of Niihau off the coast of Kauai. The area becomes increasingly dry as you continue west, and only the smaller more arid types of vegetation survive, like sisal and lantana. Lantana (*Lantana camara*) is a popular flower that blossoms almost continuously. Its flowers vary in color from yellow to orange to pink to red; infrequently, they are white with a yellow center. If you hike in the early morning or late afternoon you're likely to frighten feral goats foraging near the trail and near some of the small streams along the trail.

Although there are only a few trail-mileage markers over the rest of the route, there is no chance of getting lost. The trail is over open land and is visible ahead. There are at least five reliable sources of water between Hanakoa and Kalalau. The admonition to treat or boil the water applies.

Pohakuao (lit., "day stone") is the last small valley before Kalalau. As you ascend the west side of Pohakuao along a pali with sparse foliage and reddish earth, you reach Red Hill, as it is known to locals, from which you get your first view of Kalalau, a welcome sight after a difficult three miles from Hanakoa. There is no mistaking Kalalau, for it is a large, broad valley some two miles wide and three miles long. From the ridge, a precipitous snake-like trail drops abruptly to Kalalau Stream where rushing water and cool pools await the weary hiker.

Camping is allowed only on the beach, in the trees fronting the beach and in the caves at the far end of the beach. Try to find a spot that will shelter you from the strong winds and the hot daytime sun. Some campers find shelter in the low scrub along the beach during the day and

then sleep on the beach during the cool and usually wind-free
nights. Lantana and common guava are particularly abundant
along the trail in the beach area. You should easily find
some ripe guava to add to your meals. Don't drink the
stream water until you treat or boil the water. The falls at
the end of the beach by the caves is your best bet for safe
water although you should treat or boil the water also.

The water from the falls also serves the feral goats that
you will undoubtedly see in the morning and at dusk when
they visit to refresh themselves. Most of the campers take a
daily shower under the falls.

Kalalau abounds in a variety of life. Beach naupaka
(*Scaevola frutescens*), with small, fragrant, white flowers,
can be found near the beach, mixed with the low sisal and
lantana. Hala, ti, ferns, bamboo, bananas, mango, kukui,
monkeypod and many other species of flora can be identified.
Rock terraces where Hawaiians planted taro as late as the
1920s are also common.

Some very daring people attempt to wade and swim
around the point where the beach ends on the west side in an
effort to visit Honopu (lit., "conch bay") Valley, the so-
called "Valley of the Lost Tribe" — a reference to the legendary little people named Mu who once lived there. The
swim around the point is very risky due to the strong current
and undertow in the ocean. Occasionally, the tide is
sufficiently low so that it is possible to walk to Honopu.

Locals and visitors enjoy speculating about the exploits
and the hideouts of Kalalau's most famous citizen, Koolau.
Commonly called "Koolau the Leper," this native Hawaiian
was born in Kekaha in 1862. Three years after showing
signs of leprosy, at the age of 27, Koolau and the other
lepers of Kauai were ordered to the leper colony on Molokai,
and were promised that their wives and children could ac-
company them. When the ship sailed without his wife and
child, Koolau, realized he had been tricked, dove overboard
and swam ashore. Together with his wife and child he made
the perilous descent into Kalalau Valley to join other lepers

who sought to escape deportation. A year later, local authorities decided to round up the lepers, all of whom agreed to go
to Molokai, except Koolau. A sheriff's posse exchanged fire
with Koolau, who shot and killed a deputy. Martial law was
declared, and a detachment of the national guard was sent
from Honolulu with orders to get their man dead or alive. A
small cannon was mounted near the site where Koolau was
thought to be hiding. In the ensuing "battle" Koolau shot
two guardsmen and one accidentally shot and killed himself
fleeing the leper. The remaining guardsmen fled from the
valley to the beach. In the morning they blasted Koolau's
hideout with their cannon. Believing him dead, the guardsmen left the valley. But Koolau had moved his family the
night before the cannonading, and they lived in the valley for
about five more years, always fearful that the guard was still
looking for him. They hid during the day and hunted for food
at night. Tragically, their son developed signs of leprosy and
soon died; a year later, the dread disease claimed Koolau.
Piilani, his wife, buried her husband in the valley that had
become their home along with his gun which had enabled
them to be together to the end.

To some, Koolau is a folk hero who received unfair
treatment by the government. Indeed, locals claim that
Koolau frequently left his valley hideout to visit friends and
relatives on Kauai. Whatever the facts, it makes for an interesting story and campfire conversation.

Kalalau Beach to Big Pool, 2 miles, 1 1/2 hour.
The trail into the valley begins on the west side of
Kalalau Stream at the marked trailhead. Before heading into
the valley, hike to the top of the knoll above the beach, also
on the west side of the stream. The remains of a heiau — a
pre-Christian place of worship — lie between the knoll and
the beach and are clearly identifiable from this vantage point.
Little is known about this nameless heiau. Remember that
such places are still revered by many people, and a rock
wrapped in a ti leaf and left on a heiau site is believed to
protect the traveler.

From the trailhead, the trail parallels the stream for a short distance and then ascends an eroded rise. From here the trail alternately passes open and forested areas. In the wooded areas look for oranges, mango, common guava and rose apple. Each can be found in the valley and can supplement a backpacker's diet. At the one-mile point Smoke Rock is a convenient place to pause in an open area from which the entire valley can be viewed. This is the place where the valley marijuana growers and residents used to meet to smoke and to talk stories. The rest of the trail to Big Pool is under the shade of giant mango and rose apple trees. Before reaching Big Pool, a side stream crossing must be made. Heading into the valley, the next stream crossing is Kalalau Stream. Big Pool, a short distance from this crossing is easily identified. Two room-sized pools are separated by a natural water slide which is a joy to slip down into the cool water below. It's a delightful place to enjoy the sights and smells of Kalalau, Kauai's most precious treasure.

Kalalau Valley

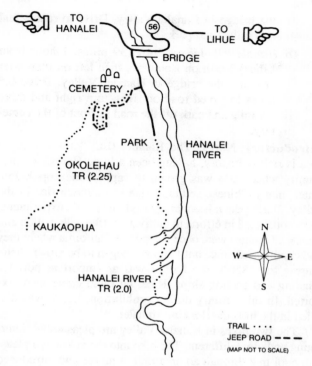

HANALEI RIVER

(Hiking Area No. 10)

Rating: See individual hikes.

Features: Swimming, bamboo forest, fruit, views, historical sites.

Permission: None.

Hiking Distance and Time: See individual hikes.

Driving Instructions:

> *To Hanalei River Trail* (31 miles, 1 hour from Lihue)
> North on Route 56, then left on road after crossing

the bridge in Hanalei Valley. Drive to road's end
(1.9 miles) and park.

To Hanalei/Okolehau Trail (30 miles, 1 hour from
Lihue) North on Route 56, then left on road after
crossing the bridge in Hanalei Valley. Drive 0.5
miles to paved road on right, turn right and drive
0.1 mile and park off the road in front of the cemetery.

Introductory Notes: The Hanalei (lit., "crescent bay")
area is rich in history, having been a large Hawaiian community where taro was grown to support the population.
Later, many Chinese settlers came to cultivate rice in the
valley. During the missionary period, numerous experiments
were conducted in efforts to cultivate coffee, silk, cotton and
oranges. Oranges were once shipped to California where they
had commercial value until oranges began to be grown there.
During the 1850's, the harbor was an important port for
whaling and trading ships. Rice, taro and cattle were exported. In this century during prohibition, liquor was distilled in the hills overlooking Hanalei.

The two hikes in Hanalei Valley are pleasurable, interesting and quite different. The hike into the valley is a pleasant, cool trek through an area rich in native and introduced
plants with a generous variety of fruits to enjoy. It is possible to traverse the two miles only if the water level in the
river is sufficiently low to allow crossing. DO NOT attempt
to cross the river during times of high water or when rain is
falling in the upper river valley.

The Hanalei/Okolehau Trail is much different. It ascends
about 1,300 feet along a ridge line to several vista points
from which picturesque views of Hanalei and the coastline
are possible. It is a hot, strenuous hike but worth every foot
of effort.

Hanalei River Trail, 2 miles, 1 hour, (hiking rating: hardy family).

As you approach the trailhead, you are passing through taro fields that have been cultivated for many years. The route follows a jeep road used by hunters. In the early morning it is common to meet pig hunters with their dogs hunting the small pig which is a popular sport with locals. A number of large mango trees border the road. Also look for oranges, guavas and delicious pomelo (*Citrus maxima*) trees which yield a large cantaloupe-sized fruit that has the aroma and taste of both grapefruit and orange. Both locals and tourists seek out these tasty treats, so the pickings are sometimes lean. Additionally, you will find a variety of flowers, particularly the small, delicate, purple mountain orchid and the aromatic ginger. Yellow ginger (*Zingiber zerumbet*) is prolific along the road, and is easy to identify by the delicately fragrant, light yellow blossom that rises at the end of a narrow tube just behind an olive-colored bract. The leaves are a luxuriant green.

Bear to the left off the end of the road, pass through a gate in the fence and follow the trail to the first of two streams that enter the river. A small but magnificent bamboo forest surrounds you, and a cacophony of sounds is heard when the wind rushes through the dense growth. Bamboo has long been an important product on the Islands, having been used for fuel, furniture, musical instruments, utensils, building material and paper. And bamboo sprouts are commonly eaten on the Islands as a vegetable.

Shortly, you cross another stream and go through another bamboo forest with the river a short distance beyond. At the 1 1/2-mile point it is necessary to ford the river. If the water level is high in the river or if it is rainy in the back of the valley, it is best not to proceed for safety reasons. You'll find a number of large mango trees along the river bank from which locals have suspended ropes so that the daring can swing our over the river and drop into the cool water. The river crossing is at a big bend in the river where the trail ends on the east side.

A trail of sorts continues into the valley, but it is not marked or taped. It is used largely by pig hunters. The Division of Forestry has plans to take the trail another two miles up river.

Hanalei/Okolehau, 2.25 miles, 2 hours, 1272 feet gain, (hiking rating: strenuous).

This trail gets its name from the valley and from the fact that during prohibition, Okolehau, a Hawaiian liquor distilled from the roots of the Hawaiian ti plant, was produced here. Many of the plants can still be found growing along the trail. Indeed, copper tubing was found recently in the area when the trail was being worked, according to the district forester.

The trail follows the powerline road to the left of the cemetery. The road is the most difficult part of the hike since portions of the route are approximately a 25% grade. The road, shaded by large silk oak, koa and mango trees, ends about 0.7-mile at a large powerline structure. Happily, strawberry guava can be found among the big trees and when in season this red, golf ball-sized fruit is a delightful treat. From roads end, you'll get your first view of Hanalei, the valley, the pali (cliffs), the river, and the bay. Wow! It's a sight to sooth the spirit.

From the powerline, the foot trail begins west of the road and ascends the ridge passing through a stand of Norfolk Island Pine, eucalyptus, ti and lots of strawberry guava. In 1988, the forestry service worked and taped the trail. Numerous vista points provide marvelous views of the Hanalei area. One of the best spots to pause is at the 1.7-mile point on a flat place where you'll find a geological survey marker. From here it's 0.5-mile to Kaukaopua (lit., "the horizon clouds alight") the summit marked by a "FR/TR" post. The panorama is a rich reward after a hot hike.

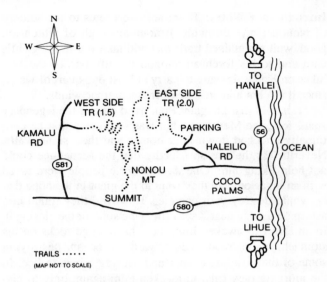

TRAILS ······
(MAP NOT TO SCALE)

NONOU MOUNTAIN (SLEEPING GIANT)

(Hiking Area No. 11)

Rating: Hardy Family.

Features: Views of Kauai, fruits.

Permission: None.

Hiking Distance and Time: Consult individual hikes.

Driving Instructions:

To east side trailhead (7 miles, 1/4 hour from Lihue)
North from Lihue on Route 56 past Coco Palms
Hotel, left on Haleilio Road for 1.2 miles, park off
road by sign "Nonou Trail."

To west side trailhead (10 miles, 1/2 hour from
Lihue)North from Lihue on Route 56, left on
Route 580, right on Route 581 (Kamalu Road) for
1.2 miles to sign "Nonou Trail" opposite 1055
Kamalu Road.

Introductory Notes: There are two routes to the summit of Nonou (lit., "throwing") mountain both of which are good, well-maintained trails that will take you to the giant's chin and to his forehead. Nonou is truly one of the best hikes on Kauai. Be sure to carry at least one quart of water, since it is a hot hike in spite of frequent trade winds.

It is said that the giant Puni lived among the legendary small folk, the Menehune, but was so clumsy that he continually knocked down their homes and their stone walls. Nevertheless, he was so friendly that the Menehune could not help liking him. One day the little people were faced with an invasion, and they went to the giant in the hope that he would destroy their enemies. However, they found him asleep on a ridge near Kapaa (lit., "the solid or the closing"). In an effort to awaken him, they threw large rocks on his stomach, which rebounded toward the ocean, destroying some of the invading canoes and causing others to flee. In the morning they tried to awaken Puni again, only to discover that some of the rocks they had thrown at him had landed in his mouth. Tragically, he had swallowed them and died in his sleep.

East-side Trail, 2 miles, 1 1/2 hours, 1,250 feet gain.

Walk up the driveway about 20 yards to the trailhead sign on the left side. The trail is a series of well-defined switchbacks along the northeast side of the mountain. Pause frequently and enjoy the vistas overlooking the east side of Kauai. Below you lie the Wailua Houselots, while the Wailua River and the world famous Coco Palms resort are to your front right. There are 1/4-mile trail markers along the entire route.

The large trees that flourish in the area not only offer a relatively shady trail, but also provide some shelter from showers. You will find strawberry guava, passion fruit, ti, tree ferns, a variety of eucalyptus, and other flora that deserve special note.

The hau (*Hibiscus tiliaceus*) tree is of particular interest not only because of its pretty bright-yellow blossom but also because of its long, sinuous branches that interlock to form an impenetrable barrier. Locals jokingly note that the tree is appropriately named (hau, pronounced "how") because where they are plentiful, no one knows "hau" to pass through!

On a spacious overlook at about the one-mile point, you can rest in the shade of the ironwood (*Casuarina equisetifolia*) tree, which resembles a pine because of its long, slender, drooping, dull-green needles. It is an introduced tree that has a long life and is very useful as a windbreak or shade tree.

Just beyond the 1 1/2-mile marker, the west-side trail merges with ours for the ascent to the summit. Alii (lit., "chief") Shelter and picnic table at the 1 3/4-mile marker is a pleasant place to picnic and to enjoy the panorama of the island and the solitude. There are a number of benches near the shelter that provide comfortable places to meditate. You should see a white-tailed tropic bird (*Phaethon lepturus*) as it soars along the mountain side with its conspicuous 16-inch tail streamers.

From the shelter, walk south through the monkeypod trees to survey the trail to the giant's "chin," "nose" and "forehead" that leads a short 1/2-mile to the summit. Be cautious as you walk across the narrow ridge above a nearly vertical 500-foot cliff, scramble up about 50 feet on your hands and knees to the "chin" and walk on a narrow ridge about 150 yards to the "forehead." From all points of the giant's anatomy, the views are outstanding. Look below the giant's chin for a hole through which the wind rushes.

West-side Trail, 1.5 miles, 1 hour, 1,000 feet gain.

The west-side trail is a bit shorter and not as steep, and offers more shade than the east-side trail. This trail passes by Queen's Acres and across a cattle range before entering the forest reserve. You will hike through a variety of introduced trees much like those found on the east side.

Look for the wild, or Philippine, orchid (*Spathoglottis plicata*). The wild variety is usually lavender with what appear to be five starlike petals, but are actually two petals and three sepals.

The east and west trails join at the 1 1/2-mile marker for the short trek to Alii Shelter and on to the summit (see East-side Trail description for details).

Shower time!

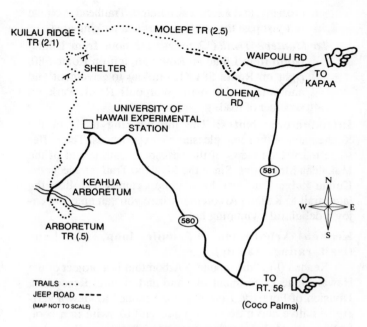

KEAHUA TRAILS

(Hiking Area No. 12)

Rating: See individual hikes.

Features: Swimming hole, native and introduced plants, fruits, picnic shelters.

Permission: None.

Hiking Distance and Time: See individual hikes.

Driving Instructions:

To Keahua Arboretum and Kuilau trails (12 miles, 1/2 hour from Lihue) North on Route 56, left on Route 580 to University of Hawaii Agriculture Experiment Station, left on paved road (1.8 miles) to Keahua Stream. Kuilau Ridge Trailhead is on the right at a small turnout just before the stream

crossing, and Keahua Arboretum Trailhead is on the
left just past the stream opposite a parking area.

To Moalepe Trail (12 miles, 1/2 hour from Lihue)
North from Lihue on Route 56, left on Route 580,
right on Route 581 (1.6 miles) to pavement end
and intersection with Waipouli Road. Park on
shoulder of road.

Introductory Notes: The three hiking trails in the
Keahua area offer some pleasurable experiences. They offer
some marvelous views of the eastside coastline and of the
Makaleha Mountains. Since the Moalepe Trail intersects the
Kuilau Ridge Trail, you have an opportunity to follow the
latter trail to Keahua Arboretum where you can hike and enjoy a delightful swimming hole.

**Keahua Arboretum, 0.5 mile loop, 1/2 hour
(trail rating: family).**

Keahua (lit., "the mound") Arboretum is a project of the
Hawaii State Department of Land and Natural Resources,
Division of Forestry. Here is a good chance to view a variety of native and introduced plants and to swim in a cool,
fresh-water pool. The arboretum receives an annual average
rainfall of 95 inches. The State Forest Reserve area extends
west to the top of Mt. Waialeale ("overflowing water"), the
highest spot on Kauai and the wettest place on earth, with
an average annual rainfall of 460 inches. It once received a
record 628 inches!

The trail begins opposite the parking lot under a canopy
of painted gum (*Eucalyptus deglupta*) trees with a colorful
bark. This tree species is native to the Philippines and New
Guinea. Behind the painted gum trees are rose gum
(*Eucalytpus grandis*), a tree from Australia and less colorful
than the painted gum. Several other trees are easy to identify
here. Two of them are kukui (*Aleurites moluccana*) and milo
(*Thespesia populnea*). Kukui trees, also called candlenut
trees, had several uses. The most noteworthy use was the
burning of its oily nuts for a light source. Kukui is

Hawaii's State Tree and identifiable by its pale green leaf and its walnut-size nuts. Today, as in old Hawaii, the wood of the milo tree is prized for its use in making beautiful umekes, or calabashes.

The trail passes several picnic shelters and parallels the stream and several good swimming holes. The Makaleha mountains to the west are the source watershed for the domestic water supply. Rain falling on the mountains percolates into the soil and is collected in tunnels for distribution into the county water system. Good forest cover increases infiltration of water into the soil. This not only helps to increase the ground water supply but it also helps prevent soil erosion and floods caused by surface run-off.

One of the most conspicuous trees along the trail is the hau (*Hibiscus tiliaceus*) whose dense tangle of limbs prohibits entry. This yellow-flowered hibiscus was an early introduced plant. Here, you will also find the most common native tree species in Hawaii, the ohia lehua (*Metrosideros collina*). Early Hawaiian uses for the wood of the ohia included house timbers, poi boards, idols and kapa beaters. In the early 1900's, railroad ties hewn from ohia logs were exported for use on the mainland. A favorite of Madame Pele (the goddess of volcanoes) the ohia is easily identifiable by its tufted red stamens that remind the visitor of the bottle-brush tree.

Streams in this forest reserve provide a home for native and introduced fish. The native Hawaiian oopu lives here as well as smallmouth bass. Fresh-water Tahitian prawns, esteemed as a delicious food, can also be found here.

As you climb the hill, notice the native hala tree commonly called "tourist pineapple." Its stiltlike trunk and its fruit that resemble a pineapple make this tree easy to identify. The trail descends the hill where you can return to your car or, better yet, return to the stream for a swim. There is usually a rope suspended from a mango tree on the bank. It's fun to swing out and to drop into the pool below.

Moalepe Trail, 2.5 miles, 1 1/2 hours (trail rating: hardy family). Elevation gain 500 feet.

Do not attempt to drive beyond the Olohena-Waipouli Road intersection because the road is deeply rutted and, when wet, very slippery. The first part of the trail is on a right-of-way dirt road over pasture land. The usually cloud-enshrouded Makaleha (lit.,"eyes looking about as in wonder and admiration") Mountains rise majestically to the northwest. In fact, the State of Hawaii, Division of Forestry, which is in charge of the area, has plans to extend the trail to the top of the Makalehas. Be sure to pause to enjoy the panorama of the coastline, from Moloaa on the north to Lihue on the south. There are some guavas along the fence and even more in the pasture, which is private land. The trail is a popular equestrian route of riders who rent horses from the ranches in the area: evidence of this fact can be found on the trail!

The first mile is a gentle ascent in open country. Then the trail enters the forest reserve. Thereafter, the trail is bordered with a variety of plants and trees, including the wild, or Philippine, orchid, different types of ferns, eucalyptus trees and the popular ohia lehua, with its pretty red blossoms. In the forest reserve the road-trail narrows and begins to twist and turn along the ridge, with many small and heavily foliated gulches to the left and Moalepe (lit., "chick with comb") Valley to the right. You can expect rain and, therefore, a muddy trail to the end of the hike. The trail reaches a junction with the Kuilau Ridge trail on a flat, open area at the 2-mile point. The ridge trail to the south (left) descends to two trail shelters and eventually ends at Keahua Arboretum, 2.1 miles from the junction. There is a sheltered picnic site 0.2 mile south of the junction along the Kuilau Ridge Trail. From the junction the Moalepe Trail is a footpath that snakes northwestward for 0.4 mile along Kuilau Ridge to a lookout point from which an enchanting panorama awaits the hiker.

Kuilau Ridge Trail, 2.1 miles, 1 1/2 hours (trail rating: hardy family).

One of the most scenic hiking trails on the island, the Kuilau (lit., "to string together leaves or grass") Ridge Trail climbs the ridge from Keahua Arboretum to two vista-point picnic sites. From the trailhead to trail's end, an abundance of native and introduced plants greets the hiker. The ascent of the ridge is on a well-maintained foot and horse trail lined with hala, ti plants, from which hula skirts are fashioned, and the very pretty lavender wild, or Philippine orchid. But the best prize is a couple of mountain apple trees on the left side of the trail a short distance up from the trailhead. Perhaps you'll find some apples, which are red or pink when ripe.

At the 1 1/4-mile point the trail reaches a large flat area with a trail shelter and a picnic site. It is a delightful place to pause to enjoy views of the many gulches and the Makaleha Mountains beyond. However, if you plan to picnic, continue on for 0.8 mile to the second trail shelter and picnic area. The trail to the second shelter passes through one of the most beautiful places on the whole island. The Kuilau Ridge Trail twists and turns on a razorback ridge past a number of small waterfalls. It is a treasure to savor. Before reaching the shelter, the trail crosses a footbridge at the bottom of a gulch and then ascends the ridge to a large flat area and the picnic spot. From here, the trail continues 0.2 mile to its junction with the Moalepe Trail.

KOKEE STATE PARK/WAIMEA CANYON

(Hiking Area No. 13)

Rating: See individual hikes.

Features: Views of Waimea Canyon, Na Pali Coast and Kalalau Valley, swimming, camping, waterfalls, iliau plant, rain forest, wilderness hiking, and fruits.

Permission: Camping permits from State Parks and cabin reservations from Kokee Lodge (see Appendix).

Hiking Distance and Time: See individual hikes.

Driving Instructions:

> *From Lihue* 38 miles, 1 1/2 hours to Kokee State Park Headquarters. South on Route 50, right on Route 550 (Waimea Canyon Drive) past Waimea to park.

Introductory Notes: Kokee (lit., "to bend or to wind") State Park and Waimea (lit., "reddish water") Canyon are the most popular hiking and camping areas on the island, for obvious reasons. Waimea Canyon has been called the "Grand Canyon of the Pacific." Kokee has numerous hiking trails and untold hunting trails that snake along the pali (cliff) to otherwise remote and inaccessible places. Everyone is quite taken by the beauty and grandeur of Waimea Canyon. It is about one mile wide, 3600 feet deep, and 10 miles long. While it does not match the magnificence of the Grand Canyon in Arizona, it has its own unique magic, with its verdant valleys, its lush tropical forest and its rare birds and flora.

Technically, this northwest corner of the island is under two state agencies, the Division of State Parks and the Division of Forestry, both of which are under the Hawaii State Department of Land and Natural Resources; and Kokee Lodge is operated by a private concessionaire. While the accommodations are not luxurious, they are very comfortable and in keeping with the surroundings.

The state cabins at Kokee, very popular with locals and tourists, require reservations. Kokee Lodge is not really a lodge but rather 12 rustic cabins completely furnished with refrigerator, water heater, range, cooking utensils, shower, linens, blankets, beds and fireplace. All you need bring is food, which is not available at Kokee but 20 miles away in Waimea. There is, however, a restaurant and cocktail lounge a short walk from the cabins, open 8:30 a.m. to 5:30 p.m. and on Friday and Saturday evenings for dinner 6–9 p.m.

Each cabin will accommodate 3–7 persons at a very modest cost from $35–45 per day. The cabins are very popular with locals, so make reservations early — even one year in advance is not too soon. Write to the lodge for complete information and reservations (see Appendix).

At the north end of a shady, picturesque meadow, tent and trailer camping are available in the shade of tall eucalyptus trees. Camping, limited to five days, is free. Water, tables, barbecues, restrooms and cold-water showers are available. There are a number of wilderness camping areas and shelters available (see the map and the trail descriptions) under the jurisdiction of the Division of Forestry.

In recent years a controversy has existed over the future of the Kokee-Waimea area. Conservationists have sought Federal legislation to establish a national park so that the wilderness can be preserved in relatively pristine condition. Opponents of this proposal seek to retain the present status, because a national park would probably prohibit hunting, leasing land for vacation cabins and taking plants.

Whatever the future, whether your interest is hiking, hunting or sightseeing, no trip to Kauai is complete without a visit to Kokee and Waimea Canyon. Kokee is also the home of the rare mokihana berry (see the Pihea Trail below), and the even rarer and beautiful iliau tree (see the Iliau Nature Loop Trail below) and the delicious Methley plum, which is ready for picking throughout the park in late May or early June. The picking season is short because local people flock to the park and carry off buckets full of this

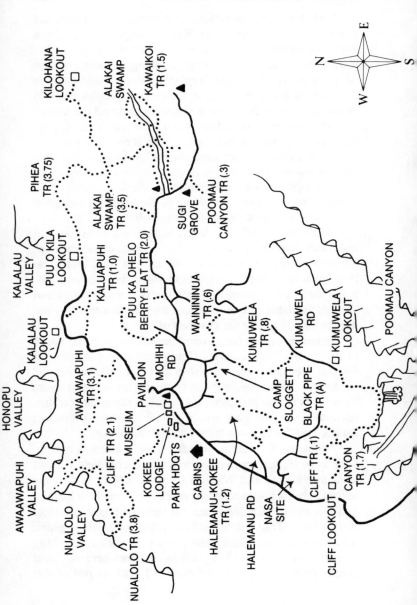

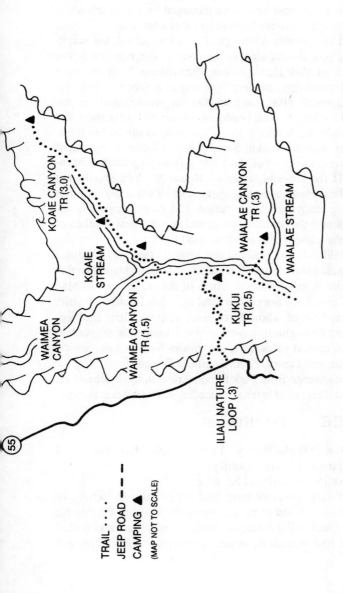

KOAIE CANYON TR (3.0)

KOAIE STREAM

WAIALAE CANYON TR (.3)

WAIALAE STREAM

WAIMEA CANYON

WAIMEA CANYON TR (1.5)

KUKUI TR (2.5)

ILIAU NATURE LOOP (.3)

55

TRAIL · · · ·
JEEP ROAD — — —
CAMPING ▲
(MAP NOT TO SCALE)

delectable fruit. Since 1986, pickings have been poor because so many trees have been damaged by harvesters while others have been overwhelmed by other vegetation.

On the Trail: Although it is not required, for safety reasons you should sign in and out in the registry at the Kokee State Park Headquarters when hiking. Your interests, physical condition, and length of stay at Kokee will help determine which hike you take. On the whole, trails in the general vicinity of park headquarters are relatively short and easy, while trails into Waimea Canyon, to the valley overlooks or into the Alakai Swamp are full-day or overnight trips. Access to most of the trails is from jeep roads that radiate off the main highway — Route 55. You should not travel these roads in a passenger car even when dry, because many are steep and deeply rutted. The ranger at park headquarters and the museum personnel are the best sources of information about road and trail conditions.

In 1987–8, the trails in the Kokee State Park/Waimea Canyon area were worked, brushed, posted, and taped so that they were in top condition. Much of the credit goes to Mac Hori, Kokee Park Supervisor, and to Ralph Daehler, District Forester, both of whom have since retired. Their trail improvement programs have involved hundreds of student workers, unpaid volunteers, the Hawaii Sierra Club, and the State National Guard, 227th Engineer Company.

The mileage from Park Headquarters to the trailhead via the most direct road is noted preceding each trail description.

KOKEE — Southwest

Puu Ka Ohelo/Berry Flat Trail, 1.3 miles, 1 hour (trail rating: family).
Park HQ to trailhead 0.9 mile.

An easy, pleasant loop trail off Mohihi (a variety of sweet potato) Road combines the Berry Flat and the Puu Ka Ohelo (Ohelo hill) trails. In 1990, the trailhead was posted and the trail was clear, broad and easy to follow. You will cross a couple of small streams along this verdant trail. The banana passion fruit (*Passiflora mollissima*) is found here draping from the trees. It is a wild vine that produces a pretty, light-pink blossom and a small, yellow, banana-shaped fruit. The Park Service regards the vine as a pest because it smothers native trees.

Both trails pass through scenic forest containing mostly introduced trees that should be easy to identify. Particularly noteworthy is a stand of California redwoods (*Sequoia simpervirens*) that will excite the senses. These wondrous giants tower over the other trees adding a certain majesty to the grove, and their droppings provide a luxuriant carpet on which to walk. They are found as you begin the Berry Flat Trail.

In addition, there are stands of Australian eucalyptus, Japanese Sugi pines and the native koa (*Acacia koa*), which grows to a height of more than 50 feet. The koa has a light gray bark that is smooth on young trees and considerably furrowed on mature trees. The leaves are smooth, stiff, and crescent-shaped. Often called Hawaiian mahogany, the wood is red with a wavy grain that makes it popular for use in furniture, woodwork and ukuleles. In older times it had nobler purposes, having been used for war canoes, surfboards and calabashes.

The prize to be sought here is the Methley plum that flourishes in the Kokee area. However, plum picking has been poor in recent years because of storm damage to the trees. Look for plum trees whose fruit ripens at the end of May or the first part of June.

There is also a variety of birds along both trails. (All bookstores on the island have small, pocket-sized, inexpensive bird books featuring the most frequently seen birds). Introduced from the mainland, the cardinal (*Richmondena cardinalis*) is a commonly seen bird on the island. The male, with it's all-red body and pointed crest, has been seen along the trail as well as throughout the park.

Black Pipe Trail, 0.4 mile, 1/2 hour (trail rating: hardy family).

Park HQ to trailhead 2.5 miles.

This is a short spur trail that connects the Canyon Trail with the middle fork of the Halemanu Road. The trail descends into a small overgrown gulch and then climbs to follow the cliff to the Canyon Trail. It is along the pali that the rare and beautiful iliau (*Wilkesia gymnoxiphium*) grows. A relative to the rare silversword that grows on Maui, the iliau is endemic to Kauai and found only in the western mountains. It grows 4–12 feet high, it is unbranched, and the stems end in clumps of long, narrow leaves 6–16 inches long. Once in its life, the plant flowers in a flourish of hundreds of tiny yellow blossoms.

Canyon Trail, 1.7 miles, 2 hours, 800-foot loss (trail rating: strenuous).

Park HQ to trailhead 2.1 miles.

Although the Canyon Trail is steep in parts and requires some stamina, it offers some of the best views of Waimea Canyon. The trail begins at the Halemanu Road and runs south along the east rim of the canyon. It is somewhat precipitous in places, so be careful. At the Cliff Lookout, which is 0.1 mile beyond the end of the Halemanu Road, you get not only a view of the canyon but also a view of the trail as it descends and snakes along the cliff.

The Canyon Trail is a popular hike. The trail descends into a gulch and snakes along the cliff to Kokee Stream and Waipoo (lit., "head water") Falls, where you can picnic in the shade and swim or splash in the stream. The best swimming hole is at the base of Waipoo Falls No. 1.

A common plant on the high, dry ridges is the lantana (*Lantana camara*), which blossoms almost continuously. Its flowers vary in color from yellow to orange to pink or red; infrequently they are white with yellow centers. It is a low shrub with a thick, strong wood.

A small, pretty, yellow-green bird, the anianiau (*Loxops parva*), is common in the high forests of Kauai. In truth it is difficult for the less-than-expert to tell the difference between the anianiau and the amakihi (*Loxops virents*), which is the same size and yellow. However, if you get a close look, the amakihi has a dark loral (space between the eye and bill) mark that joins the eye and the curved dark bill. No matter, however, for they are both pretty birds.

From the falls, the trail makes a steep climb out of the gulch and ascends the pali, from which some of the best vistas of Waimea are had. Once again, be careful for while the trail is broad and easy to follow, at some places steep walls drop to the canyon below. There are numerous places to pause in some shade to enjoy the view through the canyon to the sea on the south side.

After a steep climb, the trail ends at Kumuwela Lookout, from where you can return on the Canyon Trail or connect with the Kumuwela Road or the Ditch Trail.

Cliff Trail, 0.1 mile, 10 minutes (trail rating: family).

Park HQ to trailhead 2.1 miles.

The Cliff Trail provides a scenic vista of Waimea Canyon and a convenient departure point for the Canyon Trail. It begins after a short walk or drive down the Halemanu Road. Be quiet as you approach the lookout so that you do not frighten any goats that might be browsing there. Feral goats are commonly sighted here or walking along the pali area opposite the lookout.

Halemanu-Kokee Trail, 1.2 miles, 1 hour (trail rating: hardy family).

Park HQ to trailhead 0.6 mile.

This trail starts just before entering Camp Slogget near the old ranger station and ends on Halemanu Road. It's a hike for those who are interested in a short, pleasant, easy walk with the prospect of seeing some native birds and plants. The trail, linking Mohihi and Halemanu roads, is an enjoyable hike in itself and also a route to hiking areas on Kokee's west side.

Tall trees dominate the area, such as lehua and the majestic koa. There are three red birds that you can expect to see along the trail. The cardinal has a pronounced crest, which is the most prominent feature distinguishing it from the apapane (*Himatione sanguinea*), a deep-crimson bird with black wings and tail and a slightly curved black bill, and the iiwi (*Vestiaria coccinea*), a vermilion bird with black wings and tail and orange legs. The latter also has a rather pronounced curved salmon bill. Unless you get a good look at these birds, it is difficult to identify them, but they can be enjoyed without being identified. One other bird that is common throughout the forest is the elepaio (*Chasiempis sanwichensis*), an endemic bird that is grey-backed with a rather long, blackish tail and white rump. It is a somewhat noisy bird, giving forth with what is best described as a sort of "wolf-whistle."

Iliau Nature Loop, 0.3 mile, 1/4 hour (trail rating: family).

Park HQ to trailhead 6.3 miles.

The nature loop is a good place to see some 20 endemic plants including the rare iliau (*Wilkesia gymnoxiphium*). A relative to the equally rare Maui silversword, the iliau is endemic to Kauai. It grows 4–12 feet high, it is unbranched, and the stems end in clumps of long, narrow leaves 6–16 inches long. Once in its life, the plant flowers in a flourish of hundreds of tiny yellow blossoms. At one time, the plants were identified by name plates, but they all have been destroyed or become impossible to read because of weather damage. There is no missing the iliau, however, since hundreds flourish in this small area.

The trail provides a number of vistas for viewing the canyon and Waialae (lit., "mudhen water") Falls on the opposite, west wall of the canyon.

Kaluapuhi Trail, 1.0 miles, 1 hour (trail rating: family).

Park HQ to trailhead 1.9 miles.

Access to the trail is a few feet off the main road where a trail marker identifies the trailhead.

Even though the Park Service claims that this trail is "2.0+" miles, the last mile is overgrown with berry bushes and is not passable (1990). The first mile of the trail is wide and flat and easy to follow. At the 0.5-mile point, an equally wide, flat trail goes left and emerges 0.5 miles later, 0.2 miles northeast (right) of the Kalalau Lookout. This is a pleasant hike for the entire family with the prospect of sweet plums along the trail.

Kaluapuhi (lit., "the eel pit") Trail is a favorite during the plum season. If it is a good year (poor 1986–90) for the delicious Methley plum, this trail will take you to some of the best trees. The pickings are generally good here due to the fact that the only access to the trees is on foot.

Plum picking is regulated by the state and is limited to 25 pounds of the fruit per person per day. Pickers must check in and out at the checking station, usually located near park headquarters. Many local people bring the whole family and stay overnight to get an early start.

Koaie Canyon Trail, 3 miles, 2 hours (trail rating: strenuous).

Trail is in Waimea Canyon.

Koaie Canyon is a favorite of hikers and backpackers, for it is an easier trail than Waimea Canyon Trail and it leads to a secluded wilderness shelter. The canyon's name comes from the koaie (*Acacia koaia*) tree, which is endemic to the islands and is much like the koa tree. The wood, however, is harder than koa wood, and was once used the make spears and fancy paddles.

If the water is high in Waimea Stream, you should not hike up-river, since it is necessary to cross the river to the east side to get on the Koaie Canyon Trail. You cross the river (posted in 1990) just below Poo Kaeha, a prominent hill about 500 feet above the river, pick up Koaie Stream a short distance later, and follow the south side of the stream into Koaie Canyon.

The canyon is a fertile area that was once extensively farmed, as is evidenced by the many terraced areas you'll observe and the rock walls and the remains of house sites. You can usually find ample pools in the stream to swim in or at least to cool off in. During the summer months, the water is usually low, but sufficient for some relief from the hot canyon. The Division of Forestry has a number of wildland campsites here. At trail's end, you find Lonomea Camp, an open shelter with a table alongside the stream near a generous pool for swimming. The Lonomea (*Sapindus cahuensis*) is a native tree with ovate leaves which reaches heights of up to 30 feet. It grows only on Kauai and Oahu.

Don't forget to pack out your trash.

There is ample water in the canyon, but it should be treated or boiled before drinking.

Kukui Trail, 2.5 miles, 2 hours, 2000 feet loss (trail rating: strenuous).

Park HQ to trailhead 6.3 miles.

The Kukui (candlenut lamp) Trail is the only trail into Waimea Canyon. A Division of Forestry sign marks the trailhead both at the state highway and at the departure point off the Iliau Trail. Sign in and out on the trail register located near the trail's beginning. You may hike and camp in the canyon for three days.

The trail drops over 2000 feet into the canyon, and in 1990 it was in good condition. The first half of the trail is open so that sun protection and a hat are advisable. If you hike during the heat of the day, I am certain you would rather be standing under Waialae Falls which can be seen tumbling from the pali across the canyon. About 0.3 mile down the trail, look for a wooded gulch on the left where several hibiscus (*Hibiscus waimeae*) trees are growing. This variety is an endemic tree that bears large white flowers that are so fragrant you can smell them from a distance.

You'll probably find numerous half-gallon plastic jugs along the trail. They are left by pig and goat hunters as they descend so they will have fresh water on their return. For safety reasons you should stay out of the brush so that you won't be mistaken for a goat or pig by hunters.

The first part of the hike offers some spectacular views of Waimea Canyon and the second part passes through heavy growth until it emerges at Wiliwili (a native tree bearing red seeds that make pretty necklaces) Camp along the boulder-laden banks of Waimea River. It is a delightful spot to camp in shade with ample water. Many hikers make a base camp at Wiliwili and then hike on the canyon trails and in the side canyons. If you are in good hiking condition, it is possible to make the hike in and out in one day.

There is ample water in the canyon, but it should be treated or boiled before drinking.

Kumuwela Trail, 0.8 mile, 1 hour, 300 feet gain (trail rating: hardy family).

Park HQ to trailhead 1.0 mile.

At the end of the short spur road off Mohihi Road (see map) turn left into the forest for the beginning of the Kumuwela Trail. The trailhead is marked (1990) and the trail is well-maintained. The trail dips abruptly into a luxuriant, fern-lined gulch where kahili ginger (*Hedychium coronarium*) flourishes. The size, fragrance and light-yellow blossoms overwhelm most visitors. You should find many places on and off the trail where feral pigs have been digging to get at roots.

Along this verdant trail there are also specimens of lantana, lilikoi (passion fruit) as well as handsome kukui and koa trees. The last 0.3 mile requires a 300-foot elevation to Kumuwela Road, where you can connect with the Canyon Trail.

Waialae Canyon Trail, 0.3 mile, 1/2 hour.

Trailhead in Waimea Canyon.

This short, undeveloped trail takes you south along Waimea River from the campground at the terminus of the Kukui Trail. A marker identifies the point where you can ford the river and enter lower Waialae Canyon. The trail follows the north side of Waialae Stream for a short distance to "Poacher's Camp," where a shelter, table and pit toilets are located. You're likely to meet hunters in Waialae Canyon and you're likely to see evidence of their success by the bones and the carcasses of animals left along the trail.

There is ample water in the canyon, but it should be treated or boiled before drinking.

Waimea Canyon Trail, 1.5 miles, 2 hours.

Trailhead is in Waimea Canyon.

You reach the Waimea Canyon trail by hiking down the Kukui Trail to the river. The Waimea Canyon Trail provides access to Koaie trail and to the inner recesses of the canyon.

The Waimea Canyon Trail travels north from the end of the Kukui Trail through the canyon to the junction of Koaie Stream and Waimea River. Well-maintained, it leads up the river on the west side to a point where a plantation ditchman's house is located. The trail was originally constructed for access to the canyon to construct and maintain a powerhouse up river.

There is ample water in the canyon, but it should be treated or boiled before drinking.

Waininiua Trail, 0.6 mile, 1/2 hour (trail rating: hardy family).

Park HQ to trailhead 2.2 miles.

Mostly a short, flat, scenic forest walk, the Wainininua Trail with the Kumuwela Trail completes a loop off the Kumuwela Road. There are a variety of native and introduced plants, the most notable being aromatic ginger with its lovely, light-yellow blossoms. Many local girls like to put a fresh ginger blossom in their hair, not only for its beauty but also for its fragrance.

KOKEE — NORTHWEST

Alakai Swamp, 3.5 miles, 4 hours (trail rating: difficult).

Park HQ to trailhead 3 miles.

Few will disagree that the Alakai (lit., "to lead") Swamp is the most interesting and exciting place on the island. For interest, there is the beautiful mokihana berry — Kauai's flower — and the native rain forests; and for excitement, there is the swamp with its bogs, where a false step puts you knee-deep in mud and water. I recommend a lightweight, gore-tex or cloth hiking boot for this trail. You can bet on getting very wet and muddy.

The trail begins deceivingly easily off Mohihi (Camp 10) Road, which should be traversed by a four-wheeled vehicle because parts are steep and deeply rutted. (An alternative route is off the Pihea Trail — see below). A forest-reserve marker identifies the trailhead while the trail follows an old pole line constructed during World War II for Army communications. The trail is in good condition (1990) and taped so that it is not difficult to follow unless a heavy cloud cover is present.

The first bog is near the one-mile marker. After the Alakai-Pihea Trail junction, bogs become more frequent, wetter and deeper until the 2 1/2-mile marker, from where it is all bog until trail's end. Your nose will be your guide to the mokihana (*Pelea anisata*) tree, which emits a strong anise odor. It is a small tree whose small berries are strung and worn in leis. Native to the islands, the mokihana berry is frequently twined with the maile vine to make a popular wedding lei. The maile (*Alyxia olivaeformis*) vine is common along the trail, with its tiny, glossy leaves and tiny, white flowers. Unlike the Mokihana tree, the maile vine must be cut or its bark stripped before its musky, woodsy scent or anise is noticed.

After the first two miles of ascending and descending a number of small, fern-laden gulches, the broad, flat expanse of the swamp lies before you. There is little chance of getting off the trail if you follow the poleline route, even though many of the poles have been cut down. You may have to loop here and there to avoid the wetter, deeper bogs. At the 2 3/4-mile marker you must make a left turn, leaving the poleline to follow white pipe markers. Be alert and cautious and you will find your way.

At Kilohana ("lookout point" or "superior") Lookout one has a magnificent view into Wainiha (lit., "unfriendly water") Valley, which extends from the sea to the base of Mt. Waialeale. Beyond Wainiha lies Hanalei (lit., "crescent bay") with its conspicuous wide, deep bay. It's an enchanting place to picnic, rest and reflect. If the cloud cover prevents a view, just wait and it is likely to clear.

Awaawapuhi Trail, 3.1 miles, 3 hours (trail rating: strenuous).

Park HQ to trailhead 1.5 miles.

The trail begins north of Highway 55 at telephone pole No. 1-4/2P/152, about halfway between the Kokee Museum and the Kalalau lookout. There is a forestry trail marker at the trailhead. The trail is well-maintained, and mileage markers show the way. In 1988, the Division of Forestry identified and posted with white PVC pipe 58 plants found along the trail. The white pipe with numbers on the side are mile markers. The Division of Forestry's guide, *Awa'awa'puhi Botanical Trail Guide*, is available at the forestry office in Lihue (see Appendix). Learning about these native and introduced plants will add a dimension to your experience.

In 1988, the Hawaii State Division of Forestry completed cutting, brushing, posting and taping the Nualolo Trail and the Nualolo Cliff Trail (see map) so that a marvelous 9-mile hike is possible by following the Awaawapuhi-Cliff-Nualolo Trails. I would begin such a trek on the Nualolo Trail and end traversing the Awaawapuhi Trail since the latter is a more gradual ascent.

Of the trails that extend to points high above the Na Pali Coast and the extraordinarily beautiful valleys of the north shore, this is the best. You should be in good condition before attempting this hike and be prepared with water and food. The rewards are great as you pass through tropical forests to view the extremely precipitous and verdant valley of Awaawapuhi (lit., "ginger valley") and Nualolo.

The first part of the trail passes through a moist native forest, dominated by koa trees, for a pleasant, cool hike. Koa trees grow to a height of more than 50 feet. The koa has a light gray bark that is smooth on young trees and considerably furrowed on mature trees. The leaves are smooth, stiff and crescent-shaped. Often called Hawaiian mahogany, the wood is red with wavy grain that makes it popular for use in furniture, woodwork and ukuleles. In older times it had nobler purposes, having been used for war canoes, surfboards and calabashes. A variety of ferns, the beautiful kahili ginger, and edible passion fruit, thimbleberries, and blackberries are also found along the trail.

The trail descends gradually through a moist native forest which becomes drier scrub as it reaches the ridges above the valley. You are likely to see feral goats forage while you pause on any one of a number of lookouts about 2500 feet above the valley. Additionally, you will probably sight helicopters flying tourists in, out, and over the pali, since the Na Pali Coast is a favorite for those who are unable or unwilling to make the trip on foot.

Just before reaching the 3-mile marker, a white PVC-pipe post identifies the Cliff Trail that goes northeast (left) 2.1-miles to the Nualolo Trail, which leads to the main road between the ranger's house and the housekeeping cabins.

The Awaawapuhi Trail continues for 0.3 mile from the junction to a vertical perch above the Na Pali Coast. This is the best place to lunch and to look for goats while enjoying enchanting views into Nualolo and Awaawapuhi valleys. It is a startling and exciting place.

Kawaikoi Stream Trail, 2.5 (loop) miles, 1 1/2 hours (trail rating: hardy family).

Park HQ to trailhead 3.8 miles.

Access to the Kawaikoi (lit., "the flowing water") Stream Trail is off the Mohihi (Camp 10) Road, which is passable only in a four-wheel-drive vehicle. A 2 1/2-mile loop trail hike was made possible in 1975 when the Forest Service and the Hawaii Chapter of the Sierra Club connected the Kawaikoi Trail with the Pihea Trail.

The route begins opposite a planted forest of Japanese sugi pines and follows the south side of Kawaikoi Stream along an easy, well-defined trail in heavy vegetation. During rainy periods, this is a muddy trail. A short distance past the 0.5-mile point, a trail sign indicates a place to cross the stream to join the Pihea Trail on the north side of the stream. If the rocks are not visible, the water is too high for safe crossing. The Kawaikoi Trail itself continues east on the south side of the stream to a point 100 yards past the 3/4-mile marker, where a trail sign marks the loop portion of the trail. During the 1-mile loop it is necessary to cross the stream twice.

In recent years, there has been a good deal of grass planting and herbicide work in the area in an effort to control blackberry, which is threatening to take over not only this area but also a number of other areas in the park. There are many swimming holes in this generous stream and places to spend some peaceful moments. You may agree with Ralph Daehler, retired District Forester, who regards Kawaikoi as the most beautiful place on Kauai.

Nualolo Trail, 3.8 miles, 3 hours, 1500 feet loss (trail rating: strenuous).

50 yards west of Park HQ.

In 1988, the Hawaii State Division of Forestry completed cutting, brushing, posting, and taping the Nualolo

Trail and the Nualolo Cliff Trail so that a marvelous 9-mile hike is possible by following the Nualolo-Cliff-Awaawapuhi trails. The Nualolo Trail starts between the ranger station and the housekeeping cabins in Kokee, and if you follow the 9-mile hike suggested above, you exit the Awaawapuhi Trail on Highway 55, 1.5 miles from park headquarters. From here it is easy to walk or hitch a ride back to your car.

The first part of the trail passes through a native forest of koa trees with their crescent-shaped leaves for a pleasant, cool hike. After an initial ascent of about 300 feet, the trail then descends about 1500 feet to a number of viewpoints overlooking Nualolo Valley. In 1988, the trail was cleaned so that the first 1.5 miles are broad, posted and easy to follow. A variety of ferns, the beautiful kahili ginger, and edible passion fruit, thimbleberries and blackberries are found along the trail.

The trail narrows somewhat at the 1.5-mile marker, but then opens again at the 2.25-mile post. After this point, you're certain to see the rare, endemic iliau plant. You are also likely to find ripe strawberry guava, a small, red golf ball-sized fruit.

There are several steep parts on the trail in the last mile so be cautious. At the 3.4-mile marker, the Cliff Trail goes right for 2.1 miles until it reaches the Awaawapuhi Trail and the Nualolo Trail goes straight to numerous vista points about 2800 feet above the valley. It is a marvelous place to picnic and to enjoy the solitude. If you walk out to the end of the ridge, you will have a view of the Na Pali Coast to the north (right) and a view of the beach in Kalalau Valley.

Nualolo Cliff Trail, 2.1 miles, 1 1/2 hours (trail rating: strenuous).

Reached via Nualolo or Awaawapuhi Trails.

If you have reached the Nualolo Cliff Trail junction from the Awaawapuhi or Nualolo Trail, you should take the Cliff Trail for the views into Awaawapuhi and Nualolo valleys are outstanding. Additionally, you're likely to see feral goats here as well as the rare, delicately beautiful Kauai hibiscus.

From the Nualolo Trail, the Nualolo Cliff Trail is mostly level until just before reaching the Awaawapuhi Trail, where it makes an easy ascent. One-fourth-mile markers identify the way along which you are certain to see goats foraging for food and bounding on the steep slopes in the upper valley. In 1988, the trail was cut to provide hikers with a crossover trail between two marvelous trails and to offer some of the best views of the Na Pali Coast.

At the 1.5-mile point, the trail emerges on a flat area used by campers. Here, the trail is not clearly marked. Hike up the ridge away from the valley lookout and you will locate the trail and shortly, a white PVC-pipe-marker.

Between the 0.5 and 0.25-mile markers, look for the rare, endemic Kauai hibiscus (*Saint johnianus*) with its small, delicate, orange blossom. It's a find.

After an easy uphill, the Nualolo Cliff Trail joins the Awaawapuhi Trail where you can go 0.3 miles left to the end of the trail or go 2.8 miles right to Kokee Road.

Pihea Trail, 3.75 miles, 3 hours (trail rating: strenuous).

Park HQ to trailhead 3.8 miles.

Pihea ("din of voices crying, shouting, wailing, lamentation") Trail begins at the end of the Highway 55 at Puu o Kila (lit., "Kila's Hill") overlooking Kalalau Valley. A hiking trail registry identifies the trailhead.

The first 3/4 mile follows the remains of a county road project which was begun in a cloud of controversy and which terminated literally in the mire when money ran out, along with the willingness to continue. A road through the Alakai Swamp and down the mountain to Hanalei would have been a great tourist attraction and an engineering feat, but an ecological disaster.

From the lookout, you can usually see the white-tailed tropic bird (*Phaethon lepturus*) soaring along the cliffs of Kalalau Valley. This bird is white with large black wing patches above and 16-inch tail streamers. A similar bird that is all white except for red tail streamers is the red-tailed tropic bird (*Phaethon rubricauda*).

After enjoying the breathtaking views into Kalalau, your trail follows the rim of the valley to Pihea, the last overlook into Kalalau before the Alakai Swamp. The trail makes an abrupt right turn as it enters the swamp and then drops in and out of a number of gulches to the junction with the Alakai Swamp Trail.

The Pihea Trail can be used as part of a loop trip from Kalalau into the Alakai Swamp, with a return to park headquarters via the Alakai Swamp Trail or the Kawaikoi Stream Trail and the Camp 10 Road.

Both the maile vine and the mokihana tree (see the Alakai Swamp Trail for description) are common along the trail and are favorites of both locals and visitors. The mokihana's powerful anise aroma attracts immediate attention.

Also common in this area is the ohia lehua (*Metrosideros polymorpha*), with its tufted red stamens that remind the visitor of the bottlebrush tree. A variety of tree ferns abound along the trail, the hapu'u (*Cibotium chamissoi*) and the amaumau (*Sadleria cyatheoides*) being most common. The latter grows to 10 feet. Its pinnate fronds were once used for huts and the juice from it for a reddish dye.

From the junction with the Alakai Swamp Trail, our trail continues over the newest portion passing through native forests, crossing small streams, and winding through verdant gulches until it joins the Kawaikoi Stream Trail.

Poomau Canyon, 0.3 mile, 15 minutes (trial rating: hardy family).

Park HQ to trailhead 4.5 miles.

About 0.5 mile past the trailhead for the Kawaikoi Stream Trail on the Mohihi (Camp 10) Road is a marker identifying the Poomau (lit., "constant source") Canyon Trail. This short, easy trail passes through a small stand of Japanese sugi trees, enters a native rainforest, and ends overlooking Poomau Canyon, the largest and northernmost side canyon in Waimea Canyon. Across the canyon on the west rim, the high prominence is Puu Ka Pele (lit., "Pele's Hill") and Highway 55. Legend records that Pele, the fire goddess, left Kauai unable to find a suitable home. The caldera was created when Pele brought down her foot for the leap across the channel to Oahu. The caldera has since been filled with small stones by visitors as an offering to the goddess — or so some say. The lookout is an excellent place for pictures of the canyon and for picnicking.

Aaah!

LANAI

LANAI—TRAILHEADS, CAMPING

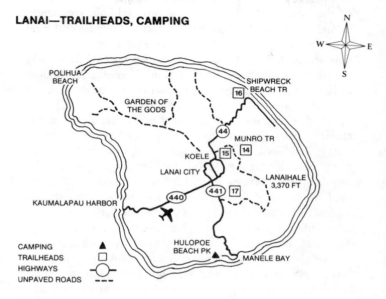

POLIHUA BEACH

SHIPWRECK BEACH TR

16

GARDEN OF THE GODS

44

MUNRO TR

14

KOELE

15

LANAI CITY

LANAIHALE 3,370 FT

KAUMALAPAU HARBOR

440

441

17

HULOPOE BEACH PK

MANELE BAY

CAMPING ▲
TRAILHEADS ☐
HIGHWAYS ⟲
UNPAVED ROADS ---

(MAP NOT TO SCALE)

The Island

Lanai is mostly owned by the Dole Pineapple Co. (Castle & Cook, Inc.) which cultivates pineapple on about 16 percent of the island. Lanai is small — just 17 miles long and 13 miles wide — with adequate to posh visitor accommodations. It does not have many hiking trails, but it does have one of the best swimming and snorkeling beaches anywhere. Hulopoe Beach was once a dream place to "kick back" and a good basecamp from which to explore the island until 1989, when construction was begun on a hotel-resort complex.

Although Lanai is known quite properly as the "Pineapple Island" today, its past belies this innocent nickname. Historically, Lanai was a place where kapu (taboo)

violators were banished and where life was once difficult on
this wild, mostly arid land (42 inches of rainfall in the center
of the island). Additionally, the aliis (chiefs) frequently
brought their dead to Lanai to be buried. Consequently, legends abound regarding ghosts who inhabit the island today.
One legend tells of Kaululaau, who for his evil deeds was
exiled by his uncle, the king of Maui. Kaululaau is thought
to have made Lanai safe for human habitation by fighting
the ghosts and driving off the evil spirits.

Today, this tiny island, which was created by a single
crater volcano, Palawai, has entered tourist-oriented Hawaii.
Castle and Cook developed the island to attract tourists.
Lanai is no longer a peaceful stopover for the person who
can do without luxury. Lanai City is in the center of the island in the foothills of a small mountain range that is
topped by Lanaihale (3370 feet), the highest place on the island. Politically, the 2200 residents are part of Maui county.
The island has a couple of grocery stores, a snack shop, and
the usual assortment of government buildings. The only
restaurants are in the hotels. The hotels aside, there are no
shopping centers, no gift shops, no bars, no nightclubs, and
no public transportation. Why would they need public transportation? There are no public roads to speak of. The
"paved" roads are narrow and in poor condition.
Consequently, although expensive to rent, a jeep is advisable to travel the pineapple and mountain roads. However,
local people are friendly, so that rides are not difficult to get
on the main roads.

Camping

Camping on Hulopoe Beach was allowed as of
December 1990. The campground may, however, be relo-
cated once the resort hotel located above the camping area
(under construction at the time of this publication) is
opened. The campground is privately owned by the Koele
Company. There is a $5.00 (1990) one-time registration fee
and a $5.00 (1990) fee per day per person regardless of age.

Reservations and applications should be made at least one week in advance, since there are only three (3) campsites in a shaded Kiawe-tree area and the stay is limited to seven days. There are clean restrooms, fire pits, tables and showers. The latter are "cold water." However, the pipes are so close to the ground surface that the sun heats the water. Be certain to bring snorkeling equipment, for there are few places to compare with Hulopoe.

Address is in the Appendix for Koele Company.

Hiking

There are three notable hikes on the island — one beach hike and two in the mountain range above Lanai City. The Luahiwa Petroghyphs Trail is included here for interest and not because it is a hiking trail. With the exception of the Munro Trial, there is no backpacking experience, although you can hike Shipwreck Beach and camp. However, no water is available. Most of the island is flat, with a modest cluster of hills above Lanai City. A major consideration is that most of the trailheads are accessible only by jeep.

On the trail?

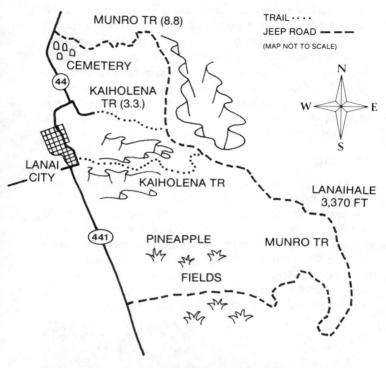

MUNRO TRAIL
(Hiking Area No. 14)

Rating: Difficult.

Features: Viewpoints, fruits, Lanai's highest point —
Lanaihale, 3370 feet.

Permission: None.

Hiking Distance and Time: 17–18 mile loop,
overnight, 1400 foot gain/loss.

Driving or Hiking Instructions:

From the Post Office on Lanai Avenue drive or walk 2
miles north on Route 430 out to the end of town

past Lanai Lodge. Turn right on a paved-graveled road and go 0.4 mile past a cemetery on the right to the trailhead.

Introductory Notes: Do not attempt to drive a conventional vehicle on the Munro Trail. It begins innocently, but it soon becomes wet and rutted. It is possible to travel the entire trail in a four-wheel-drive vehicle or to hike it. George C. Munro, after whom the trail is named, was a naturalist who is credited with reforesting this part of Lanai with exotic tropicals in an effort to restore a watershed area.

On the Trail: From the trailhead, the jeep road-trail crosses a flat, grassy place. After 200 yards bear left at a junction with a faint road which bears right. The trail descends into Maunalei (lit., "lei mountain") Gulch, which is shaded for about a mile by large eucalyptus trees. Maunalei was so named because the clouds over the mountain suggest a lei. Edible thimbleberries (*Rubus rosaefolius*) are plentiful for the entire length of the trail. They grow on a small, thorny bush with white flowers. The trail begins an ascent on the east side of the mountains, from which views of Maui (east) and Molokai (northeast) are possible. At the head of Maunalei Gulch (southeast) is the place where in 1778 the king of Hawaii massacred many Lanai natives who sought shelter in this stronghold. Beyond the gulch, the trail passes alternately through open areas and forested areas in which Norfolk Island pines (*Araucaria excelsa*) dominate. These tall, perfectly symmetrical trees were chosen by Munro and others to increase Lanai's ground water, since the trees collect moisture from low-hanging clouds. After a steep climb along the east side of the range, the trail reaches some flat areas. At 6.6 miles a spur road turns right onto a small clearing, on which you will find an abandoned rain gauge and a house site. This road is part of the Kaiholena Gulch Trail (see map).

Along the upper Munro Trail there are numerous flat, grassy places to camp. Legally, you should get a permit to camp from the Department of Land and Natural Resources in

Lanai City, but I doubt if anyone does. Lanaihale (lit., "house of Lanai") is reached at 7.7 miles. At 8.3 miles look for a turnout on the right, a good spot to view Lanai City and the west side of the island. It is also a good place to camp, although it can be a bit wet. One-half mile beyond, the Munro trail makes an abrupt descent and from a number of clearings provides views of Maui (east), Kahoolawe (southeast) and Hawaii beyond on a clear day. The trail ends when you reach the pineapple fields. Stay on the main roads (24 feet wide) bearing to the right to reach Lanai City.

Beach camping

KAIHOLENA GULCH
(Hiking Area No. 15)
(see map page 128)

Rating: Strenuous. Elevation gain 1050 feet.

Features: Forested, views.

Permission: None.

Hiking Distance and Time: 3.3 miles, 2 hours.

Driving Instructions:

From the Post Office on Lanai Avenue drive north (1.5 miles) on Route 44 to the end of town and bear right to the lodge. Take a right before the entrance to the lodge and drive to the end of the parking area from where you can see the trailhead southeast at the telephone poleline above a gulch and a grove of Norfolk Island pines.

Introductory Notes: Kaiholena (iholena is a type of banana) Gulch is a pleasant mountain hike which provides some outstanding views of the west side of Lanai. It could also serve as a shortcut to the Munro Trail, which it joins at the 3.1 mile point of the latter.

On the Trail: The trail follows the poleline up the hill and passes through the twin poles at the top of the rise. It then swings right, into a grove of eucalyptus trees, and begins an ascent on a ridge between Kaiholena Gulch on the right and Hulopoe (named after a man) Gulch on the left. The trail is in good condition and easy to follow to the Munro trail-road about one mile distant. Throughout the hike, but particularly on the higher parts, be on the lookout for ripe common and strawberry guavas. The former are soft, yellow and lemon-sized when ripe, and the latter are crimson and cherry-to-plum-sized when ripe. Both can be quite sweet and both are high in vitamin C. The tall trees that dominate the first part of the trail are all introduced trees, the result of reforestation programs. Eucalyptus (many species), Norfolk Island Pine and ironwood are abundant here and throughout

Hawaii. The ironwood, with its long, slender, drooping, dull-green needles, makes a good windbreak and the fallen needles make a soft mat for a camper.

After one mile the trail meets the Munro Trail road, and we turn right onto it. Views of the west side of Maui are possible along the road, which is bordered with Norfolk Island and sugi pines. Walk southeast along the road for about 1/2 mile until you come to a vehicle turnout on the right and a small clearing on which you will see an abandoned rain gauge and a housesite. All that remains of the house site is a set of stairs which lead dangerously into a gulch. From the "staircase" and the abandoned housesite, the trail goes northwest, then shortly turns south to a flat area. This section was marked with trail tape in 1989 and was easy to follow, although staghorn ferns and the thimbleberry bushes with their thorns reached across the trail in many places. The result was a lot of scratches if you were wearing shorts. Along the trail on the flats, there are a couple of short spur trails which lead to the left to lookouts into the gulch below. Be cautious at these vista points for they are at the tops of nearly vertical walls.

The trail continues up the ridge to its highest point, Puu Alii (lit., "royal hill") from which views of Lanai City are good. The northwestward descent from the hill is at first gradual, but then you reach a steep, eroded area and the rest of the descent is more abrupt. Molokai should be visible to your front right. This section is not marked, but stay on the flat land and head for the highest point while trying to avoid the staghorn ferns and thorny thimbleberry bushes that reach across the trail in many places. Continue into a eucalyptus grove for a short distance to where the trail turns sharply left and follow a relatively steep and eroded ridgeline to a large communications reflector and to the pineapple fields a short distance beyond. Once on the pineapple road, follow the shortest route to Lanai City, which is clearly distinguishable about one mile distant.

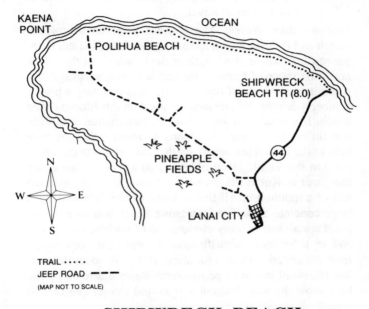

KAENA
POINT   OCEAN

POLIHUA BEACH

SHIPWRECK
BEACH TR (8.0)

PINEAPPLE
FIELDS

44

LANAI CITY

N
W · E
S

TRAIL · · · · ·
JEEP ROAD — — —
(MAP NOT TO SCALE)

SHIPWRECK BEACH
(Hiking Area No. 16)

Rating: Family to strenuous.

Features: Shipwrecks, beachcombing for wreckage, shells, glass floats, petroglyphs.

Permission: None.

Hiking Distance and Time: 1 to 8 miles one-way, 1/2 hour per mile.

Driving Instructions to Shipwreck Beach: 10.3 miles, 1 hour.

> *From the Post Office on Lanai Avenue* drive north on Route 44 to the end of town, bear right on Keomuku Road and drive to the end of the paved road. Just before reaching the beach, turn left on a

dirt-sand road and go 1.8 miles, which is as far as even a jeep can travel.

Introductory Notes: The 8 miles between Shipwreck Beach and Polihua Beach are a long, hot hike, but not without rewards. The entire length of the beach along the north-northeast shore of Lanai is littered with shipwreckage, sea shells, and a variety of ocean debris. It is certainly a beachcomber's delight; the pickings are good on this little-traveled beach. If you take the entire hike, transportation is a problem unless you retrace you steps. Certainly, the one-mile hike to the largest shipwreck on the coast is worth the hike.

On the Trail: The trail begins on a rocky ledge above the water at Kukui (lit., "candlenut lamp") Point, once the site of a lighthouse. All that remains of the lighthouse is a large concrete slab. The interesting beach houses near the point are almost entirely constructed of timbers from ships and an assortment of driftwood. A spur trail goes inland from the concrete pilings for about 100 yards to an interesting but small group of petroglyphs. Painted arrows on the lava show the way. Human and animal shapes can be discerned.

The trail-beachfront is only a few yards wide even at low tide, and the rotting timbers of ships tend to block your passage. It is fun to examine the wreckage and to splash in the shallow water for relief from the heat. There is no good swimming beach, for the surf bottom here is largely rough lava and beach stones. However, it is a good fishing area where locals may be observed pole fishing or throwing a net. From Kukui Point to a place opposite the rusting hulk of a large ship about 150 yards offshore is one mile.

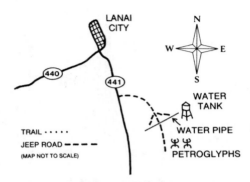

LUAHIWA PETROGLYPHS
(Hiking Area No. 17)

Rating: Family.

Features: Petroglyphs.

Permission: None.

Hiking Distance and Time: 50 yards

Driving Instructions: 2.8 miles, 15 minutes.

From the post office on Lanai Ave. drive south, right on Route 440. Left on Manele Road (Also Route 440) for a total of 1.5 miles to a wide cane (dirt) road on the left. Follow the cane road for 0.8 mile to a handprinted sign "Petroglyphs." Continue for 0.5 mile and park.

Introductory Notes: By any definition, this is not a hike, but your effort will take you to a fine collection of petroglyphs.

On the Trail: On the hill to your left you'll see a cluster of boulders under some large trees. The petroglyphs are on the rocks. No trail exists so you must make your way through the tall grass uphill to the rocks. There are at least three rocks with discernable pictures of human forms, animals, boats and abstract images. What do they mean? When were they chiseled? Your guess is as good as anyone's.

MAUI—TRAILHEADS, CAMPING

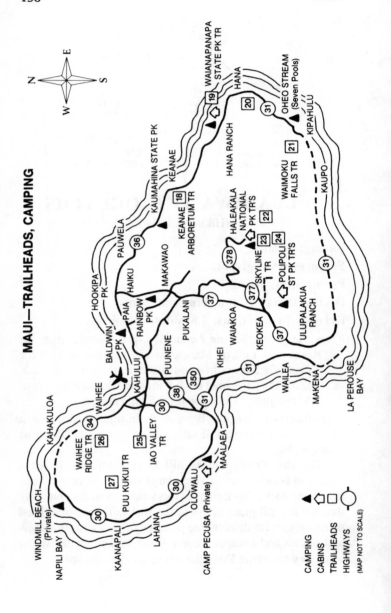

CAMPING ▲
CABINS ⬦
TRAILHEADS □
HIGHWAYS ◯

(MAP NOT TO SCALE)

MAUI

The Island

Adventurers come in all shapes, sizes and dispositions. Some enjoy the challenge of trudging through a quagmire in wind and rain in order to stand atop a mountain whose name is unknown to most people. Others find wonder in a crater conformed like the surface of the moon, with no familiar sights or sounds except the sounds made by the wind. Still others prefer a leisurely walk to a fern-rimmed pool and a cool swim beneath a waterfall.

All these options are possible within 729 square miles in a land of contrasts, in a land of unmatched beauty, in a land often equated with paradise by the casual visitor as well as the native-born. It's the Valley Isle — Maui. As the familiar stenciled T-shirt proclaims, "Maui No Ka Oi" — "Maui is the best." Maui has 150 miles of coastline, with 33 miles suitable for swimming. The Valley Isle possesses more beach area than any other Hawaiian island, which probably accounts for its exceptional popularity.

The island of Maui is the result of eruptions of two large volcanoes, which first formed separate land masses that were later joined by succeeding eruptions. Although some debate exists over the origin of the name, many people believe the island was named after Maui, a legendary superman, who lassoed the sun to bring daylight to the island. In spite of this male giant's influence, locals refer to Maui as "our beautiful lady" because of the island's curvaceous physical appearance. Topped by 10,023-foot Haleakala, the lady's shirt fans out in multitudinous pleats in the form of valleys and gulches. Some are usually dry, awaiting the seasonal rains. Others are usually wet and abound with introduced and native flora and fauna.

Maui is not only the second largest of the Hawaiian Islands in land size (Hawaii is the largest) but also the second most visited. More and more tourists are departing from the tour-bus route and becoming familiar with a Maui previously known only to natives. Campers, bicyclists and hikers are now more numerous and visible. There are hikes on Maui to satisfy the tenderfoot as well as the backpacker: short, easy hikes for the family, which reveal the beauty of the valleys, and more strenuous hikes, which do not necessarily reveal more but which fulfill the spirit of the more adventurous.

Camping and Cabins

Camping on Maui will add a dimension to your visit. Campgrounds and state rental cabins on Maui range from adequate to good and contain most of the amenities. Fees are modest and assure an inexpensive stay on the island. The camping map locates the county, state and national campgrounds, camping shelters, and cabins.

The county of Maui provides two tent and mobile (auto camper) campgrounds. H.A. Baldwin Park is 10 miles from Wailuku, and Rainbow Park is 12 miles. Neither park is recommended because of the poor facilities. Of the two, Baldwin has the better, more convenient location. Permits are required in county parks and are limited to 15 days per year. Camping fees are $3 for adults and $.50 for persons under 18. Each park has water, tables, and portable restrooms. For reservations, write the Maui Department of Parks and Recreation.

The State of Hawaii provides three campgrounds. Two are located on the east side of the island. Kaumahina State Wayside Park is 30 miles from Wailuku, and Waianapanapa State Park is 51 miles from there. Both parks are in beautiful settings. The former is on a cliff overlooking the east coast, while the latter is on a bluff overlooking a black-sand beach. If you are looking for solitude, the third state campground, at Polipoli State Park, will satisfy you. Polipoli is 31 miles from Wailuku, in Maui's upcountry at 6200 feet elevation. A four-wheel-drive vehicle is necessary to travel the road off the main highway. The maximum length of stay is 5 nights. There is no fee for any state park, but a permit is required from the Division of State Parks.

In addition to the campgrounds, the State of Hawaii also operates rental cabins at two locations. Each of the 12 cabins at Waianapanapa accommodates up to 6 people and is completely furnished with bedding, towels, cooking and eating utensils, electricity, hot water, showers, electric stoves and refrigerators. The one Polipoli cabin has similar facilities except that it has no electricity and has a gas stove and a cold shower only. The Polipoli cabin accommodates up to 10 persons. The cabins at both locations are comfortable and inexpensive. The maximum cost at Waianapanapa per cabin per day is $30 and at Polipoli is $50. For reservations or permits for the cabins and campgrounds, write or contact the Division of State Parks.

The National Park Service operates campgrounds and rental cabins in Haleakala National Park. One campground is located outside the crater at Hosmer Grove, a short walk from park headquarters at 7000 feet. Two other campgrounds are located in the crater — at Paliku Cabin on the east side and at Holua Cabin on the north side. Wilderness permits are required only for the crater campgrounds, where tenting is limited to three nights and four days (two nights at one site). Tenting is further limited to 50 persons per day, with 25 only per camping site. There is no fee for any of the campgrounds. Permits are available at park headquarters. There is one other campground in the park, located at sea level in the Kipahulu (formerly Seven Sacred Pools) section of the park. It is a primitive camping area without water. No permit is required at Kipahulu.

Use of the crater cabins presents a definite problem because of their popularity with visitors and locals. There are three cabins available in the crater — at Paliku, at Holua and at Kapalaoa (see the Haleakala map). Each cabin is equipped with water, pit toilet, wood-burning cook stove, firewood, cooking and eating utensils, 12 bunks, mattresses and blankets (pillows and sheets are not supplied). You must bring a warm sleeping bag. Use is limited to 12 persons per group, and, as with tenting, limited to three nights — two nights at any one site. Rates are $8 per night and $5 for children under 12, with a $20 nightly minimum. A lottery is conducted to determine cabin users. To participate, you must write to the Superintendent, Haleakala National Park, two months prior to the month for which you are requesting use, forwarding an outline of your proposed trip, including the number in your group, the exact dates and which cabin you want to use each night. You will be contacted only if your request is drawn. Don't pass up hiking and camping in Haleakala. It is one of the best places for both in the islands.

Two private campgrounds are available on the westside of the island. The Maui Land & Pineapple Company allows camping by permission (tel. 669-6201) on their property at Windmill Beach, which is 16 miles north of Lahaina. Windmill is a good swimming and snorkeling beach, but has no water or facilities.

Camp Pecusa is an Episcopal Church Camp located on the beach near Olowalu, 7 miles southeast of Lahaina and 14 miles southwest of Wailuku. A small sign identifies the highway turnoff. Camping is on a first-come, first-served basis at a rate of $3 per person, per night. The camp has an outdoor, solar heated shower, portable toilets, picnic tables, water and campfire pits.

Cabin facilities are also available at Camp Pecusa for rent by organized groups. Six A-frame cabins with six cots each, a fully equipped kitchen and dining hall, and bathrooms with hot showers are provided at a cost of $7 per person, per night ($100 minimum charge). Users must provide their own bedding (four inch foam mattresses are included), transportation, and food.

Addresses for all of the campgrounds and cabins above are in the Appendix.

Campers are advised to bring their own equipment because there are no reliable rental companies on Maui.

A SPECIAL NOTE: Camping has always been an enjoyable and inexpensive way to experience the Islands. Recently, however, some campers have been beaten and a few killed. Most of the beatings have been committed by local men, according to the victims. Most of the assaults have taken place at campgrounds that were close to cities or towns where locals congregate. There has been little violence in remote and wilderness areas of the national parks. The best advice is to avoid contact with groups of people.

Hiking

The island provides a great variety of hiking experiences. The verdant coastline and the valleys on the east side contain some fine hiking trails and places to find solitude. Haleakala National Park, particularly Haleakala Crater, has some outstanding hiking trails which provide the hiker with unique experiences.

The island provides short, easy hikes to suit the short-term visitor, and longer, more ambitious hikes for the visitor with more time and energy to expend. The hiker becomes familiar with a different Maui and views this beautiful lady from a perspective unknown to the ordinary tourist. It is with mixed feelings that I reveal her secrets, for the result may be an intrusion on heretofore pristine areas. Some parts of the island have not yet felt the impact of the visitor, with his frequently careless habits and the resulting pollution and abuse. I proceed under the assumption that the hiker is of a special breed: one who loves and cares for the land, one who tends to minimize his impact on the land, and one who does not violate the earth without feeling he has violated himself. Hike Maui for a week or two and you too will say, "Maui No Ka Oi."

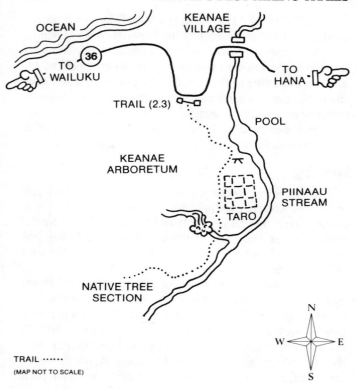

TRAIL ······
(MAP NOT TO SCALE)

KEANAE ARBORETUM
(Hiking Area No. 18)

Rating: Hardy Family.

Features: Swimming, fruits and native flora (identified).

Permission: None.

Hiking Distance and Time: 2.3 miles, 1 1/2 hours.

Driving Instructions:

From Lahaina (53 miles, 2 hours) southeast on Route 30, right on Route 380, right on Route 36 to the arboretum.

From Wailuku (34 miles, 1 1/2 hours) east on Route 32, right on Route 36 to the arboretum.

Introductory Notes: Keanae (lit., "the mullet") Arboretum provides an excellent introduction to native and introduced plants in a setting much like old Hawaii. Three distinct sections feature cultivated Hawaiian plants, native forest trees, and introduced tropical trees. You can enjoy all this and a swim in a fresh water pool.

On the Trail: From the turnstile, a jeep road (0.2 mile) leads to the arboretum entrance, and from there 0.5 mile through a cultivated section to road's end. Introduced ornamental timber and fruit trees located in this area are all identified for the visitor. The fruit of the pummelo (*Citrus maxima*) tree is of particular interest and good taste. It is a large, melon-sized fruit that has the aroma and taste of both grapefruit and orange. There are numerous banana and papaya plants. The area features several patches of irrigated taro, representing many of the varieties planted by the Hawaiians. Poi, a native staple, is produced from the taro root. Picnicking is available and encouraged in the grove alongside Piinaau (lit., "climb, mount") Stream which is an inviting place to swim.

At the far end of the domestic-plant section and taro patches and from the end of the jeep road, a trail (1 mile) leads to a large, forested flat that is representative of a Hawaiian rain forest. The trail winds through some heavy growth in places and crosses the stream 10 times, offering some welcome relief from the heat. Bear left at the first stream crossing and follow the trail, which parallels the stream below. About 100 yards from the first stream crossing, you will find the best pools and even a few relatively smooth, short water slides.

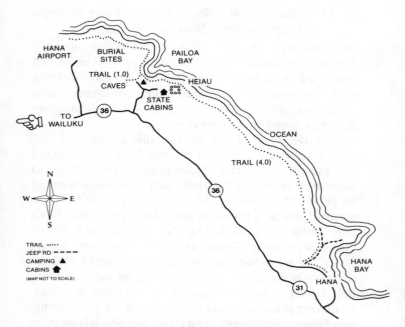

WAIANAPANAPA STATE PARK

(Hiking Area No. 19)

Rating: Hardy Family.

Features: Lava flows and formations, heiaus, burial sites, swimming, camping, blowholes, caves, black-sand beach.

Permission: For tenting and cabin reservations and permits write Hawaii State Department of Land & Natural Resources, State Parks Division (address in Appendix, see "Camping" for details).

Hiking Distance and Time: 4 miles, 3 hours.

Driving Instructions:

From Lahaina (70 miles, 3 hours) southeast on Route 30, right on Route 380, right on Route 36, left on road to Waianapanapa State Park.

From Wailuku (51 miles, 2 1/2 hours) east on Route 32, right on Route 36, then as above.

Introductory Notes: A round trip from Lahaina or Wailuku to Hana in one day is exhausting. To enjoy the beauty and serenity of the area, take a couple of days to experience the Hana Highway, camp at Waianapanapa (lit., "glistening water") State Park, swim at the black-sand beach, and hike the lava flows to the airport and to Hana.

Cabins situated along the beach are fully furnished and very comfortable. Each has beds, linen, utensils, water and an electric stove. All you need to bring is food. (See "Camping" for details).

On the Trail: The trail begins on a cliff above Pailoa (lit., "always splashing") Bay, with its black-sand beach, and follows the coastline — at times coming precariously close to the edge — to the enclosed bay at Hana.

Just below the campground you'll find burial sites decorated with artificial flowers and overlooking a rather fragile lava formation. The lava flow is undoubtedly honeycombed with tunnels and caves, evidenced by the many pits and holes and by the sound of rushing, crashing surf underfoot. Indeed, one blowhole is just a few hundred feet beyond the burial grounds.

The white substance on the lava is called Hawaiian "snow." A lichen, it is the first plant to grow on fresh lava. Other plants along the hike include the hala (*Pandanus odoratissimus*), which produces a large pineapple-shaped fruit. It is also called "tourist pineapple," since locals jokingly identify it as such to visitors. Beach morning glory (*Ipomoea pesca-prae*), with its pretty, delicate blue or purple flowers, plays an important role in preventing wind and water erosion of beaches by forming a large carpet. Also, a bush form of sandalwood (*Santalum ellipticum*) which grows less than three feet high is rather profuse in most areas.

You'll find rental cabins nestled among the hala trees at 0.5 mile, with a number of trails leading from them to the beach. At 0.6 mile a small bridge crosses a natural arch in the lava under which the surf pounds and crashes as small crabs scurry about. Just before the bridge, you may be sprayed by a small blowhole that is particularly active when the surf is up.

Overlooking the sea from its volcanic perch (0.7 mile) is a heiau (a place of worship). Heiaus played an important part in pre-Christian Hawaiian culture. There are hundreds of known heiaus on the islands that served specifically to ensure rain, good crops, or success in war, while others were used for human sacrifice. Some believe that if you wrap a stone in a leaf and place it on the walls of a heiau, you will be protected from harm. From the heiau, you pass a generous growth of hala, follow the coastline at its very edge, and reach a point about 50 feet above the surf. From here, about midpoint in the hike, you can see the cross on Mt. Lyons erected in memory of Paul Fagan, founder of the Hana Ranch and Hotel. You can also see tree-covered Kauiki (Lit., "glimmer") Head, an imposing buttress on the south side of Hana Bay.

The trail is no longer clearly identifiable. However, you should not have any problem if you follow the coastline and avoid "ankle twisters" on the broken lava. You will find numerous caves and pits caused by gas that was trapped under the lava as the surface cooled. Later, the brittle surface collapsed, leaving some interesting holes.

A sign marks the trail's end just before you reach a boulder-laden beach. From here, you can take any of the roads leading to the Hana Highway for a return trip to Waianapanapa, continue along the beach for 1/2 mile to Hana Bay, or return to the park via the lava flows. It is worth the extra hike to Hana Bay for lunch and a swim at its calm, gray-colored beach. The water at Hana Bay is not dirty but simply discolored by decomposed lava.

Waianapanapa Caves

Before you leave Waianapanapa, be sure to take the short, 1/4-mile hike to the caves, where it is possible to swim underwater to a chamber with a rock ledge. Legend recounts that a Hawaiian princess hid in the cave from her jealous husband, who, while resting by the cave, saw her reflection in the water. Since the ledge in the cave was a reputed meeting place for lovers, he promptly slew her by smashing her head against the walls of the cave. Consequently, it is said, the water in the pool turns blood-red every April, and her screams can be heard. If you cannot accept this legend, you may choose to believe that the red color of the water is the result of the tiny red shrimp that frequent the pool, and the screams are the result of the water and wind sweeping into the lava tube from the ocean.

Give it a try. The water is cool but refreshing, particularly after an ocean swim. A flashlight in a plastic bag will enable you to find the infamous ledge. It's fun.

North to the Airport.

The trail north from the black-sand beach is particularly rough because of the lava rocks underfoot. After passing two small bays, look for Hawaiian burial grounds and a heiau on your left where the terrain levels somewhat. The gravesites on top of the rough *aa* rock are rather prominent mounds. As you hike, you will be aware of the pounding surf and the interesting formations in the lava rock. Children enjoy assigning names to these strange forms. Be careful, as the trail is often precariously close to the surf. You are hiking over an early Hawaiian shoreline trail extending to the Piilanihale Heiau some three miles north of the airport.

You may choose to return to Waianapanapa via the shoreline route or to take the paved road by the airport to the Hana Highway and follow it to Waianapanapa.

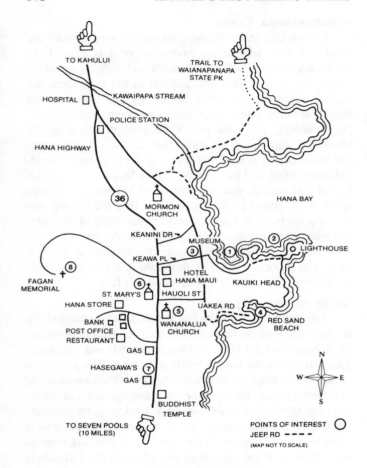

HANA TOWN
(Hiking Area No. 20)

Rating: Family.

Features: "A bit of old Hawaii," museum, historical sites, churches, swimming.

Hiking Distance and Time: 4 mile loop, 3 hours.

Driving Instructions:

From Lahaina (73 miles, 3 hours) southeast on Route
   30, right on Route 380, right on Route 36 to Hana
   Bay.

From Wailuku (54 miles, 2 1/2 hours) east on Route
   32, right on Route 36 to Hana Bay.

Introductory Notes: I recommend that visitors spend at
least one night in Hana so that they may enjoy the Hana
Highway with its many delights, but, more importantly, so
that they may enjoy Hana Town, one of the very special
places anywhere. You need to spend at least three hours to
enjoy just the highlights of this largely Aloha-spirited,
Hawaiian community.

On the Road:

(1) HANA BAY. This is a logical departure point for
exploring the town especially if you have driven the Hana
Highway. Lunch at Tutu's snack shop offers a lot of local
specials like a teriaki-burger or saimen (noodle soup) and, of
course, haupai (coconut) ice cream for dessert. Yum ! Yum!
After lunch you may opt to swim in the bay or snooze on
the soft gray sand beach.

(2) SNORKELING. (200 yards from Tutu's). From
Tutu's walk the road toward the pier and follow a dirt path
toward the lighthouse (beacon). Just before the beacon, a
plaque commemorates the birthplace of Queen Kaahumanu,
the favorite wife of King Kamehameha. Just past this place
climb over the rocks to a small alcove with white sand and a
calm ocean. It's a good spot to snorkel.

(3) HALE WAIWAI O'HANA. ("House of Treasures of
Hana") (0.2 mile from Tutu's). It may be the tiniest museum in the world but it's fine. Built in 1983, it stands on
the grounds of the refurbished, hundred-year-old former
county courthouse. Here you'll find many old, rare pho-
tographs of Hana, Hawaiian quilts, poi boards, kapa, stone
mortars, Hawaiian games, and most importantly, a large
measure of "Aloha" from the friendly staff. Look for my favorite exhibit, "A'i'Ai," a special pohaki (stone) donated by

Hawaiian authoress, Inez Ashdown. "He" has perfect little ears, nose, mouth, and eyes. Note also the very beautiful koa wood doors to the museum.

(4) RED SAND BEACH. (0.5 mile from museum). Walk south on Uakea Road past Hotel Hana-Maui on the right to the end of the pavement to the parking area for the hotel's beach units. Turn left across an open field, past a small cemetery, and descend to the shoreline where you'll find a trail leading to the popular red sand beach. It's still popular with nudists, so be forewarned if nakedness is offensive. It is also a fair snorkeling spot.

(5). WANANALUA CHURCH. (0.3 mile from Red Sand Beach). This interesting, century and a half old church on Hauoli Street was built by hand of lava rock over a 20-year period.

(6) ST. MARY'S CATHOLIC CHURCH. (Across the street from Wananalua Church). A very beautiful, brightly painted church. As you face the church, the conspicuous cross on the hill above the town is a memorial to Paul Fagan, the founder of the Hana Ranch.

(7) HASEGAWA GENERAL STORE. (0.1 miles from St. Mary's). Until 1990, if you visited Hana and didn't stop at Hasegawa's store, you made a BIG mistake. Sadly, an arsonist burned the store in August, 1990. The Hasegawas have opened a store in the old theater until a new store is completed in 1993 on the old site. Expect a warm "Aloha" from the employees and from owner, Harry Hasegawa. The generosity of the Hasegawa family over the years is legendary.

Take every opportunity to talk to local people as you stroll through town. They are quick to discuss their island as well as your home. Many locals have traveled extensively or have relatives on the mainland and they always seem to have a relation or friend in your town. In any event, be assured that "Aloha" lives in Hana.

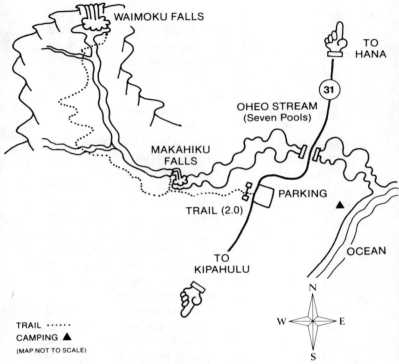

TRAIL ······
CAMPING ▲
(MAP NOT TO SCALE)

HALEAKALA NATIONAL PARK
(Waimoku Falls)

(Hiking Area No. 21)

Rating: Hardy family.

Features: Waimoku Falls, Makahiku Falls, bamboo forest, ancient Hawaiian agricultural sites, swimming, fruit, Oheo Stream, free camping.

Permission: None.

Hiking Distance and Time: 2 miles, 2 hours, 900-feet gain.

Driving Instructions:

> *From Lahaina* (82 miles, 4 hours) southeast on Route
> 30, right on Route 380, right on Route 36 to
> Hana, right on Route 31 to Oheo Stream (formerly
> called Seven Sacred Pools) and Haleakala National
> Park, Kipahulu Section.

> *From Wailuku* (63 miles, 4 hours) east on Route 32,
> right on Route 36 to Hana, then as above.

Introductory Notes: The Hana Highway and the pools in
Oheo ("something special") Stream (formerly Seven Sacred
Pools) are two of the most popular tourist attractions on the
island. To avoid a tiring return trip to Central Maui the
same day, you should consider staying at the cabins or
campgrounds outside Hana at Waianapanapa State Park (see
"Camping" for details). The Park Service campground here
in the park is located on pasture land south of the pools on a
bluff overlooking the rugged coastline. There is no water
available. Chemical toilets are placed throughout the parking
area. Camping is free and no permits are required.

On the Trail: The route begins opposite the parking
lot south of the bridge, ascends through pasture, and then
parallels the stream below. A few hundred yards from the
trailhead stands a 10-foot-tall concrete support, which is all
that remains of a water-flume system that once spanned
Oheo Gulch and carried sugar cane to a now abandoned sugar
mill one mile away in Kipahulu. The first highlight along
the trail, however, is at the 0.5 mile point, where the 184-
foot Makahiku Falls drops into a stunning gorge below.

To the left of the lookout, an abandoned irrigation ditch
cut in the cliff allows you to hike to the top of the falls. Be
cautious as you walk in the ditch. You may encounter a
cow, and there is not enough room for the both of you!
Retrace your steps to the pasture land and to the trail to
Waimoku Falls (lit., "flash flood").

While hiking through the pasture land, sample the yellow, lemon-sized guavas. They were relatively sweet the last
time I hiked to the falls. Grazing cattle do not seem dis-

turbed by your presence in this pastoral setting. As you hike toward the mountains, a number of waterfalls are visible.

At the one-mile point, a trail marker directs you into the woods and to the first stream crossing. As a sign notes, if the water is high in the stream and crossing is not easy, do not attempt to continue. At the stream crossing, there are several generous pools suitable for swimming. After the stream crossing and on to the falls, the trail is always wet and muddy. It is well-defined, but expect to make two more stream crossings, to hop over slippery rocks, and to carefully avoid the exposed roots on the trail. The Park Service recently placed some sections of boardwalk in the muddiest places.

The trail takes you through two marvelous bamboo forests. If the wind is up, you'll be serenaded by a discordant symphony of rattling bamboo. Beyond this "musical" forest are the remains of old taro patches, evidenced by walled terraces and shelter sites. Additionally, there are edible thimbleberries and guavas. Coffee plants are abundant also. With luck you will also find ripe mountain apples (*Eugenia malaccensis*). Before the falls there are numerous trees that bear a small, deep-crimson fruit with a pure white pulp and a large, round seed.

Shortly, Waimoku Falls comes into view. It's an idyllic spot to picnic after a pleasant hike. Before you shower under the falls, remember that most of the rocks in the stream fell from above.

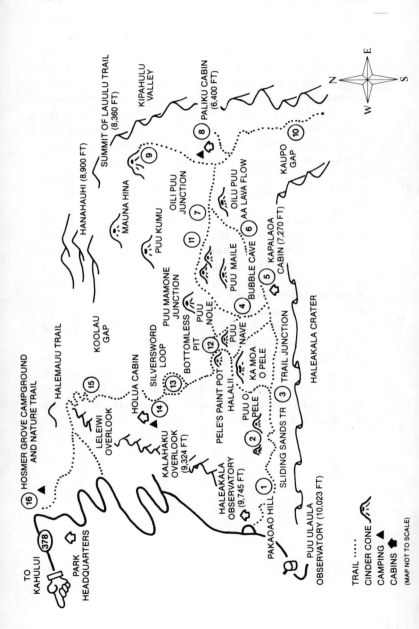

TRAIL ....
CINDER CONE
CAMPING
CABINS
(MAP NOT TO SCALE)

HALEAKALA NATIONAL PARK
(Crater)
(Hiking Area No. 22)

Rating: Difficult.

Features: "Moon" hiking, silversword, nene (a goose which is the Hawaiian state bird), lava tubes, lava formations, camping, rental cabins.

Permission: Hiking and cabin permits from Haleakala National Park. (See "Camping" for details).

Hiking Distance and Time: See the mileage tables in the text below.

Driving Instructions:

> *From Lahaina* (59 miles, 2 hours) southeast on Route 30, right on Route 380, right on Route 36, right on Route 37, left on Route 377, left on Route 378 to the summit (Park Headquarters is 11 miles before the summit). Entry fee.

> *From Wailuku* (40 miles, 1 1/2 hours) east on Route 32, right on Route 36, right on Route 37, left on Route 377, then as above.

(As you drive to the summit of Haleakala look for the large [three-foot] ring-necked pheasant [*Phasianus colchicus torquatus*] and the smaller chukar [*Alectoris graeca*] with its brownish black markings and a black band extending through each eye and joining at the lower throat. Both flush along the road and may also be seen in the crater.)

Introductory Notes: "Give me my life," pleaded the sun after Maui, the demigod, had lassoed it. "I will give you your life," replied Maui, "if you promise to go more slowly across the sky so the women may dry their cloth." To this day, the sun seems to pass more slowly over Haleakala, the House of the Sun. Such legends are still repeated by locals when they speak of nature's cauldron of power and destruction that helped create their island.

Recent evidence, however, credits other forces. Scientists believe that a hot spot exists beneath the earth's crust in the Pacific area and, as a consequence of periodic eruptions of this hot spot, a chain of volcanoes, the Hawaiian Islands, has been created. Centuries of submarine volcanic eruptions piled up successive layers of lava. Finally, this undersea volcano burst through the ocean's churning surface, and eventually reached a height of 12,000 feet above the Pacific Ocean. Nature then began to work her wonders from above, as wind, rain and the sea eroded the new rock, and streams ripped away at its surface, creating valleys. Ultimately, in the Haleakala area, two major valleys grew until they met, forming a long depression. Subsequent volcanic activity then filled the depression, while vent eruptions created symmetrical cones.

The persistent trade winds, carrying over 300 inches of rain per year, had an equally dramatic effect on Haleakala crater. Because these winds blow consistently in one direction, the crater has eroded unequally, and the vegetation differs correspondingly. Erosion has created two gaps in the crater: the Kaupo Gap on the south side, and the steeper Koolau Gap on the north side. Although it is possible to hike down both gaps, the Koolau Gap is not recommended because it is steep and treacherous in the lower elevations and no trail exists.

According to volcanologists, Haleakala Crater does not qualify as a volcanic caldera because erosion has caused it to shrink about 2,000 feet to its present 10,023 feet. Nevertheless, Haleakala is not extinct but only dormant, and it can be expected to erupt again some day.

Statistically, the "House of the Sun" is a large dormant volcano, covering an area of 19 square miles. It is 7 1/2 miles long, 2 1/2 miles wide, and 21 miles in circumference. Some 30 miles of well-marked trails invite the hiker to enjoy the awesome yet delicate beauty, and the unmatched serenity and solitude of the crater.

Hiking into the crater is serious business because of the distance involved, the terrain, and the altitude. Experienced hikers can plan a trip from the information contained herein. For others, I recommend the following hikes.

Part-day Hikes

Sliding Sands Trail to Kaluu o Ka oo

An enjoyable 3–4 hour, 5-mile round-trip hike can be made by good hikers partway into the crater via the Sliding Sands Trail. From the trailhead, you descend 1,700 feet in 2 miles into the crater to a posted junction where you'll find numerous silversword plants. A 0.5-mile spur trail leads to Kaluu o Ka oo (lit., "the plunge of the digging stick"), which is the only place in Haleakala that you can stand atop a cinder cone and look into the depression on the top. Remember that the return ascent to the summit is demanding at this altitude.

Full-day Hikes

Halemauu Trail to Holua Cabin.

This is a vigorous, eight-mile-round-trip, 1,400 foot-gain hike over a foot and horse trail to the floor of the crater. Food and water are a must on the trail, although water is available at Holua Cabin.

Sliding Sands Trail to Holua Cabin, exit by Halemauu Trail.

If you have only one day and if you want to hike into the crater and if you are a good hiker in good physical condition, then this is the hike for you. It's a difficult 12-mile, 1,400-foot-gain hike, but it will take you down the marvelous Sliding Sands Trail, across the crater floor, and up the Halemauu Trail. Whew! Better yet, plan an overnight stay at Holua Cabin or campground.

Overnight Hikes

Sliding Sands Trail to Holua Cabin, exit by Halemauu Trail.

This is a pleasant hike, and moderately strenuous when it includes an overnight stay in a rustic cabin. Tenting in the campground near the cabin is permitted. Remember, advance reservations are necessary to secure Holua cabin.

Sliding Sands Trail to Kapalaoa Cabin, exit by Halemauu Trail.

This hearty, 13.5-mile hike features an overnight visit at Kapalaoa Cabin. In the morning you can traverse the crater floor, visiting the Bottomless Pit, Pele's Paint Pot and the Silversword Loop.

Sliding Sands Trail to Paliku Cabin to Kaupo Village.

Hikers in good condition can take this 17.5-mile hike from the highest point on Maui to sea level. It covers the sparsely vegetated crater and the lush foliage of the Kaupo Gap. An overnight visit at Paliku is particularly rewarding, since the rich flora there is in marked contrast to the rest of the crater.

If you are able to spend more than one night in the crater, I recommend staying at Holua or Paliku Cabin. Time permitting, spend a night at each cabin. This will certainly enable you to enjoy the crater at a leisurely pace.

On the Trail: The following description of trails and highlights encountered along the way correspond to the numbers on the map. Six interconnected trails in the crater are listed on the hiking chart.

1. Sliding Sands Trail

The trail begins just above the visitor center on the south side of Pakaoao (lit., "sun comes through the portals of heaven") Hill at 9,745 feet. Pause before descending for a broad panorama of the crater. With the map, a number of prominent points can be identified. Koolau (lit., "windward") Gap is to the north and Kaupo Gap is south of Paliku.

Pakaoao Hill has an interesting history as a place used by wayfarers and by robbers who waylaid them. The southwest slope is covered with stone-walled enclosures used by the Hawaiians as sleeping shelters and for protection from the elements.

TRAIL MILEAGE	
Sliding Sands Trail Summit at 9,745 feet to:	
Holua Cabin	7.4
Kapalaoa Cabin	5.8
Bubble Cave	6.5
Paliku Cabin	9.8
Kaupo Village	17.5
Haleamauu Trail Park road at 8,000 feet to:	
Holua Cabin	3.9
Silversword Loop	4.8
Bottomless Pit	6.2
Kapalaoa Cabin	7.7
Paliku Cabin	10.2
Kaupo Village	17.9
Lauulu Trail Paliku Cabin (6,400 feet) to:	
Kalapawili Ridge (8,630 feet)	2.3

As you begin your hike, you will agree that the Sliding Sands Trail is appropriately named. The cinders and ash that make up the area around the trail were expelled from vents during eruptions and were carried by the wind to line the inner crater. As you descend, the contrasts of the crater become evident. The lush forest of the Koolau Gap to the north and the usually cloud-enshrouded Kaupo Gap southeast stand in marked contrast to the seemingly barren terrain around you.

After 2 miles and a 1,700-foot descent, you reach a trail marker which identifies a spur trail that leads to Kaluu o Ka oo, a cinder cone. At the end of this short spur trail, you stand atop a cinder cone and examine its design close up.

You will find some common crater plants in this area. The pukiawe (*Styphelia tameiameiae*) has tiny, evergreen-like leaves with reddish-white berries. The plant with yellowish flowers on upright stems is the kupaoa (*Dubautia menziesii*) which, literally translated, means "fragrant." A few isolated silversword plants (see Haleakala Trail Description No. 13) are located just off the trail.

2. Puu O Pele ("Hill of Pele")

Although legend has it that Pele, the Hawaiian goddess of fire, lives in Kilauea Volcano on the island of Hawaii, this hill was named in her honor. The building visible to the north is not Holua Cabin but a horse corral used by maintenance crews.

3. Trail Junction

You have hiked 3.9 miles and are now on the crater floor at 7,400 feet.

TRAIL MILEAGE (From the Junction)	
East to: Kapalaoa Cabin	1.9
Paliku Cabin	6.0
Kaupo Village	13.7
North via Ka Moa O Pele Trail to:	
Bottomless Pit	1.7
Bubble Cave	2.7
Holua Cabin	3.5
Paliku Cabin	5.9
Kaupo Village	13.6

Flora in the area includes a native grass (*Trisetum glomeratum*) that grows in tufts or bunches and is known locally as mountain pili (lit., "cling, stick"). Mountain pilo (lit., "bad odor") (*Corrosma montana*) is common and may be identified by its orange berries and handsome bush.

4. Bubble Cave

This is a natural shelter created when a portion of a bubble collapsed in the center, providing a convenient entrance. The bubble was blown by gases that held its shape until the surrounding lava cooled.

5. Kapalaoa Cabin (7,270 feet)

Kapalaoa (lit., "the whale or whale tooth") Cabin is one of three comfortable cabins maintained by the Park Service. There is no tent camping permitted in this area. Behind the cabin and about 1,000 feet above on a ledge on a ridge are the remains of a heiau constructed by early Hawaiians and used for religious purposes. There are also a number of platforms and shelters along the ridge, but the climb is difficult and should be approached with CAUTION. There are no markers or trails to lead the way. The views are superb, particularly that of the south coast of Maui.

6. Aa Lava Flow

The hike to Paliku Cabin (3.5 miles) crosses a lava flow composed of aa (lit., "rough") lava, a Hawaiian term that is accepted today by geologists to identify lava whose surface cooled, hardened and fractured into rough pieces. The trail is difficult, with extremely rough underfooting.

Hawaiian "snow," a whitish lichen is very common on the aa lava. About midpoint, Paliku Cabin is visible straight ahead across the lava flow, nestled in a grove of native trees.

7. Oli Puu ("hill to appear") Junction

Get out the poncho, if you have not already, for the rainy portion of your crater experience usually begins at this point if you are going on to Paliku Cabin. A different type of lava (pahoehoe) appears in this area. It is a smooth variety that frequently forms lava tubes when the outside chills and hardens and then the still-molten interior flows out of the cool shell.

TRAIL MILEAGE (From the Junction)	
East to:	
Paliku Cabin	1.3
Kaupo Village	9.1
Northwest to:	
Bottomless Pit	2.7
Holua Cabin	5.0
Halemauu Trail to Park Road	8.9

Very pretty mamane (*Sophora chrysophylli*) trees are conspicuous with their yellow blossoms, a favorite of feral goats. But the favorite of hikers is the ohelo (*Vaccinium reticulatum*) bush, which bears a tasty red, edible berry in the late summer. It is rather prolific in this section of the crater.

Although the jet-black berries of the kukaenene (lit., "goose dung") (*Coprosma ernodeoides*) bush are eaten by the nene, the Hawaiian goose, they are used as an emetic by Hawaiians. You are well-advised to avoid them.

8. Paliku Cabin (6,400 feet)

Unless you have cabin reservations or a water-repellent tent and sleeping bag, you won't spend too much time enjoying Paliku (lit., "vertical cliff"). The rain and wind blow for a while, stop, and then start again. It is precisely this yearly 300-plus inches of rain, however, that creates a lush garden of native and introduced plants and makes Paliku the most enchanting spot in the crater. The cabin is located at the base of a pali (lit., "cliff") that towers 1,000 feet above. The campground is in a grassy area to the front-right of the cabin.

Behind the cabin and surrounding the pit toilet, the akala (lit., "pink") (*Rubus hawaiiensis*), a Hawaiian raspberry, grows profusely. It bears a large, dark, edible berry that is rather bitter to eat but makes a delicious jam. In addition to the mamane described above, other native trees include the ohia (*Metrosideros collina*), the island's most common native tree, with its gray-green leaves and red flowers that look like those of the bottle-brush plant. The kolea (lit., "boast") (*Myrsine lessertiana*) is conspicuous around Paliku, since it grows to a height of 50 feet and has thick leaves and dark purplish-red or black fruit. Hawaiians used the sap of the bark to produce a red dye for tapa cloth. Several Methley plum trees are mixed in with the foliage. When ripe, usually May–June, these deep purple, ping-pong-ball-sized fruits are a special treat. In recent years, however, the area has become overgrown and some of the branches of the plum trees have been broken so that fruit has been scarce.

Around all three cabins you're likely to see the nene (*Branta sandvicensis*), the Hawaiian state bird. After disappearing, this native bird was reintroduced on Maui in 1962 and has since done well. The Park Service has a program to raise goslings at the park headquarters and to return them to the wilds in due course. The natural breeding cycle is difficult, owing in part to a number of introduced predators such as mongooses, pigs, and feral dogs and cats, for whom the eggs and the young goslings are easy prey.

The nene has adapted to its rugged habitat on the rough lava flows far from any standing or running water. The most noticeable anatomical change has been a reduction of webbing between the toes, creating a foot that better suits its terrestrial life.

If you spot a nene, don't be surprised if it walks up to you. It is a very friendly bird and has been known to enjoy a petting!

9. Lauulu Trail and Kipahulu Valley

The trail begins behind Paliku Cabin and zigzags up the north wall 2.3 miles. Although the trail is not maintained, a "good" hiker can make it. Kipahulu (lit., "fetch from exhausted gardens") Valley lies beyond the pali and extends to the ocean and the Seven Sacred Pools. It is a genuine wilderness area that has been explored by a few daring souls who have hiked the difficult Lauulu (lit., "lush") Trail to Kalapawili (lit., "twisting") Ridge. From the ridge there are excellent views of the Hana coast, the Kaupo Gap and the crater. Hiking into Kipahulu Valley, however, is prohibited by the Park Service.

10. Kaupo Gap

Kaupo (lit., "night landing") Trail follows Kaupo Gap and is a popular exit from the crater, but one that presents a transportation problem from Kaupo Village to central Maui or to Lahaina and Hana. Although the road has been improved around the south side to Kaupo Village, it remains rugged and bumpy. Hitchhiking from Kaupo is only a remote possibility, since few cars are found on the road. However, if you are up to a nine-mile hike to the Oheo Gulch (Seven Sacred Pools), a ride from there to your destination is more likely.

The trail is well-defined and initially follows the base of the pali, from which a number of waterfalls and cascades are visible, as well as views of the coastline and the Kaupo area. You are using some muscles you didn't use in the crater, for your descent is 6,000 feet in eight miles, which means you will be "braking" all the way. You may hear goats and pigs along the trail, although they may not be visible in the heavy brush.

About halfway, the trail becomes a jeep road, used by the Kaupo Ranch, which may be used by four-wheel-drive vehicles with permission.

11. Aa Lava Flow

On the connecting trail between the east and west sides, you are crossing the ancient divide between the Koolau and Kaupo valleys, in addition to one of the most recent lava flows (500–1000 years old) in the crater. Just before the trail junction, on the north side, is a prominent wall constructed of lava rock which was once used to corral cattle being driven into the crater to graze on the lush, rich grasses at Paliku.

At the junction, the vertical, slablike columns of rock protruding from the ridge are volcanic dikes that are remnants of the ancient divide between the valleys. Puu Nole (lit., "grumbling hill") opposite the dikes is a small cinder cone with a number of silversword plants on its slopes.

12. Bottomless Pit

In recent years a safety railing has been built around this pit, which is 10 feet in diameter and 65 feet deep. Some locals claim the pit extends to the sea. The pit was formed by superheated gases that blasted through from beneath.

In an earlier period, Hawaiians threw the umbilical cords of their newborn children into this pit-among others — to prevent (they believed) the children from becoming thieves or to ensure them strong bodies later in life. The Hawaiians' motive for this practice varied.

As you continue on the trail northwest about 100 yards beyond the pit, look for Pele's Paint Pot-a colorful area that was created by the many different minerals present in the magma. Many volcanic "bombs," hunks of lava in spherical shapes, are identifiable.

13. Silversword

Don't fail to hike this short (0.4 mile) loop trail to view some of the best examples of silversword in the crater. Silversword (*Argyroxiphium sandwicense*) is probably the single most popular attraction in the crater. The plant is endemic to the islands and, thanks to protection by the Park Service, it is recovering and thriving. Its enemies are the feral goats, who eat the plant, and "feral" visitors, who pick the firm, silver-colored leaves for souvenirs.

A relative of the sunflower, the silversword has stiff, stiletto-shaped leaves and a brilliant flower stalk. Typically, the plant will grow from four to twenty years, its age marked by the size and number of silverswords at the base. Then in a brilliant burst, the flower stalk will grow from one to nine feet in height, sometime between May and October, and will produce hundreds of purplish sunflowerlike blooms. After flowering only once, the entire plant dies and the seeds are left to reproduce. The crater species does surprisingly well, surviving on 16–50 inches of rain annually. Viewers familiar with the yucca blossom of the Southern California desert will find the silversword a familiar sight, although the two plants are not related. Please stay on the trail when viewing the silversword.

14. Holua Cabin

A day or two stay is particularly enjoyable at Holua (lit., "sled"). It is fun to explore the cave and lava tube in the area.

Behind the cabin, about 25 feet up the cliff, is a cave that Hawaiians once used as a campsite. About 100 yards to the front-right of the cabin is a lava tube through which you may walk with the aid of a flashlight. To locate the tube, follow the trail from the cabin toward Paliku for about 100 yards to a 10-foot-deep pit on the left and a faint trail that goes right. Walk up to the right about 40 yards to the tube's entrance marked by a sign and a metal ladder. The tube is about 150 feet long and exits through a hole in the roof. A recent archeological survey found the remains of an adult male and two young children entombed in the portion of the tube between the entrance and spatter vent — known as Na Piko Haua (lit., "the hiding place of the navel cords"). Ancient Hawaiians hid the umbilical cords of their newborn in such pits. It was regarded as unlucky for the child if the cords were found.

At dusk, be certain to listen for the strange call of the dark-rumped petrel (*Pterodroma phaeopygia*), which sounds like the barking of a small dog. This white-and-black sea bird makes its nest on the crater slopes where it produces one white egg annually. For six months afterward, it flies in from the ocean each day to tend the nest, arriving after sundown. Its "bark" seems to assist it in finding the nest after nightfall. This rare creature is now threatened by rats which have invaded the crater.

TRAIL MILEAGE (From Holua)	
East to:	
Silversword Loop	.9
Pele's Paint Pot	2.2
Bottomless Pit	2.3
Bubble Cave	3.3
Kapalaoa Cabin	3.8
Paliku Cabin	6.3
Kaupo Village	14.1
Observation Point at summit	7.4
Haleamauu Trail to Park Road	3.9

15. Halemauu Trail

Halemauu (lit., "grass hut") Trail, constructed by the Civilian Conservation Corps in the 1930s, remains in good condition. Horse and mule pack trains enter and exit the crater via Halemauu on a series of switch-backs for most of the 3.9-mile course, ascending 1,400 feet to the park road.

From Holua Cabin, the trail crosses a flat, grassy area before ascending. It's an enjoyable hike with spectacular views of the crater and the east side-when the weather is clear. There are a number of comfortable spots at which to rest in the morning shade. Keep a sharp eye out for the Maui wormwood shrub (Artemisia mauiensis), which is two to three feet high and usually grows on the cliff. It has aromatic silvery leaves and small orange flowers. Hawaiians still pound the leaves to use in treating asthma.

16. Hosmer Grove

The grove contains a small campground and picnic area with six tables, fire grills, shelter, water and a tenting area. It is a delight for an overnight visit. It's a good, convenient spot to camp if you wish to see the sunset or the sunrise from the summit of Haleakala. Camping is free and permits are not required.

A short, self-guiding trail is adjacent to the campground, and trail pamphlets are available to assist in identifying the native and introduced plants. Many of the introduced plants were established by Dr. Ralph S. Hosmer, the first Territorial Forester of Hawaii. There are excellent examples of sugi (Japanese cedar), cypress, cedar, juniper, Douglas fir, eucalyptus spruce and a number of pines. Native plants include sandalwood, mamane, aalii, mountain pilo, ohelo and kupaoa.

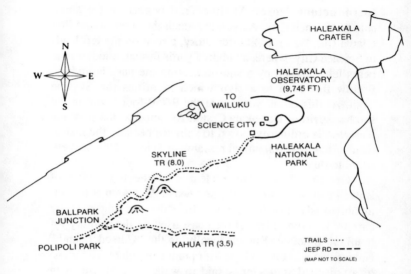

SKYLINE TRAIL
(Hiking Area No. 23)

Rating: Strenuous.

Features: Views of Lanai, Kahoolawe and Hawaii, and West Maui Mountains, cinder cones, historical sites, Polipoli Park, and native and imported flora.

Permission: None.

Hiking Distance and Time: 8 miles, 4 hours (to Polipoli Park), 3,800-foot descent.

Driving Instructions:

From Lahaina (59 miles, 2 hours) southeast on Route 30, right on Route 380, right on Route 36, right on Route 37, left on Route 377, left on Route 378 to the summit (Park headquarters is 11 miles before the summit). Entry fee.

From Wailuku (40 miles, 1 1/2 hours) east on Route 32, right on Route 36, then as above.

Introductory Notes: Skyline Trail begins on the south side of Science City. As you approach the summit and Puu Ulaula (lit., "red hill") Observatory, a road on the left leads to Science City, where, a hundred yards farther, another road bears left, marked by a sign indicating the park boundary. Follow this road to a sign which identifies the Skyline Trail. At this point, you are at the 9,750-foot level on the southwest rift of Haleakala Crater. As noted on the sign, the jeep road is ordinarily closed to vehicles because the instruments used in astronomical research at Science City are sensitive to dust.

On the Trail: On a clear day, the big island of Hawaii can be viewed to the southeast. Also seen is the uninhabited island of Kahoolawe (lit., "the carrying away by current"), seven miles off the coast used by the military for bombing practice. Known locally as the "Cursed Island," Kahoolawe was once a base for opium smugglers. The ghost of a poisoned smuggler is said to walk at night. Between Maui and Kahoolawe, tiny, U-shaped Molokini (lit., "many ties") appears. The pineapple-producing island of Lanai is to the northwest.

On this trail you will descend a total of 3,800 feet. The first 1,000 feet is your "moon walk" over rugged and barren terrain, with several cinder cones and craters along the rift. You are compensated, however, by a spectacular panorama of the island. The eye easily sweeps the offshore islands, the West Maui Mountain range, central Maui and the east side. The Maui "neck" is clearly visible from the trail.

The mamane (lit., "sex appeal") tree line begins at the 8,600-foot level, and the native scrub becomes denser and more varied. A mamane tree (*Sophora chrysophylla*) in full bloom is a beautiful sight, with its bright yellow flowers. It is a favorite of feral goats, who eat them greedily and quickly exterminate them in an area. The gate across the jeep trail at the 8,200-foot level marks the halfway point to Polipoli. When you reach this point, you will have hiked four miles.

An additional two miles brings you to the Papaanui-Kahikinui (lit., "large, parched-great Tahiti") Junction at 7,000 feet. On the left of the trail is a large open area that was used as a baseball field by members of the Civilian Conservation Corps during the 1930s. The area is referred to as "Ballpark Junction" by locals. From the junction, it is a one-mile trek to a point where a sign identifies the Haleakala Ridge Trail. After 0.3 mile from the sign, take the Polipoli Trail to the camping area some 0.6 mile farther, passing through dense stands of cypress, cedar and pine.

Polipoli Park provides camping facilities, water, flush toilets and a stand of redwood trees. There are also numerous easy family hiking trails in the vicinity (see Hiking Area No. 24). Between May and July, delicious Methley plums are a favorite of locals, who swarm over the area with baskets and pick them. All along the trail, you can expect to be surprised by California quails with their curved head plume, ring-necked pheasants, and chukars, which are brownish-black ground-dwelling partridges.

NENE — Hawaii's state bird

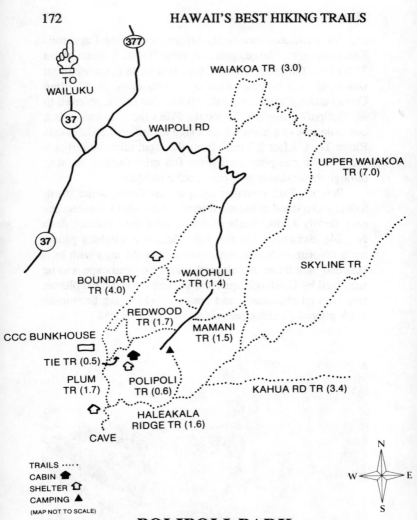

POLIPOLI PARK

(Hiking Area No. 24)

Rating: See individual hikes.

Features: Plums, redwoods, solitude, fresh and crisp air, birds, camping, cabin.

Permission: Tenting or cabin permits from Hawaii State Department of Natural Resources. (See Appendix). Trail shelters are first come, first served; no fee or permit required.

Hiking Distance and Time: Consult individual hikes.

Driving Instructions (Four-wheel-drive only):

> *From Lahaina* (50 miles, 2 hours) southeast on Route 30, right on Route 380, right on Route 36, right on Route 37 past Kula, left on Route 377 for 0.4 mile, right on Waipoli Road to end (10.5 miles).
>
> *From Wailuku* (31 miles, 1 1/2 hours) east on Route 32, right on Route 36, then as above.

Introductory Notes: The Waipoli Road to Polipoli (lit., "mounds, bosom") is a winding, bumpy route. The first three-and-one-half miles are paved, but the next seven miles are difficult and not recommended for passenger cars. A four-wheel or front-wheel drive vehicle is best.

Polipoli Park is an enjoyable hiking and camping area for the whole family. Although the road is difficult, it is well worth the effort for an overnight visit. On weekends, usually in the early morning hours, you may be treated to some local hang-gliding enthusiasts "doing their thing" on the slopes of Haleakala. These daring people, harnessed to kites that measure about 12 by 20 feet, take off around the 6,000-foot level for a fifteen-minute glide to the Forest Reserve entrance below.

Polipoli Park is only a part of 12,000 acres that also comprise the Kula (lit., "open country") and Kahikinui (lit., "great Tahiti") Forest Reserve on the upper west and south slopes of Haleakala Crater. Native forests of koa, ohia and mamane have been largely destroyed since the 1800s by cattle, goats, fires and lumbering. During the 1920s a major reforestation and conservation project was begun by the state, and it was continued in the 1930s by the Civilian

Conservation Corps. The result was the planting of hundreds of redwood, Monterey cypress, ash, sugi, cedar, and numerous types of pine.

Early mornings and evenings are usually clear, but fog, mist and light rain arrive during the day. Annual rainfall is 20–40 inches, and the nights are generally cold — unexpected by visitors to Hawaii. Indeed, winter nights frequently have below-freezing temperatures. But don't be discouraged: at least those pesky mosquitoes are absent!

A number of birds may be found in the park along the trails. With the aid of a small booklet, *Hawaii's Birds*, published by the Hawaiian Audubon Society, I have been able to identify the ring-necked pheasant (*Phasianus colchicus torquatus*), the chukar (*Alectoris graeca*), the California quail (*Lophortyx californicus*) with its distinctive head plume, the skylark (*Alauda arvensis*), and the ever-present mynah (*Acridotheres tristis*), which is probably the noisiest bird known to man. Indeed, the mynah, one of the most common birds on the island, is both intelligent and entertaining. One clue to recognizing it is that it walks rather than hops.

On the Trail:

Redwood Trail, 1.7 miles, 1 hour, 900-foot gain/loss (trail rating: hardy family).

Aptly named, this trail is my favorite at Polipoli because of the hundreds of redwoods (Sequoia sempervirens) that were planted as part of the reforestation program in 1927. Since that time, these wondrous giants have grown to a height of about 90 feet, and some measure four feet or more in diameter at the base. The hike is a particular joy for those familiar with the California redwoods. To walk among these majestic trees, to delight in their fragrance, to feel the soft sod from accumulated needles underfoot, and to view the sun trying to force its way through their dense foliage is an overwhelming experience.

The trail begins at the camping area at 6,200 feet and follows a circuitous route through stands of redwoods and other conifers to the 5,300-foot level. Markers identify many of the trees along the way, such as Mexican pine, tropical ash, Port Oxford cedar, sugi, and some junipers. A state park cabin is located a couple of hundred yards from the camping area along the Redwood Trail. The view from the cabin is exciting and the sunsets can be very beautiful. Don't miss either.

At trail's end, you are met by a generous garden of hydrangeas that seem to engulf the ranger's cabin, which is occupied only when the area is being serviced. However, flowers are not the main attraction here. Locals flock to this part of the park yearly to pick the Methley plum, which grow abundantly just below the cabin. The plums usually ripen in June, although they may be sweet by the end of May.

Tie Trail, 0.5 mile, 1/2 hour, 500-foot gain (trail rating: hardy family)

A trail shelter located at the junction of the Tie Trail and the Redwood Trail contains four bunks. The Tie Trail does what the name implies: it connects the Redwood Trail with the Plum Trail, descending 500 feet through stands of sugi, cedar and ash. The Tie Trail junction is 0.8 mile down the Redwood Trail. The Tie Trail joins the Plum Trail 0.6 mile south from the ranger's cabin.

Plum Trail, 1.7 miles, 1 hour (trail rating: hardy family)

The trail begins at the ranger's cabin and the old Civilian Conservation Corps (CCC) bunkhouse and runs south until it meets the Haleakala Ridge Trail. The trailhead is a favorite spot to pick Methley plums during June and July. Both the ranger's cabin and the old CCC bunkhouse may be used for overnight shelter, but both are rough and weathered and do not provide drinking water or other facilities. Often, during late afternoon, the trail becomes shrouded by fog or mist, which makes for wet, damp, cool hiking. You should be prepared with rain gear.

Although the plums attract hikers, there are stands of ash, redwood and sugi trees as well. The trail terminates on a bluff overlooking the Ulupalakua ranch area of Maui. An overnight shelter sleeping four is located here.

Polipoli Trail, 0.6 mile, 1/2 hour (trail rating: family)

This trail connects the camping area of the park with the Haleakala Ridge Trail. From the park it passes through rather dense stands of Monterey pine, red alder, cedar, pine and cypress, all of which emit delicious fragrances. Many fallen and cut trees provide an abundant supply of firewood for campers.

Haleakala Ridge, 1.6 miles, 1 hour, 600-foot gain (Trail rating: family)

For a full panorama of the island, the Ridge Trail provides the best views, since it is not as heavily forested as other portions of the park. It begins at the terminal point of the Skyline Trail, at 6,550 feet, and follows the southwest rift of Haleakala to join with the Plum Trail at 5,950 feet.

Monterey pine, cypress, eucalyptus, blackwood, hybrid cypress and native grasses are identified by markers along the trail. At trail's end, be certain to investigate a small ten-by-twenty-foot dry cave located in a cinder cone and used as a trail shelter. An eight-by-ten-foot ledge in the cave provides a relatively comfortable kingsized bed. A spur trail to the cave is clearly marked and easy to follow.

Boundary Trail, 4.0 miles, 2 1/2 hours (trail rating: strenuous)

The Kula Forest Reserve boundary cattle guard on the Polipoli Road marks the trailhead for the Boundary Trail. This trail descends gradually along switchbacks to follow the northern boundary of the reserve to the ranger's cabin at the Redwood-Plum Trail Junction.

The trail crosses many gulches that abound in native scrub, ferns and grasses as well as stands of eucalyptus, Chinese fir, sugi, cedar and Monterey pine. About 1/2 mile below the cabin, fuchsia bushes proliferate to the point of obscuring the trail. As you pass through this garland of delicate red, lanternlike flowers, a clearing encircled by eucalyptus trees appears across the fence. Hikers wishing to connect with the Kula road must jump the fence and cut across the pasture to Kula Sanitarium about four miles below. Numerous points along the trail provide views of central Maui.

Waiohuli Trail, 1.4 miles, 1 hour, 800-foot gain/loss (trail rating: hardy family)

The rough, poorly maintained Waiohuli (lit., "churning water") Trail begins on the Polipoli Road at 6,400 feet and goes straight down the mountainside to meet the Boundary Trail at the 5,600-foot level. Indeed, rather than looking for the trail, simply follow the ridge line. The trail first passes rough, low, native scrub, young pine plantings and grasslands, and then wanders through older stands of cedar, redwood and ash.

You will eventually join the Boundary Trail, which is well-maintained and clearly identifiable. At this junction, another overnight shelter is conveniently located.

Kahua Road, 3.5 miles, 3 hours (trail rating: strenuous)

Used primarily by hunters, this road begins at Ballpark Junction where the Skyline Trail joins the road at 7,100 feet. It leads east on the contour through very rough lava country to the cinder cone called Kahua (lit., "jealousy"). Even a four-wheel drive vehicle has difficulty traversing this road. An overnight cabin here is maintained by the state, and arrangements can be made in Wailuku for its use. It accommodates four people and has potable water. The primary attraction is the view of the east side and the rugged coastline. On clear days it is possible to see across Kahikinui to the Kaupo Gap. This is a very hot and difficult hike.

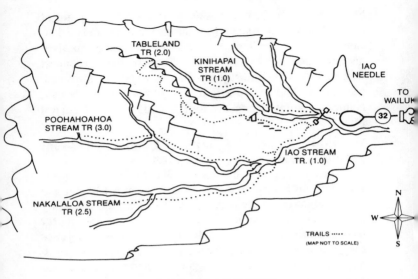

IAO VALLEY
(Hiking Area No. 25)

Rating: Consult individual hikes.

Features: Strawberry and common guavas, swimming, native flora, and views of central Maui, Iao Valley and Iao Needle.

Permission: None.

Hiking Distance and Time: See individual hikes.

Driving Instructions:

From Lahaina (24 miles, 1 hour) southeast on Route 30 to Wailuku, left on Route 32 to end.

From Wailuku (3 miles, 1/4 hour) west on Route 32 to end.

Introductory Notes: Few people dispute that Iao (lit., "valley of dawning inspiration") Valley is one of the most beautiful valleys on Maui. It has long been a favorite of locals and tourists, who come to see the Iao Needle, the John

Kennedy Profile, and the splendid tropical gardens and streams.

The area surrounding the state park is owned by the Maui Land and Pineapple Company; however, trails and paths have been "established" by locals and visitors and are used without securing permission. Use extreme caution when hiking off the trail in the stream, for the mossy rocks are treacherous. I have lost count of the twisted ankles and bruised knees I have received there, not to mention the times I have fallen into the stream. On all but the tableland hike, you can expect to get wet, since the trail frequently crosses the stream.

The whole family can enjoy Iao. There are casual family walks as well as more difficult hikes to challenge the adventurer. However, do not hike the streams when it is raining in the higher areas because of the possibility of flash flooding. Each year the streams are altered considerably by the seasonal rains and resulting floods; therefore, pools, small waterfalls and other such features mentioned here may no longer exist. You can expect, however, that other pools and waterfalls will have been created.

ON THE TRAIL

Tableland Trail, 2 miles, 1 1/2 hours, 500-foot gain (trail rating: hardy family).

From the parking lot at the end of the road, cross the bridge and follow the paved walk to the lookout shelter. The trail to the tableland begins behind the shelter. The first 1/2 mile is relatively steep, with a gain of 500 feet. At this point, the Needle is all but indistinguishable as you view its west side across Kinihapai Stream. As you continue, watch for a short trail on the left that leads to the top of the ridge. Follow this spur trail and continue along the razorback for a spectacular view of Iao Valley and Wailuku. The razorback detour then rejoins the Tableland Trail, which is level to the tableland. Between August and October, strawberry guavas flourish along the trail. This red, walnut-sized fruit may be eaten whole or after removing the small seeds inside. Sample them, but for the most succulent selections do your picking on the tableland.

In addition to the profuse guavas, ti plants and ferns abound in this area. As you approach the tableland, the strawberry guavas become more abundant. The tableland is identified by the tall, chest-high grass on a large flat area ringed by guava trees. Pick, eat and enjoy the varieties of guavas. The common guavas may be eaten whole, although some prefer to eat the inner portion, which is sweeter without the skin. Local people complain that it is no longer possible to find truly sweet guavas like those they ate when they were young; however, to a visitor these fruits are delicious.

A tasty drink may be concocted from the guavas you bring back from your hikes if you have a blender. Wash the whole guava and place in the blender. Add one cup of water. Reduce by blending to a syrup, and strain. Mix this syrup with your favorite base (orange, grapefruit, passion fruit) to taste. Serve with ice or after chilling.

The trail passes straight through the tableland and into moderately heavy growth and continues on a winding, ascending course for about 1/2-mile to a marvelous viewpoint — when it's not cloudy — from which you can view the dramatic pali (cliffs) here. USE CAUTION on the last 100 yards of the trail because it is steep, muddy, and overgrown. Usually, several waterfalls can be sighted from trail's end.

When you return to the parking lot, be sure to walk to the stream below for a swim. There are a number of sizeable pools. You'll probably share the pools with local children who frequent the area; better yet, find your own private pool.

Iao Stream, 1 mile, 1/2 hour (trail rating: family)

After crossing the bridge at the parking lot, take the path to the left, which descends to Iao Stream. A well-defined trail extends for 1/2 mile along the stream and sometimes along the cliff above the stream and abruptly ends at a

large pool. Since it is not possible to continue on the north
(right) side of the stream, you must cross the stream and
continue on the south side where the trail is no longer distinguishable. From then on, it is necessary to make your
way by walking in the stream, or over the rocks, or along
the bank if the water level is low.

At the one-mile point, the stream divides, with
Nakalaloa Stream to the left and Poohahoahoa Stream to the
right. The relative seclusion and the inviting pools make
this area a favorite of skinnydippers and nude sun bathers. If
you blush easily, you had better wear blinders.

BE CAUTIOUS if you elect to explore beyond this
point since both valleys narrow considerably and there is the
ever-present danger of flash flooding.

**Poohahaohoa Stream, 3 miles, 2 hours (trail rat-
ing: strenuous).**

Above the stream junction, it is unlikely that you will
find other people. USE EXTREME CAUTION, since
Poohahoahoa (lit., "heads getting together") Stream on the
right narrows in places, making it necessary to swim the
stream or to crawl over rocks in order to proceed. Indeed,
there are places where ropes are needed to negotiate narrow
canyons. This is a very rugged area where flash flooding is
common. The canyons are extremely beautiful in this remote wilderness.

I do not recommend that any but the most experienced
hikers continue beyond the stream junction. The terrain is
rugged and the rocks treacherous. Bear in mind that even the
largest rock or boulder may roll or shift if enough weight is
applied to it. If you continue, don't get careless. Make your
way carefully and cautiously and always take the easiest
path.

**Nakalaloa Stream, 2.5 miles, 2 hours (trail rat-
ing: strenuous).**

Nakalaloa (lit., "complete forgiveness of sin") Stream
on the left from the junction is not as narrow nor as difficult

to hike as is Poohahoahoa. More delights await the hiker upstream. There are not only a number of large pools in which to swim but also a natural slide that drops the slider into a large pool. Only the most experienced hikers should continue beyond this point, for the terrain is rugged and the pitfalls many. Remember, most stream rocks are worn smooth and may be wet and mossy, making them treacherous. Don't be careless.

Maui's Silversword

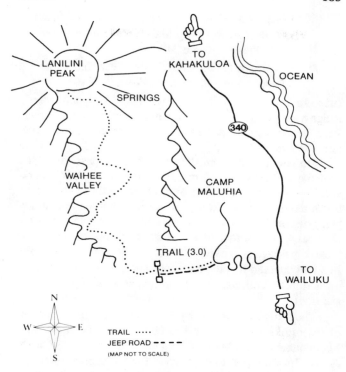

WAIHEE RIDGE

(Hiking Area No. 26)

Rating: Strenuous.

Features: Views of Waihee Canyon and Valley, central Maui, the north side.

Permission: None.

Hiking Distance and Time: 3.0 miles, 3 hours. Elevation gain 1,500 feet.

Driving Instructions:

From Lahaina (32 miles, 1 1/4 hour) southeast on Route 30 toWailuku, right on Route 32, left on

Route 340, (Kahului Beach Road) through Waihee,
left on road to Camp Maluhia to trailhead on left
0.8 mile from Route 340.

From Wailuku (11 miles, 1/2 hour) east on Route 32,
left on Route 340, then as above.

Introductory Notes: The Waihee (lit., "slippery water")
Ridge trail and area are under the management of the Hawaii
State Department of Land and Natural Resources and are reg-
ularly maintained.

On the Trail: From the parking area, pass through a
turnstile and cross the pasture, following red "R/W" markers. You may be surprised by grazing cattle in the heavy
brush along the road. Relatively sweet common and strawberry guava abound along the trail. Shortly, a gate across the
road marks the border of forest-reserve land. If the gate is
locked, passage is provided 20 feet to the right of the gate.
In a few hundred feet the road ends and a foot trail begins. It
turns right and climbs a ridge through an area of grass, ferns
and trees.

The trail is marked every 1/4 mile. There are a number
of overlooks into Waihee Canyon and to the north into
Makamakaole (lit., "not without intimate friends") Gulch.
At the 3/4-mile point and beyond for a distance, there are
superb views of the valley. Thereafter, the trail switchbacks
and ascends the narrow ridge that is heavily foliated, wet,
muddy, and in places quite steep so that it is necessary to
use the trees and bushes for support. After two miles, the
trail reaches a flat, grassy tableland that may or may not be
passable if it is too wet and boggy.

Be on the lookout for edible thimbleberries (*Rubus
rosaefolius*), which grow profusely in this area. These red
berries grow on a small bush with white flowers.

From the tableland, it is about a mile to Lanilili (lit.,
"small heaven") Peak and breathtaking views of the north
side of the island and of the surrounding valleys.

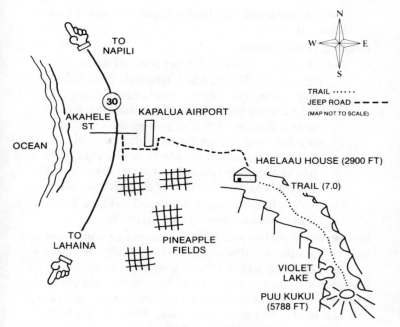

PUU KUKUI

(Hiking Area No. 27)

Rating: Difficult.

Features: Rare silversword and greensword plants, fern forest, views of the west side and offshore islands, Violet Lake, and the highest point on the West Maui Mountains.

Permission: The Maui Land & Pineapple Co. is reluctant to grant permission to hike Puu Kukui, but they may do so. They are reluctant because the area is of ecological importance and is very fragile. Call 877-3351 for permission and for the gate keys if you plan to drive to Haelaau House.

Hiking Distance and Time: 7 miles, 6 hours, 3,000-foot gain from Haelaau House at 2,900 feet. Add 7 miles, 3 hours, and 2,900 feet if departure point is from Route 30.

Driving Instructions:

From Lahaina (13 miles, 1 hour) north on Route 30 to the Kapalua Airport Road, turn right (you MUST have a four-wheel drive vehicle to continue) and make a quick right on the plantation road, left on the next road, and left after passing the airport runway and continue on the road that parallels the runway until reaching the telephone pole road. Turn right and continue (about 7 miles) on the main road until reaching the forest reserve and Haelaau House.

From Wailuku (34 miles, 1 1/2 hours) south on Route 30 past Lahaina, then continue as above.

Introductory Notes: Puu Kukui is the most exciting and interesting hike on the island and certainly the most difficult. This is a hike for those who don't mind getting soaked to the skin and chilled to the bone by rain and thirty-mile-an-hour trade winds. Meanwhile, a false step would put you in a muddy bog up to your waist. The rewards, however, are great. In no other place in the world do the exotic greensword and silversword thrive so abundantly.

On the Trail: A spectacular view of the west side and of the offshore islands is possible on clear days from Haelaau (lit., "wild forest") House, atop Kaulalewelewe (lit., "candlenut hill"). From the trailhead you can see the halfway point of the hike, marked by four prominent trees some three miles away in the northeast. The trail is relatively dry and easy to that point. Make frequent stops along the razorback for breathtaking views deep into Honokowai (lit., "bay drawing water") Valley on your right.

The first few miles from the trailhead are mostly through a thick native forest area containing a variety of ferns. The prettiest and the most common is the Hawaiian tree fern (*Cibotium chamissoi*), which grows from three to nine feet in height. The midpoint, at Nakalalua (lit., "to gather herbs") rain gauge, is a good spot for a snack or lunch break. A few fallen trees and a small clearing provide a comfortable setting.

A few hundred feet from the rain gauge are three successive overlooks, a short distance apart, from which you can view Honokahua (lit., "bay drawing dew") Valley and a spectacular waterfall. Caution: the winds are strong and the overlook is precipitous. From here to the summit, you can expect to find many silversword (*Argyroxiphium sandwicense*) plants and the rare greensword (*Argyroxiphium virescens*). Each is readily identifiable by its green or silver swordlike leaves. The silversword leaves (as described in Trailmark 13 of Hiking Area No. 22) are stiff and stiletto-shaped, while the greensword leaves are soft and pliable. Related to the sunflower, each is magnificent when in bloom.

Some Mauians still insist — in spite of the facts — that the only place in the world to find the silversword is on the slopes and in the crater of Haleakala. But in recent years the silversword has been found on the big island of Hawaii — on Mauna Loa and Mauna Kea. Actually, two species of the silversword are found on Maui. One grows in the West Maui Mountains and thrives on 200–300 inches of rain. The other flourishes on the bare cinder slopes of Haleakala, surviving on 16–50 inches of rain per year. The leaves of the Haleakala species contain a gel that enables them to retain water. This gel is not necessary to — and therefore absent from — the plant that grows on the slopes of Puu Kukui, where it thrives in bogs.

The rarer greensword has all but vanished from the island. It once flourished in very wet areas from 6,000 to 9,000 feet, but is now found in any quantity only in the West Maui Mountains. A few plants may still be found on the wet slopes of Haleakala, in the Koolau Gap and on the edges of the cliffs at Kaupo Gap. Over the years, feral goats, grazing stock and tourists have taken a heavy toll, particularly in the Haleakala region. To its credit, the National Park Service has made a concentrated effort to protect these plants. Both plants are found in most unusual places. Some grow in cracks between rocks and others on the remains of fallen trees. They can also be found growing in clusters of 10–15 in three successive clearings. The clearings also provide views of Napili (lit., "the joinings") Bay and the island of Lanai.

If you're from the Great Lakes region, tiny Violet Lake will be a surprise. Although it's not much of a lake, measuring about 15 by 30 feet depending on the season, it should be approached cautiously because of the uncertain footing. Indeed, the trail for the remainder of the hike is wet and boggy and should be approached carefully.

From Violet Lake, a little more than a mile remains, but do not continue if visibility is poor. The trail is obscured by the growth, but if you continue to walk up to the high ground, you will reach the top. At the summit, you will find the remains of a shelter that has been used over the years by hikers. With a whole lot of luck, you will be rewarded for your hike with an overwhelming view of Iao Valley, central Maui, Haleakala, and perhaps the big island of Hawaii beyond the summit. Be prepared for disappointment, however, for each time that I have hiked to the summit, the visibility has been about six feet! A ranger with the Hawaii Department of Land and Natural Resources is one of the few people with whom I've compared notes who was at the summit on a clear day. He reported a sight to stir the senses.

Your return trip, as expected, will be quicker. Somehow you don't mind getting wet and muddy, and you seem to slip into all the holes and bogs about which you were cautious and missed on the hike up.

Congratulations! You have completed the most difficult hike on the island.

MOLOKAI

The Island

Molokai is the island for a person who feels that Hawaii is overdeveloped and over commercialized and is looking for outdoor experiences. The fifth largest island in the Hawaiian chain — 37 miles long and 10 miles wide — Molokai was once known as the "Lonely Island" because the native sufferers of Hansen's disease (leprosy) were once banished here by the monarchy. Today, perhaps in response to an effort to change the island's image and to reflect more accurately its character, Molokai is known as the "Friendly Island." Locals still wave to passing motorists, shout greetings across the street to friends, and congregate in the few bars and restaurants in Kaunakakai, Molokai's town, to "talk stories" with friends and visitors. The slow-paced, relaxed life style is infectious.

Politically a part of Maui County, Molokai was created by three volcanoes. Mauna Loa is a shield volcano on the west side rising to 1381 feet; Kamakou, on the east side, is the island's highest point at 4970 feet; and about 2 million years after most of the island was formed, Kauhako (405 feet) erupted and formed the Kalaupapa peninsula. It is along the range of mountains and valleys on the east and north sides of the island that the best hiking trails are to be found. Indeed, the four valleys on the north coast, Waikolu, Pelekunu, Wailau and Halawa, offer outstanding outdoor experiences. Practically speaking, only Halawa is accessible on foot. Pelehuna and Wailau can be reached on foot but only by skilled hikers and outdoors people who are able to deal with hardships particularly the descent into these valleys. I strongly recommend hiring a local guide for either trek. The others can be reached by helicopter or, in summer during calmer seas, by boat.

MOLOKAI—TRAILHEADS, CAMPING

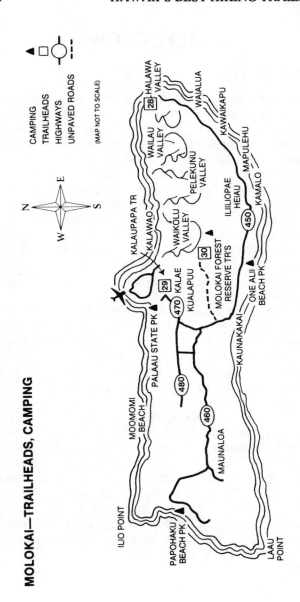

Although Molokai has retained a "nontourist," "low-key" style, it still offers adequate accommodations. There are a couple of hotels and a couple of condominiums offering satisfactory-to-first-class rooms and apartments, a number of car-rental agencies offering a wide range of vehicles, and a few good restaurants. A problem for the visitor is the lack of public transportation. Presently, hitchhiking in Maui County is illegal (check the law for any change) but a person may stand on the roadside. Most drivers understand, and I haven't had any problems getting rides on Molokai.

Camping

Palaau State Park, located nearly in the center of the island at 1600 feet elevation and eight miles from Kaunakakai, is an adequate camping site. Restrooms, picnic tables, grills and water are available, at the usual state park fee — free! The campground is located in a heavily wooded portion of the park where it is always cool and sometimes wet and damp. It is a short walk to the Kalaupapa trailhead.

The county offers two beach camping areas on Molokai. One campground is at One Alii County Beach, 3.3 miles east of Kaunakakai and the other is at Papohaku, 23 miles west of Kaunakakai. Each has the same amenities as Palaau State Park, but a fee ($3 in 1990) is charged. Reservations may be made through the County of Maui (see Appendix). Of the two, only Papohaku located near the Sheraton Molokai Hotel on the west side has a good swimming beach.

Wilderness camping is allowed in the Molokai Forest Reserve without a fee by permission of the Division of Forestry (tel. 553-5019). At Waikolu Lookout in the reserve there is a pavilion, water, restrooms, and barbecue pits. It is located 13.4 miles from Kaunakakai, but 10 miles of this distance is on a rough forest road which is passable in a four-wheel drive vehicle. All addresses are in the Appendix.

Hiking

Molokai offers some particularly interesting hiking and backpacking experiences. With the exception of Halawa Valley, the trails included are infrequently traveled. Kalaupapa does entertain many visitors daily, but few hike the trail — most fly to the peninsula or ride in on mules.

The Wailau Valley on the north shore and the Wailau "trail" require special note. Wailau Valley is one of the few nearly pristine places in Hawaii that is accessible on foot — almost. The trailhead is 15 miles east of Kaunakakai behind Iliiliopae Heiau (look for highway marker), but the trail from the heiau up the valley to the pali (cliffs) is not clearly defined. The 3000-foot descent of the pali is very difficult. On it, the trail is where the hiker can manage. The Wailau Trail should not be attempted by anyone who is not experienced in Hawaiian terrain or does not possess considerable outdoor skills. I suggest that you join a hiking group, such as the Sierra Club, which usually makes an annual trek into Wailau, or else hire the services of a local person who will guide you. There are a number of persons on the island who will serve as guides, particularly in Halawa Valley. Ask around. There are also a number of local boatmen who take people in and out of Wailau in the summer when the ocean allows safe passage. In any event, Wailau is an exciting experience. There are a number of camping spots along the beach and others on a 50-foot rise above the beach on the east side of the valley. The valley abounds with bananas, plums, mountain apples, guava, thimbleberries, and freshwater prawns and shellfish.

Permits to camp in Wailau Valley are required and may be obtained from the Forestry & Wildlife Office, Department of Land & Natural Resources, on Molokai. The office has announced emphatically that permits will not be issued "to those whom the Ranger deems inexperienced or otherwise unfit to safely negotiate this difficult and dangerous trail."

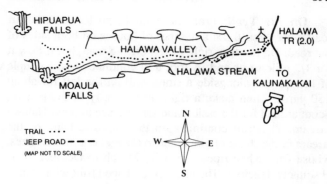

HIPUAPUA FALLS

HALAWA VALLEY

HALAWA STREAM

MOAULA FALLS

HALAWA TR (2.0)

TO KAUNAKAKAI

TRAIL · · · ·
JEEP ROAD — — —
(MAP NOT TO SCALE)

N
W — E
S

HALAWA VALLEY
(Hiking Area No. 28)

Rating: Hardy family.

Features: Waterfalls, swimming, fruits.

Permission: None.

Hiking Distance and Time: 2 miles one-way, 1 hour.

Driving Instructions:

> *From Kaunakakai* (28 miles, 1 1/2 hours) drive east on Route 450 to Halawa Valley. When the roads levels in the valley, locate a small church and a dirt road on the left. Park in the turnouts near the church or in the parking area at Halawa Beach Park, a short distance away. The trailhead is at the church.

Introductory Notes: Halawa (lit., "curve") Valley would most certainly be on anyone's list of the best places to visit in Hawaii. It contains all that a person expects in Hawaii — a good, pleasant hiking trail, fruits, and a generous pool in which to swim at the base of Moaula (lit., "red chicken") Falls. The valley is about 1/2 mile wide at the beachfront and about three miles deep. It was once heavily populated, but a tsunami in 1946 and almost annual flooding have discouraged permanent residents.

On the Trail: From the church, go left on the dirt road where you'll see a number of houses on both sides of the road. Do not turn right or left off the road, but follow it for 1/2 mile to its end. A foot trail continues past a couple of houses and alongside a stone wall on the left for about 150 yards. Then make a right turn directly to the stream. Scout around for the easiest and safest place to cross Halawa Stream. The trail continues on the opposite bank of the stream in the shade of giant mango (*Mangifera indica*) trees, whose fruit when ripe — usually March to October — is absolutely delicious. The large, pear-shaped fruit with orange pulp is quite sweet and juicy. The wood from these large, beautiful trees has been used for craftswood, furniture and gun stocks. From the stream, the trail passes under the mango trees and up a short rise to where it intersects a trail paralleling the stream. The fork to the right goes to the beach over private land. The fork to the left, our trail to the falls, passes more mango trees and countless noni (*Morinda citrifolia*), or indian mulberry, from whose roots and bark a yellow and a yellowish-red dye were produced. The small, warty-looking fruit was eaten in times of famine. It is a small evergreen with large, shiny, dark-green leaves. From here to the next stream crossing, the trail parallels a water pipe. It also passes by and bisects the remains of numerous taro terraces which once yielded great quantities of taro, from which the Hawaiian staple, poi, is produced. After you cross the north fork of Halawa Stream, Moaula Falls is about one hundred yards distant. Before you swim at Moaula, you should know about the legend of the moo (lizard) who lives here. It is safe to swim only if moo is happy, which can be determined by placing a ti leaf in the pool. If it floats, all is well; but if it sinks, well, you're on your own!

About 75 yards from the north fork stream crossing and just before the falls, a spur trail bears off to the right and up the cliff. The trail levels and is soon lost in the brush. If you continue through the brush, Hipuapua (lit., "tail flowing") Falls is about one-fourth mile distant. Be extremely cautious here. The trail to Hipuapua is not clear, and a rockslide before reaching the falls makes passage difficult. The best route is to scramble down the pali to the stream and to rock hop to the falls. But be cautious, the rocks are wet and slippery. Be certain to mark your route. Look for mountain apples (*Eugenia malaccensis*) on your way to Hipuapua. These lemon-sized apples, when ripe, are deep-crimson with a pure white pulp and a large round seed. They make an ideal snack after a swim at Moaula.

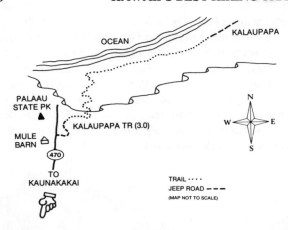

KALAUPAPA
(Hiking Area No. 29)

Rating: Strenuous. Elevation loss 1600 feet.

Features: Historical sites, views.

Permission: None to hike, but arrangements must be made to be met at trail's end by Damien Tours. No one is allowed to travel unescorted on the peninsula. Persons under 16 years may not visit Kalaupapa. If you ride the mules, a peninsula tour is part of the cost. If you wish to make your own arrangements, contact Damien Tours, 567-6171. Advance reservations are not necessary, but I suggest you call for the peninsula tour as soon as you arrive on Molokai.

Hiking Distance and Time: 3 miles one-way, 2 hours.

Driving Instructions:

From Kaunakakai (9.6 miles, 1/2 hour) drive west on Route 450, right on Route 470 to the entrance of Palaau State Park just beyond the Molokai mule barn and park. Walk right on a dirt road at the Park's entrance to the trailhead.

Introductory Notes:

> "To see the infinite pity of this place,
> The mangled limb, the devastated face,
> The innocent sufferers smiling at the rod,
> A fool were tempted to deny his God.
> He sees, and shrinks; but if he look again,
> Lo, beauty springing from the breast of pain!
> He marks the sisters on the painful shores,
> And even a fool is silent and adores."

After a week on the Kalaupapa peninsula in 1889, where he spent much of the time playing with leper children, Robert Louis Stevenson left this bit of verse with the sisters when he departed. I do not believe that anyone can visit Kalaupapa without being affected, some profoundly. Certainly these 4 1/2 square miles, which are bounded by vertical 2000-foot cliffs on the one hand and a rough sea on the other, have changed a great deal since that first day that Father Damien de Veuster set foot on shore in 1873. This first white resident of the peninsula was dedicated to aiding the forsaken souls who were banished to this leper colony. Many were tossed overboard from the ships that brought them and did not survive the swim to the shore. Those who did survive found an inhospitable society where children, women and the seriously ill were exploited by other sufferers from leprosy and where survival of the fittest was clearly the rule. For 16 years, until leprosy took his life, Father Damien attended to the spiritual, medical, and material needs of the populace. He built a church, but he also built houses, a hospital, and, perhaps most importantly, a patient society where exploitation was replaced by cooperation. After Father Damien's death in 1889, Brother Joseph Dutton and many others carried on his work. Today, Hansen's disease is controlled with the use of sulfone drugs, so that it is not necessary to isolate sufferers. The peninsula is now under the authority of the National Park Service, and Kalaupapa is likely to become a national park soon. Meanwhile, the 90 (1990) patients who remain are guaranteed a home as long as they choose, but they are free to leave.

Years ago, the Catholic Church began considering the question of sainthood for Father Damien. Robert Louis

Stevenson expressed the feeling that the patients had for
Damien during his life, and many have had after discovering
this remarkable man. In 1890 Stevenson concluded a letter
to Rev. C. M. Hyde, who had been severely critical of
Damien, by writing, "Well, the man who tried to do what
Damien did, is my father, and the father of the man in the
Apia bar, and the father of all who love goodness; and he
was your father too, if God had given you grace to see it."

On the Trial: Before descending the trail, walk to the
guard rail by the U. S. Navy facility for a fine view of
Kalaupapa (lit., "the flat plain") below. The peninsula was
built long after the rest of Molokai by Kauhako (lit., "the
dragged large intestines"), a 405-foot shield volcano. It is
best to begin your hike before 8:30 a.m., when it is cool
and you won't be troubled by the tour mules. The trail is
wide and safe in spite of its abrupt descent and 26 hairpin
turns. But some places have deep holes from the mules so
caution should be exercised to avoid a twisted ankle.
Throughout the day, shade trees and trade winds offer relief
from the heat. There are numerous places along the trail to
view Kalaupapa. This is not the trail used by Father
Damien; it was farther east. The so-called Damien trail was
dynamited after the priest's death by the people who owned a
ranch in the flat country above the cliffs. It seems that some
of the patients would ascend the trail and steal and slaughter
cattle for food. After the trail reaches the beach, it is about
1/4 mile to the mule corral and a paved road which leads to
Kalaupapa town. Your tour guide will meet you at the corral. You are not allowed to wander beyond this point. It is
permissible to stroll along Puwahi (lit., "broken conch")
Beach, before reaching the coral, where you are likely to encounter patients pole-fishing or throwing nets. The patients
are very friendly and are quick to talk stories.

Hopefully, Richard Marks, the county sheriff, will be
your guide. He is a patient, resident and all-around wonderful
man whose reportoire will fascinate and cheer you in spite of
the somber surroundings.

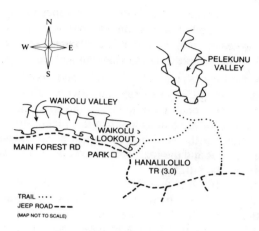

HANALILOLILO

(Hiking Area No. 30)

Rating: Strenuous.

Features: Mountain and coastal views, native flora, swamp.

Permission: Camping permits from Department of Land & Natural Resources. No fee.

Hiking Distance and Time: 1.5 miles, 1 hour.

Driving Instructions:

From Kaunakakai (13.4 miles, 1 hour) drive west on Route 450 for 3.4 miles to a dirt road on the right just before a large white bridge and opposite the "Molokai Aggregate Co." Go right on the dirt road for 10 miles to Waikolu Lookout. Do not attempt this road in a conventional car. The road is not posted, so bear left whenever you meet another road. However, do not turn left into the pineapple fields. You will be ascending a ridge and heading in the direction of tall trees. If you do not reach the forest reserve (posted) after driving 5.6 miles on the dirt road or the Nature Conservancy Camp 0.2 mile beyond, you are on the wrong road. From the camp, it is 3.2 miles to the "sandalwood boat" and from there 1.0 to the lookout and picnic area.

Introductory Notes: The "sandalwood boat," or Lua Na Moku Iliahi (lit., "pit of the sandalwood ship"), which is alongside the road one mile before the lookout, deserves a note. It is believed that a chief had this pit constructed to the dimensions of the hold of a sailing ship. Sandalwood trees were then cut and the logs were placed in the pit and sold to traders by the pitful.

Waikolu (lit., "three waters") Lookout provides a dramatic view into narrow and steep Waikolu Valley from a 3700-foot perch. During wet periods countless waterfalls burst forth from the cliffs. A recently constructed water tunnel provides most of the water for the south side of the island. On a clear day, the view is breathtaking. However, on a cloudy day you may see your shadow on the clouds — the rare Spectre of the Brocken.

On the Trail: Hanalilolilo (lit., "disappearing place") gets its name from the illusion that some experience here. They say that as they approach Hanalilolilo (the area above Waikolu Valley) it seems always to be receding.

From Waikolu Lookout walk 0.2 mile (Waikolu Valley should be on your left) on the road to the trailhead sign on the left side of the road. The entire hike is through a native forest of ohia lehua and a variety of ferns. Initially the trail climbs in the forest at the head of Waikolu Valley. Views of the valley are not good here because the ohia trees are so profuse. The ohia is a noble tree, a native tree and the most common tree in Hawaii. It has gray-green leaves and tassel-like red flowers that look like those of the bottlebrush plant. Legend holds that the flower is a favorite of Madame Pele, the goddess of volcanoes, and if it is picked without the proper incantation she will cause rain to fall. There are many varieties of ferns along the trail. The most common tree fern on the island is the Hawaiian tree fern, Hapu (*Cibotium menziesii*), whose trunks were used to make tikis, fences, pathways and orchid logs. In times of famine, the fleshy stems of the fern were eaten. The ulei (*Osteomeles anthyllid-ifolia*), or Hawaiian rose, is particularly abundant near the trailhead. It is a single, sweet-scented thornless rose usually found on a low shrub which sometimes grows to a height of 14 feet. Its hard wood, known for its pliability, has been used for bows, back scratchers, and javelins used in the Hawaiian game of pahee.

A short distance from the trailhead, you pass a water-works on the left side, from which you may get your last view of Waikolu Valley. About 1/2 mile beyond, be alert for a large lava-walled, fern-lined pit on the right. It is the type of formation that when combined with lush tropical fo-liation is one of the treasures of Hawaii. From this point to the tableland, the trail twists and turns through a heavily fo-liated native rain forest where the safest footing is on the roots of the trees. One false step and it's mud to the knee. Avoid the soft, damp mudholes in the middle of the trail.

You emerge on the tableland where you are greeted by a boardwalk constructed by the 1985 Alu Like Summer Youth Group commemorating the Hawaiian Bog Studies of 1938. The boardwalk allows for an easy walk to the center of the tableland, to the junction with the Pepeopae Trail. Make a left turn at the junction and follow the boardwalk for 0.4 mile through a rain forest to several precipitous points over-looking Pelekuna (lit., "smelly from lack of sunshine") Valley.

After returning to the tableland, retrace your steps to the trailhead, or go in the opposite direction on the boardwalk into the ohia forest on a 1/2-mile trail that will take you to a spur road off the main forest road. Continue a short dis-tance on the spur road to where it joins the main road. Turn right and follow the road to the Hanalilolilo Trailhead and the Waikolu Lookout some 2.5 miles distant. The road to Wailoku Lookout twists, turns, and drops through two gulches. Bear to the right at all intersections.

OAHU

The Island

Take a walk along Waikiki Beach any time of the day, any time of the year, and you will understand why this, the third largest of the Hawaiian Islands, is called Oahu, "the gathering place:" Everyone is here — Japanese, Chinese, Filipinos, Blacks Samoans, Germans, Canadians, Australians, Americans and others.

What is it that brings people here from all over the world? Can it be the air temperature, which seldom varies by more than 10 degrees, with a year-round average of 75 degrees F? Can it be the 80 degree water temperature at Waikiki Beach? Can it be the enchantment of precipitous cliffs and heavily overgrown valleys existing as backdrops to a city covered with asphalt and high-rise buildings? Can it be the fascinating blend of the multi-ethnic population? Can it be the life style in which individuality reigns supreme, and muumuus and cutoffs, oxfords and bare feet, tuxedos and swimsuits intermingle in the restaurants and night clubs? Can it be the surf, the music, the suntanned bodies, the Aloha spirit, the wild fruits, the hiking, the camping, the slow pace of life, the....?

The truth is that Waikiki and Honolulu are all of these things. The truth is that long before the first-time visitor arrives, Hawaii has transmitted its message via the plaudits of happy visitors, the media, and the Hawaii Visitors Bureau. The truth is that the first-time visitor has been primed for pleasure long before his jumbo 747 flies over Diamond Head and lands in Honolulu. For most people, there are no disappointments, and they return again and again.

Indeed, the crowds are sometimes so great that people spill off the sidewalk onto Kalakaua Avenue in order to get by casual strollers. Combine the 6-million-plus tourists who visit Oahu annually with the 800,000-plus permanent

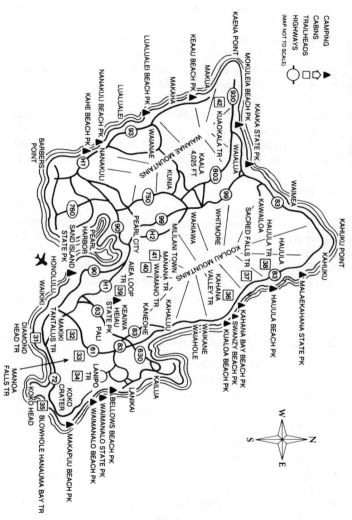

OAHU—TRAILHEADS, CAMPING

residents (about 80% of the state's population) and you have a lot of people on a rather small island.

Honolulu was not an original Hawaiian city. It was established by the followers of Captain Cook who, in search of anchorage, discovered this protected deep-water bay. Honolulu (lit., "protected bay") grew rapidly and was soon recognized as the trading and business center of the islands by King Kamehameha III. The official capital of the Kingdom of Hawaii was moved from Lahaina, Maui, to Honolulu in 1850. For the next 85 years, the southeast end of the city remained a swamp where taro was cultivated and ducks and other marsh birds roamed freely. However, in the past 40 years Waikiki has been dramatically altered from its humble beginnings to become one of the most recognized beaches in the world.

The two mountain ranges and the island of Oahu were created by volcanic eruptions. Oahu took shape as subsequent lava flows filled the area between the ranges until the present 607 square miles remained. In time, the Koolau mountain range on the east side and the Waianae mountain range on the west side were further sculpted by natural forces, so that both have gently sloping parts and steep precipitous areas.

Camping and Cabins

The camper should keep in mind that most of the campsites on Oahu are in heavily populated areas or in areas accessible to population centers. Consequently, all of the ills of urban living are present — thievery, damage to equipment, drunkenness. Campers should not leave valuables and equipment unattended or unprotected.

Hiking can be an exciting way to see Oahu, and camping can make your visit an inexpensive one. Since camping is a popular activity with local people, make your plans in advance and obtain permits as soon as you arrive on the island. There are five state campgrounds on the island and numerous county beach parks where camping is permitted. The best part is that camping is free at all parks.

Camping is permitted at five campgrounds in the state park system on Oahu. Sand Island State Recreation Area, located in Honolulu Harbor, provides close to town camping. The campground at Keaiwa Heiau State Park in Honolulu is in a shaded, wooded area near the trailhead of the Aiea Loop Trail. Waimanalo Bay State Recreation Area offers beach camping in an ironwood grove and board surfing and body surfing at one of Oahu's largest sandy beaches. It is located on Kamehameha Highway (#83) north of Hanauma Bay on the east coast. Malaekahana State Park is just north of Laie on the east coast, on a beautiful white sandy beach. It is a new park and campground, with new facilities. The fifth state campground is located on the popular and famous North Shore of Oahu where board surfing is "primo" — the best. Kaiaka State Recreation Area provides beach front camping in a landscaped coastal park. Permits are not issued earlier than two Fridays before the weekend of occupancy and are not issued for more than five (5) consecutive days. Camping begins at 8 a.m. Friday and ends at 8 a.m. on Wednesday. Campgrounds are closed Wednesday and Thursday. Reservations may be made by mail, to the Department of State Parks, at least seven calendar days in advance of the date the permit is to be in effect. (See Appendix).

The state has housekeeping cabins and camping operated by a private management company at Malaekahana State Park, located on the beach 0.9 mile from the entrance to the park. Group cabins (20 persons or less), family cabins (10 persons or less) and small cabins (5 persons or less) are available. Prices range from $25 to $80 per night. Amenities include mattresses, refrigerator, stove and hot water. Guests need to supply linens, pots and pans and cooking supplies. Camping costs $3 per night. Write or call Network Enterprises, Inc. P.O. Box 503, Kahuku, HI 96731, (808) 293-1736.

The County of Honolulu operates over 60 recreational areas located on all parts of the island. Camping is permitted at 12 places (number and location changes frequently due to heavy use), all of which are beach parks. Permits are not issued earlier than two Fridays before the weekend of occupancy and are not issued for more than five (5) consecutive days. Camping begins at 8 a.m. Friday and ends at 8 a.m. on Wednesday. Campgrounds are closed Wednesday and Thursday. Permits can be obtained from the Department of Parks and Recreation in Honolulu or at any of 10 satellite city halls located around the island. (All addresses are in the Appendix). All the campgrounds have cold-water showers, drinking water and restrooms. Most of the beach parks receive heavy use, so they are not always clean and the facilities are not always in good operating order. The campgrounds at Waimanalo, Kahana Bay, Mokuleia, Keaau, Lualualei, Nanakuli and Kahe are recommended, since they are usually clean and they have ample space for camping. Trailer camping is permitted at all of the parks where tents are allowed except Lualualei Beach Park. Trailers must be self-contained, since there are no electrical or sewer connections.

Hiking

There is more to Oahu than world-famous Waikiki, Diamond Head and Pearl Harbor. On the windward (east) side of the island are the Hawaiian communities of Hauula and Laie, where numerous valley hikes and beach camping, away from the crowds, await the outdoorsperson. The north shore of Oahu may well be the surfing capital of the world, with the Banzai Pipeline, Sunset Beach and Waimea Bay.

Although there are no hikes on Oahu to compare to the Kalalau Trail on Kauai or the trails in Haleakala Crater on Maui, there are trails to excite and to challenge the hiker. The hikes to Sacred Falls and into Makiki Valley are equal to any of the valley hikes on the other islands.

While most of the hikes on Oahu are short-distance, part-day hikes, I have included a wide selection of trips from short, easy family walks to long, difficult hikes. I have not included areas from which hikers are forbidden by law (protected watershed) or where the terrain is dangerous and unsafe even though local people may boast of their adventures into these places. Each year numerous injuries and some fatalities occur where people have hiked in spite of the prohibition. For example, a prominent sign at the end of the Manoa Falls Trail warns hikers not to climb above the falls, where the terrain is brittle and treacherous. Nevertheless, numerous injuries, rescues, and even deaths have been recorded there in recent years. However, good judgment and a regard for the time-tested rules of hiking are good protection.

The fine public transportation system on Oahu deserves a special note. Many visitors make the mistake of renting a car when "The Bus" — yes, that's what it's called — is convenient, reliable, comfortable and inexpensive. The Bus makes regular stops at most places of interest on the island. Unquestionably, The Bus is the best bargain on Oahu. For $.60 cents you can ride nearly 100 miles around the island: From Honolulu, the Bus travels along the east coast, passes across the north shore and returns through the central part of Oahu to Honolulu. The system is so reliable that I have included instructions for taking The Bus to the trailheads.

The one shortcoming of the system is that backpacks are not allowed unless they can be carried on the lap or stored under the seat. Call 531-1611 from 5:30 a.m. to 10 p.m. daily for information and schedules.

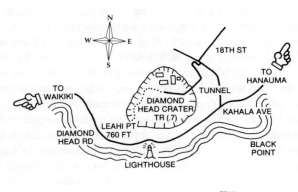

TRAIL · · · ·
(MAP NOT TO SCALE)

DIAMOND HEAD

(Hiking Area No. 31)

Rating: Family.

Features: Panorama of greater Honolulu area, historical site, extinct volcanic crater.

Permission: None.

Hiking Distance and Time: 0.7 miles, 1 hour, 550-foot gain.

Driving Instructions:

> *From Honolulu* (4 miles, 1/4 hour) drive south on Kalakaua Ave., right on Diamond Head Road and around to east side of crater, left at sign marked "Civ-Alert USPFO" opposite 18th St. Follow road through tunnel into crater to parking area on left.

Bus Instructions:

> *From Waikiki on Kalakaua Ave.*, take bus #58 (Hawaii Kai/Sea Life Park) to 18th St. and Diamond Head Road at a sign marked "Civ-Alert USPFO." Follow this road into the crater.

Introductory Notes: Although the hike to the summit of Diamond Head is hot and dry, the panorama offered from the top and along the rim trail is striking. This is a "must" hike for the whole family. Although a large portion of the crater and the surrounding area are on a military reservation, the hiking trail is under the jurisdiction of the Division of State Parks.

Without question, Diamond Head is the most photographed and the most readily identifiable place in Hawaii. Before the arrival of Western man, the area was known as Leahi (lit., "casting point"). In the early 1800s British sailors found calcite crystals in the rocks on the slopes of the crater and thought they were diamonds. Following the discovery, the tuff crater was called Kaimana-Hila (lit., "Diamond Hill), and today the world-famous place is known as Diamond Head. Geologists estimate that the crater was formed some 100,000 years ago by violent steam explosions. During World War II Diamond Head was an important bastion for the protection of the island. Gun emplacements, lookout towers, and tunnels were concealed in and on the walls of the crater. Although abandoned in recent years, these places are interesting to investigate, particularly for children. It is helpful to carry a flashlight, since the trail passes through two short tunnels and up a spiral stairway.

On the Trail: The trailhead on the northwest side of the parking area is marked, and the trail is easy to follow to the summit. Kiawe (*Prosopis pallida*) trees abound on the floor of the crater. These valuable trees with fernlike leaves and thorny branches are the descendants of a single seed planted in 1828 by Father Bachelot, a priest, in his churchyard in Honolulu. The tree is a source not only of fuel and lumber but also of honey (produced from the flower), medicine, tannin and fodder, which is produced from its bean-like yellow pods containing 25% grape sugar.

As you continue along the gently rising trail to the first concrete landing and lookout, you should be able to identify a number of birds. Two species of doves, the barred dove

(*Geopelia striata*) and the spotted dove (*Streptopelia chinensis*), are common and abundant on Oahu. The spotted dove, the larger of the two, has a band of black around the sides and back of the neck which is spotted with white. The barred dove is pale brown above, gray below, and barred with black. You should also see the beautiful, bright red, male cardinal (*Richmondena cardinalis*) with its orange beak and black face.

The concrete landing is the first of many lookout points along the trail. You have a good view of the crater and are able to distinguish some of the bunkers and gun emplacements on the slopes and on the crest of the crater. Follow the steps and the pipe railing to the first tunnel. You cannot see daylight at the end of the tunnel because it turns to the left at midpoint. A flashlight is not necessary to pass through the tunnel safely, but it is a comfort to small children since it is dark. As you leave the tunnel, investigate the rooms in the concrete building opposite the exit. They contained supplies and a power unit. Look for the bunker behind the building and hike to the left to a viewpoint overlooking the crater. A steep staircase — 99 steps — leads the hiker into a short tunnel at the end of which is an observation room and the first view of Waikiki and the greater Honolulu area. Look for the room containing a spiral stairway. Climb the stairway and then the ladder which takes you to the top and to the summit of Diamond Head. The concrete building at the summit is situated on top of Leahi Point at an elevation of 760 feet. Keep a watchful eye on children, for the summit's flanks are precipitous. The observation point at the summit provides a shady and comfortable picnic spot as well as a panoramic view.

It is possible to hike completely around the rim of the crater and to return to the parking lot by cutting through the brush, but the trail is steep and dangerous due to loose volcanic rock and ash. Only confident hikers should attempt this alternative route to the parking area. You will find numerous observation points and gun emplacements around the rim similar to those at the summit.

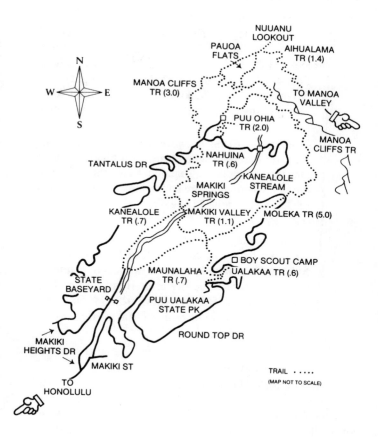

MAKIKI/TANTALUS

(Hiking Area No. 32)

Rating: See individual hikes.

Features: Mountain apples, Job's tears, native and introduced flora, valley views.

Permission: None.

Hiking Distance and Time: See individual hikes.

Driving Instructions:

To Makiki Valley — *From Honolulu* (3 miles, 1/4 hour) drive up Makiki St., turn left on Makiki Heights Dr. and continue straight on paved drive in Forestry "baseyard" (2135 Makiki Heights Dr.). Drive past a sign "Makiki Forest Recreation Area" to a parking area on the right just before a chain gate.

To Tantalus — *From Honolulu* (6 miles, 1/4 hour) drive up Makiki Street, turn left on Makiki Heights Dr., then go right on Tantalus. Drive three miles to the top, where there are a telephone-service road on the left and a trailhead marker.

Bus Instructions:

To Makiki Valley — *From Waikiki on Kuhio Ave.* take bus #2 ("Liliha-Puunui" or "School-Middle St.") to Beretania/Alapai Street. Secure a transfer and walk toward the ocean to Hotel Street. Take bus #15 (Pacific Heights) to Mott-Smith Drive and walk toward the mountains to Makiki Heights Dr. and to the trailhead.

To Tantalus — No bus service on Tantalus Drive or Round Top Drive.

Introductory Notes: There are three trails in Makiki Valley, two trails in the Tantalus area, two trails that connect the Tantalus area with Makiki Valley, one trail that joins Makiki Valley with Puu Ualakaa State Park, and one trail that connects Tantalus with Manoa Valley (see map). Consequently, there are trails to suit most hikers' interest and abilities. Your choices should be easy after consulting the maps and the trail narratives.

Tantalus and Round Top Drives combine to make a popular auto tour above Honolulu. The many turnouts, which provide panoramas of Honolulu, are favorites of visitors and locals in the daytime and lovers in the evening. The two hikes that lead into the mountains from the top of the road are a delight for the whole family. Local students named this area "Tantalus" after the mythical Greek king. Tantalus Mountain (2,013 feet) was so named, it is suggested, because as the students hiked, the peak seemed to recede. (You may recall that Tantalus was punished by being made to stand in a pool of water that receded each time he tried to drink).

You have a choice of numerous trailheads for the hikes included in this area. I suggest that you begin your hiking either at the Manoa Cliffs trailhead on Tantalus Drive or at the Puu Ohia trailhead, where Tantalus Drive becomes Round Top Drive (0.5 mile from the Manoa Cliffs trailhead on Tantalus Drive). The Manoa Cliffs trailhead on Round Top Drive is on the mountain side of the road at telephone pole #55 opposite a turnout and parking area. Two other good choices of trailheads are the Aihualama trailhead near the base of Manoa Falls in Manoa Valley and the Makiki Valley trailhead.

Kanealole Trail, 0.7 mile one-way, 1/2 hour (trailing rating: family). Elevation gain 500 feet.

The trail on the west side of Kanealole Stream is usually wet and muddy, but it is a gentler ascent than the Maunalaha Trail on the east side. The trail follows an old road that was once used by work crews to control the growth in the valley. Although the hike is uphill, there is abundant shade along the trail, which makes for a fairly cool and enjoyable hike for the whole family. Look on the left side of the trail as you ascend for surinam cherries (*Eugenia uniflora*) which, when bright red, are quite sweet. This small, ovate cherry from Brazil is a local favorite for making jelly. The Kanealole Trail ends at a junction with the Makiki Valley Trail, that goes across the valley to the right. Go left a short distance on the Makiki Valley Trail to join the Nahuina Trail, which will take you to Tantalus.

Nahuina Trail, 0.6 mile one-way, 1/2 hour (trail rating: hardy family). Elevation loss 600 feet.

Nahuina was constructed by the Sierra Club's Hawaii Chapter, which organized volunteers in 1979 to link the Tantalus and Makiki Valley hiking areas (see map). The idea was good because there is a lot of hiking pleasure to be gained from the loop hikes now possible. From the Manoa Cliffs trailhead on Tantalus Drive, the Nahuina Trail is easy to find. It is about 150 yards down the road on the left side (east), at the end of a white guard rail. From the junction with the Makiki Valley Trail, the Nahuina Trail heads north to Tantalus Road.

From Tantalus Drive, the trail is well-defined until tall grass obscures the trail. From here, be alert and cautious because the trail is overgrown and difficult to follow until you reach the Makiki Valley Trail.

Makiki Valley Trail, 1.1 miles one-way, 1 hour (trail rating: family).

This east-west trail traverses Makiki Valley. (The valley was named after a type of stone found here that was used as a weight for an octopus lure.) The trailhead on the west side is about 2 miles up Tantalus Drive from Makiki Heights Drive, north of a eucalyptus grove where the road makes a sharp turn. The trailhead on the east side is about at the midpoint of the Ualakaa Trail.

From the Tantalus Drive trailhead, the trail descends eastward through a forest into Makiki Valley, passing the Nahuina Trail on the left (north) and, shortly, the Kanealole Trail on the right (south). At this second junction, pause to look for springs in the brush to the left of the junction. The grass and brush should be matted where other hikers have made their way to the springs, 30 feet north of the junction. It is an enchanting place to pause to enjoy the beauty and the solitude. It is also a place to pick Job's tears (*Coix lacrymajobi*), which are abundant. The black, blue-gray and white, pea-sized beans of this plant are favorites with the local people, who string them into attractive necklaces, leis and rosaries. Ranging from one foot to six feet high, the plant is a coarse, branched grass with long, pointed leaves. The beans are easy for children to string with a needle and heavy thread.

From the junction, the trail turns in and out of small gulches and crosses a couple of small streams, passing through a richly foliated, forested valley. One of the many delights along this trail is the mountain apple (*Eugenia malaccensis*), which is abundant and within easy reach. What a treat! The apples are found on both sides of a stream in a very peaceful setting in which to pause and enjoy this succulent red fruit. Up the hill from the stream at an unmarked junction, the Moleka Trail goes to the left to meet the Manoa Cliffs Trail at Round Top Drive, the Makiki Valley Trail goes straight about 1/4 mile more to end where it meets the Ualakaa Trail, and the Maunalaha Trail to the right goes to Makiki Valley and the baseyard.

Maunalaha Trail, 0.7 mile one-way, 1/2 hour (trail rating: family). Elevation loss 555 feet.

From the junction with the Makiki Valley Trail, the hike on the Maunalaha Trail is an easy downhill walk. The trail contours along Makiki Ridge, passing through avocado, juniper, eucalyptus and bamboo in the lower parts. Periodically, a break in the forest provides good views of Honolulu and of Manoa Valley to the east. One of the most interesting trees in the valley is the octopus, or umbrella tree (*Brassaia actinophylla*), whose peculiar blossoms look like the long, spreading arms of an octopus. The new blossoms are first greenish-yellow, then light pink and finally deep red. As the trail levels, it crosses a footbridge over a stream, passes through the territorial nursery, and returns to the baseyard parking area.

Moleka Trail, 0.5 mile, 1/2 hour one-way (trail rating: hardy family).

Joining the Makiki Valley and Tantalus-Round Top, the Moleka Trail, like the Nahuina, was constructed in 1979 by volunteers organized under the leadership of the Sierra Club's Hawaii Chapter. Of the two trails, the Moleka is in good condition and is easy to locate and to follow. The trailhead is on Round Top Drive opposite the Manoa Cliffs trailhead, southeast of the turnout and parking area.

Descending from Round Top Drive, you step into a natural garden of ti, ginger (both white and yellow), bamboo and the delightfully beautiful heliconia (*Heliconia humilis*), or "lobster claw," so named because the bright red bracts are similar to boiled lobster claws. The trail gently contours along the valley slope, providing numerous views into Makiki Valley. Be on the lookout for edible red thimbleberries along the trail, growing on a small thorny bush with white flowers. About midway, a side trail to the left (east) will take you to Round Top Drive. Continue down and to the right to reach a junction with the Makiki Valley Trail. From the junction, the Makiki Valley Trail goes to the left to join the Ualakaa Trail and to the right across Makiki Valley. The trail ahead, the Maunalaha Trail, descends to the Makiki Valley baseyard.

Ualakaa Trail, 0.6 mile one-way, 1/2 hour (trail rating: family).

Ualakaa (lit., "rolling sweet potato"), was constructed in 1980 by volunteers organized by the Sierra Club's Hawaii Chapter. The purpose was to connect Puu Ualakaa State Park with the Makiki/Tantalus hiking area.

The trailhead is 0.1 mile from inside the entrance of Ualakaa State Park at telephone pole #9 on the right side just as the road makes a sharp turn. From here, the trail ascends, paralleling Round Top Drive for a short distance until it meets, entering from the left, the Makiki Valley Trail. The Ualakaa Trail ends shortly on Round Top Drive just opposite Camp Ehrhorn, a Boy Scout camp.

Manoa Cliffs, 3 miles one-way, 2 hours (trail rating: hardy family). Elevation gain 500 feet.

Just 3 miles up Tantalus Drive, a sign identifying the trail and a spur road that leads to a Hawaiian Telephone Co. facility mark the trailhead for the Manoa (lit., "vast") Cliffs Trail. The trail is well-maintained and easy to follow. You are likely to share the trail with students from the University of Hawaii, since the area is used as an outdoor classroom. The initial, forested part (1.2 miles) contours the hillside. A number of native and introduced plants, some of which are identified by markers, are found along the trail. According to the Division of Forestry, 33 native species of flora have been identified. You should not have any trouble finding guava and thimbleberry, two introduced plants whose fruit is edible. Guava (*Psidium guajava*) trees are particularly abundant throughout the area. The yellow, lemon-sized fruit is a tasty treat high in Vitamin C. Red thimbleberries (*Rubus rosaefalius*), which are also profuse, grows on a small, thorny bush with white flowers.

About 1 mile from the trailhead, you reach a junction. The trail to the left (north) is unnamed. At the junction with the unnamed trail, the Manoa Cliffs Trail makes a sharp right and follows switchbacks up a hill for 0.2 mile to the Manoa Cliffs/Puu Ohia trail junction (actually, a pair of junctions 30 feet apart). Puu Ohia leads north (left) down the hill and south (right) up the hill while the cliffs trail continues east.

The remaining part of the Manoa Cliffs Trail hike contours the hillside above Manoa Valley. Spectacular views of the valley are possible from a number of viewpoints. Keep a sharp eye on small children, however, for parts of the hillside along the trail are steep. There are a number of overgrown trails leading off both sides of the trail which should be avoided. One spur trail, a short distance east from the Manoa Cliffs/Puu Ohia junction, switchbacks up the hill to meet the Puu Ohia Trail. The Manoa Cliffs Trail turns south and emerges on Round Top Drive at the other trailhead

for this hike, from where it is 1.4 miles west (right) to your
car via the road or 0.9 mile west to the Puu Ohia trailhead.

Puu Ohia Trail, 2 miles one-way, 1 1/2 hours (trail rating: hardy family). Elevation gain 500 feet.

The Puu Ohia (lit., "ohia tree hill") trailhead is easy to
find. It is 0.5 mile from the Manoa Cliffs Trailhead near the
uppermost point of Round Top and Tantalus Drives, where
you will find a large parking area opposite the trailhead (the
nearest street number is 4050). The first 0.5 mile of the trail
follows a circuitous route up a hill. The trail then straight-
ens and goes along the side of the ridge a short distance to
where a number of trails lead off down to the right. Bear left
and follow the trail to where it meets a paved road, then follow the road to its end at a Hawaiian Telephone Co. facility.
The trail continues north from behind and to the left of the
telephone building and descends to cross the Manoa Cliffs
Trail. As you descend, bear to the left to avoid the somewhat
overgrown trails to the right and the one clear spur trail also
on the right. This latter trail eventually meets the Manoa
Cliffs Trail farther east. Soon you reach the Cliffs Trail, jog
right 10 yards on it, and then continue north. The Puu Ohia
Trail is wide but steep, so proceed with caution until you
reach Pauoa Flats. Although the trail over the flats is level,
it is usually wet and slippery and it has exposed roots which
are potential ankle-busters.

Eucalyptus (*Eucalyptus robusta*) and paper-bark
(*Melaleuca leucandendra*) trees dominate the flats area. The
eucalyptus has thick, pointed leaves with a capsule type of
fruit, while the distinguishing feature of the paper-bark tree
is bark that can be peeled in sheets. This tree has been
planted on the islands for conservation purposes in wet,
boggy areas. There are a number of secondary trails on the
flats where hikers have cut through the bamboo to vistas
overlooking Manoa Valley, the Pali Highway, and Reservoir
No. 4 in the Honolulu Watershed Forest Reserve. DO NOT
hike beyond the lookout into the watershed area, which is
protected by both law and good judgment.

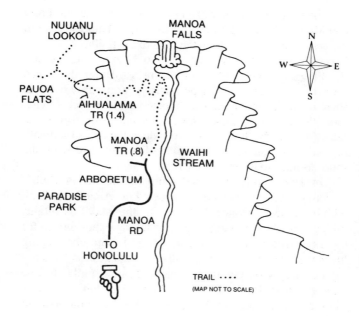

MANOA FALLS

(Hiking Area No. 33)

Rating: Family.

Features: Waterfall, swimming, fruits.

Permission: None.

Hiking Distance and Time: 0.8 mile, 1 hour, 500-foot gain.

Driving Instructions:

> *From Honolulu* (3 miles, 1/4 hour) drive north on Manoa Road past Paradise Park and Lyon Arboretum to the end of the road.

Bus Instructions:

From Waikiki to Ala Moana Center take bus #8. From Ala Moana Center take bus #5 (Moana) to Paradise Park at the end of the line. Walk up the road to the trailhead.

Introductory Notes: The trail to Manoa (lit., "vast") Falls is easily accessible from downtown Honolulu, which probably accounts for its popularity. You can expect to share the trail and the pool with local people as well as visitors. Nevertheless, pack a lunch and make the trip to the falls, for it is worth the time. To reduce the risk of a break-in, park your car in the lot at Paradise Park and walk the short distance to the end of the road.

In 1978, under the leadership of the Sierra Club's Hawaii Chapter, volunteers constructed the Aihualama Trail, which connects Manoa Valley with the Makiki/Tantalus hiking area, thus creating numerous hiking opportunities for a person who is looking for longer and more challenging hikes than the one to Manoa Falls. One suggestion for a delightful day's outing is to hike to Manoa Falls, follow Aihualama to Pauoa Flats, walk the Puu Ohia Trail to Manoa Cliffs, hike Moleka, and complete your trip in Makiki Valley or at Puu Ualakaa State Park.

On the Trail: A chain gate and a foot bridge at the end of the road mark the trailhead for the hike into Manoa Valley along Waihi (lit., "trickling water") Stream. Most of the trail is muddy and a bit slippery because heavy rains have washed away soil around trees and exposed their roots. The heavy rains also sustain a heavily foliated area where vegetation common to damp areas is abundant. The trail is easy to follow through the forest reserve. There are some fruit trees along the trail, but the likelihood of finding fruit is slim because of the popularity of the hike. The yellow, lemon-sized guava may be found as well as the popular mountain apple. This succulent apple is small and red, has a thin, waxy skin, and is usually ripe in June.

At midpoint, the canyon narrows and the footing becomes wetter. There are a number of larger pools where you may see hikers swimming or catching prawns, crayfish or frogs. The latter are particularly plentiful. You should be able to see the falls from a number of points along the trail. The junglelike setting at the falls makes for an enchanting place to swim and picnic if it is not too crowded.

The Division of Forestry prohibits entry into the closed watershed beyond the falls. Violators might damage a protected area and face the prospect of court appearances and fines. Furthermore, numerous injuries and a few fatalities have been recorded as a result of people hiking in this prohibited area.

Aihualama Trail, 1.4 miles, 1 1/2 hours, 400-foot gain (Trail rating: hardy family).

Do not mistake the precipitous and dangerous trail to the left of Manoa Falls for Aihualama. Beginning 50 feet from the falls, the Aihualama Trail follows a gentle zigzag path to Pauoa Flats. Enjoy the views provided along the first part of the trail. After 150 yards, turn for a good view of upper and lower Manoa Falls and across Manoa Valley to Waahila Ridge on the east side. A bit farther on, a view of the tip of Diamond Head and Waikiki is possible. The trail can be wet and muddy due to frequent showers throughout the year, but the rewards are great. Huge koa (*Acacia koa*) trees, with their crescent-shaped leaves, and interesting banyan (*Ficus benghalensis*) trees, with their aerial roots growing earthward from horizontal branches, combine with aromatic and delightfully beautiful ginger to excite the hiker.

After following the contour of the hill, the trail begins to switchback. Just before reaching Pauoa Flats, the trail cuts through a bamboo forest, which offers some interesting sights and sounds as the wind passes over the flatland and through the bamboo. At an unmarked junction, the Pauoa Flats trail turns right, and at the end of that trail, about 0.5 mile distant, there are views of Nuuanu Valley. The trail to the left goes to the Puu Ohia/Manoa Cliffs trail junction.

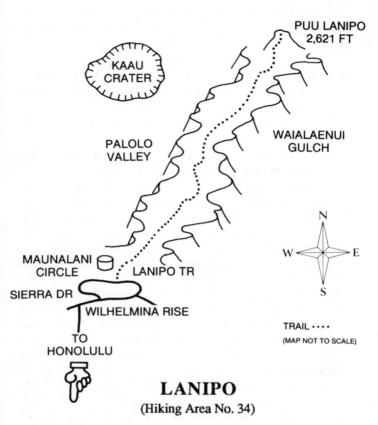

LANIPO
(Hiking Area No. 34)

Rating: Strenuous.

Features: View from Koolau Mountain Range, native and introduced flora.

Permission: None.

Hiking Distance and Time: 3 miles one-way, 3 hours, 1,600-foot gain.

Driving Instructions:

> *From Honolulu* (6 miles, 1/2 hour) drive southeast on H-1 to Koko Head turnoff. Go left over freeway toward mountains, then right on Waialae Avenue, and then take the first left, Wilhelmina Rise, to the top of the hill and 4969 Maunalani Circle, where a public-access passageway begins on the left of the driveway between fences.

Bus Instructions:

> *From Waikiki at Kalakaua/Kapahulu Avenue* take bus #14 (Maunalani Heights) to Sierra Drive/Lurline Drive. Walk up Sierra Drive to Maunalani Circle and to the trailhead.

Introductory Notes: The Lanipo and Wiliwilinui trails are parallel hikes to peaks along the Koolau Mountain Range. Indeed, an experienced and daring hiker could join the trails by hiking 1/2 mile along an extremely precipitous and dangerous ridge on the Koolau Range. Do not attempt this connecting hike alone. In any event, Lanipo, while strenuous, is worth the effort, for the views from the summit of the east side of the island are stunning.

On the Trail: The trail initially ascends along a fenced walkway for about 100 yards, to a point on Mauumae (lit., "wilted grass") Ridge. After a short descent, the trail traverses a number of saddles along the ridge. The first two saddles are a bit steep, with loose rock underfoot, so that caution is advised to avoid sore feet or a twisted ankle. The flora along the ridge is mostly low scrub and low trees, so that views of the surrounding area are unobstructed. To the west (left) Palolo (lit., "clay") Valley extends north to Kaau (lit., "forty") Crater which lies at the base of the Koolau Range ridge. The 1/4-mile-wide crater, legend holds, was formed by the demigod Maui who, wanting to join Kauai and Oahu, threw out a great hook hoping to catch the foundation of Kauai. He gave a tremendous tug and loosened a rock. The rock fell at his feet where he was standing at

Kaena Point on Oahu, while his hook sailed over his head and landed in Palolo Valley, creating Kaau Crater.

After the midpoint of the hike, the ridge narrows considerably. Thereafter, the trail is wet, muddy and steep, and it is necessary to grasp branches and roots of plants to continue. However, there are level places to rest and to enjoy a panorama of Diamond Head and the Honolulu area.

A variety of native plants can be identified. Look for ulei (*Osteomeles anthyllidifolia*), a single, sweet-scented, thornless Hawaiian rose; kawau (*Byronia sandwicensis*) a Hawaiian holly tree with white blossoms and black berries; and the common yet beautiful and interesting ohia lehua (*Metrosideros collina*), a plant that varies in size from a shrub to a tree 100 feet tall. The leaves are usually small, rounded or blunt, and grayish, and the flower appears as a tuft of red stamens emerging from close-growing petals. Visitors frequently identify it as a bottlebrush tree due to the close similarity of the two. Both the lehua and the bottlebrush are in the myrtle family. Legend says that the lehua is a favorite of Pele, goddess of volcanoes, who will cause rain unless an offering is made before a lehua flower is picked.

The last 1/2 mile is steep and requires agility to climb the precipitous ridge, to make your way around thick brush, and to avoid mud holes. But the views from the summit are ample reward for your efforts. You have a sweeping view of the east side, from the town of Waimanalo (lit., "potable water") to the northeast, to Kailua (lit., "two seas") to the north, and along the magnificent Koolau Range extending west. All this, and a plentiful supply of thimbleberries, await the hiker at the summit. Puu Lanipo (lit., "dense peak") (2621 feet elevation) is to the east (right), on the way to the Wiliwilinui Trail.

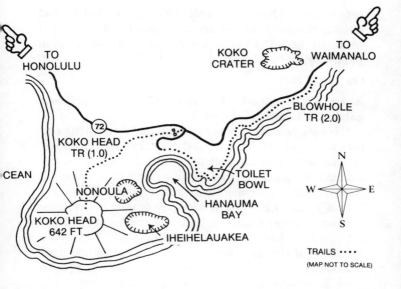

HANAUMA BAY

(Hiking Area No. 35)

Rating: See individual hikes.

Features: Swimming, snorkeling, tidepools, historical sites, blowhole, views of coastal area.

Permission: None.

Hiking Distance and Time: See individual hikes.

Driving Instructions:

> *From Honolulu* (12 miles, 1/2 hour) drive southeast on H-1, which becomes Route 72, then right on Hanauma Bay Road to parking lot.

Bus Instructions:

> *From Waikiki at Kuhio*, take the "Beach Bus" to Hanauma Bay.

Introductory Notes: To visit Oahu but fail to hike and swim at Hanauma is a mistake. Hanauma Bay is not only a strikingly beautiful place, but it also offers outstanding snorkeling.

On the Trail:

Koko Head Trail, 1 mile, 1/2 hour, 450-foot gain (trail rating: family).

For the protection of your vehicle and for convenience, park in the parking lot at the end of the bay road overlooking Hanauma Bay. To reach the trailhead, walk up the bay road to the highway. A gate across a paved road on the left (west) prevents vehicular travel to the summit of Koko (lit., "blood") Head. Climb through the gate or walk around it for the short hike to the summit. Enchanting views of Hanauma (lit., "curved bay" or "hand-wrestling bay") Bay and a panorama of the surrounding area are had along the road. Koko Head is a 642-foot-high tuff cone and, according to legend, is the last place on Oahu that Pele, the goddess of volcanoes, attempted to make a home for herself. From the summit, there are good views west to Diamond Head, north to the Koolau Mountain Range and Hawaii Kai (Henry Kaiser's 6000-acre town development) and northeast to Koko Crater and the coastline around Hanauma. Two small craters are below the summit to the east: Nonoula (lit., "red sunburned") on the left and Iheihelauakea (lit., "wide-leafed ihi-ihi" — an extinct or unknown plant that may have grown here) on the right. Look directly east and, if it is clear, you should see the island of Molokai some 20 miles across the channel. If you decide to return to the bay by crossing the two craters below, proceed with caution. There is no trail, and the slopes on the bay side of the craters are precipitous and dangerous.

Hanauma Bay to Blowhole, 2 miles one-way, 1 1/2 hours (trail rating: hardy family).

In 1967 Hanauma Bay was declared a marine-life conservation district, which meant that no marine life could be caught here or injured in any manner. Consequently, it is a delightful experience to investigate tidepools or to snorkel and to observe the variety of sea life under water. Hanauma Bay was once a crater, until the sea broke through the southeast crater wall.

From the beach, hike (left) along the shelf above the water on the east side of the bay. Be alert not only for interesting tidepools but also for waves which may splash onto the shelf. While the danger of being overcome by a wave is slight, it is wise to keep a watchful eye on the water. Be certain to visit the popular "toilet bowl" just beyond the far end of the bay. This interesting feature is a hole about 30 feet in circumference and 10 feet deep which is alternately filled and emptied from beneath as waves come in and recede. Bathers jump or slide into the bowl as it fills. Then, to escape, they scramble out when the water rises to the top of the bowl. Try it. It's different!

From the "toilet bowl" you can climb to the ridge overlooking the bay or follow the coastline around Palea (lit., "brushed aside") Point. From here to the blowhole you are likely to find many local people fishing and snorkeling, so pause to examine their catches and to exchange pleasantries. You will find that a smile and an inquisitive attitude will usually make a friend.

After the first mile, you may choose to hike to the road and to follow it to the blowhole, since the ledge above the water is narrow, and one needs some agility to climb, crawl and jump over the lava while trying to avoid the crashing surf. However, by timing the waves and by using good judgment, you can make it to the blowhole at Halona (lit., "peering place") Point. A blowhole is a narrow vent in the lava through which water is forced by the charging surf. The blowhole at Halona Point "blows" water geysers 30–50 feet into the air, depending on surf conditions. It is a happy terminus to a delightful hike.

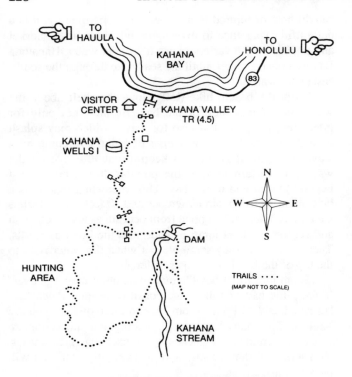

KAHANA VALLEY
(Hiking Area No. 36)

Rating: Hardy family.

Features: Mountain apples, rose apple, swimming, "living park."

Permission: Division of State Parks (see Appendix for address).

Hiking Distance and Time: 4.5 mile loop, 2 1/2 hours.

Driving Instructions:

From Honolulu (26 miles, 1 hour) drive northwest on H-1, then right on Route 61 (Pali Highway), then left on Route 83 to Kahana Valley State Park.

Bus Instructions:

From Ala Moana Center take bus #55 (Kaneohe / Circle Island) to Kahana Valley State Park.

Introductory Notes: Kahana (lit., "cutting") Valley State Park has been designated by the state legislature as a "living park." By definition, such a park is intended "to nurture and foster native Hawaiian culture and spread knowledge of its values and ways. ...This goal is to be achieved by the individuals living there, who will educate the public."

In July 1980 a committee composed of state-park officials and valley residents was formed to develop a program which will be offered to visitors. In the late summer of that year, the state completed a visitor center and a pavilion where some of the 140 valley residents and others will exhibit their skills so that visitors may learn about the traditional Hawaiian way of life in Kahana Valley. To date (1990) little progress has been made.

Kahana was once a thriving self-contained community where the people practiced the traditional concept of "ohana" — family units related by blood, marriage and adoption. Ample annual rainfall (average of 75 inches along the coast to 300 inches in the back of the valley) sustained the farms, and the ocean provided seafood for the residents. To date, the Bishop Museum has identified 120 small wet terraces and 12 irrigation canals constructed to grow taro.

The Kahana Valley hike is an enjoyable walk for the entire family. Be certain to secure a hiking permit because it will be checked by a caretaker.

On the Trail: From the visitor center, a jeep road leads into the valley for a little over a mile, to a fourth and last gate and the beginning of a hunting area and of a loop trail into the valley. Along this first mile, you pass some residences and then a couple of demonstration pavilions and public restrooms. Shortly, you pass the "Kahana Well" facility on the right, then a couple of hunter checking stations, and, just before the beginning of the loop trail, a papaya grove.

At the last gate, a large sign on the right side inside the gate identifies the entrance to the hunting area. From this junction one jeep road goes left for a couple of hundred yards and ends at the stream and a dam. The road to the right, bordered by hala trees, ends in about 1/4 mile and a foot trail continues into the valley. After crossing a small stream, the first part of the foot trail passes through a mountain-apple orchard. In season — usually between June and August here — these succulent red apples are the highlight of the trip.

Beyond a second small stream crossing, the loop trail is pleasant and easy to follow until it nears Kahana Stream. Just before the stream, a number of spur trails go in different directions. The loop trail bears to the left and descends to Kahana Stream. The trails off to the right were probably made by hunters, by hikers looking for a place to cross the stream when the water is high, and by people looking for rose apple (*Eugenia jambos*), an edible, egg-shaped golden fruit with rose-water taste and odor. Related to the mountain apple, the rose-apple tree is an evergreen with narrow, pointed leaves and large, greenish-white pompon flowers. At the stream, you should be opposite a concrete water intake that is under a tangle of branches of a hau tree. Cross the stream here and crawl under the limbs to the trail, which becomes clear a short distance beyond the hau trees. The trail ascends out of this small gulch for 0.2 mile to where it makes a sharp left and descends 1/2 mile to the stream and the dam.

Because of the heavy rainfall in the valley, it is not always easy to make the stream crossing. If you make it, be alert for the trail-marking tape on trees, which will direct you to the dam, the gauging station and the swimming holes. If the water is too high, you may retrace your steps to the junction at the last gate and from there follow the jeep road east to the dam.

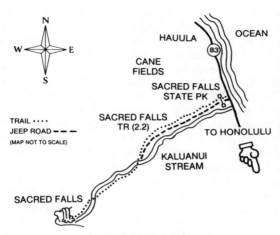

SACRED FALLS
(Hiking Area No. 37)

Rating: Hardy family.

Features: Waterfall, swimming, fruits.

Permission: None.

Hiking Distance and Time: 2.2 miles one-way, 1 1/2 hours.

Driving Instructions:

> *From Honolulu* (28 miles, 1 1/4 hours) drive northwest on H-1, turn right on Route 61 (Pali Highway), then left on Route 83 to the sign "Sacred Falls State Park" on the left.

Bus Instructions:

> *From Ala Moana Center* take bus #52 (Kaneohe / Circle Island) to Sacred Falls State Park.

Introductory Notes: Kaliuwaa (lit., "canoe hold" or "canoe leak") is the Hawaiian name for Sacred Falls. Probably the name was changed because "Kaliuwaa" is difficult to pronounce and because "Sacred Falls" sounds more romantic to most tourists. In truth, ancient Hawaiian belief regards the entire valley as sacred to the gods. Legend holds that the pool at the base of the falls is bottomless and leads to another world where a demon lives. The waves in the pool are thought to represent the struggle between the demon and the thrust of the falls, which prevents him from entering this world. Interestingly, another Hawaiian name for the falls and pool is Kaluanua, which literally means "the big pit." To pacify the gods thought to live in the area, believers wrap a stone in a ti leaf and place it along the trail. They believe this act will protect them from falling rocks. Don't miss this hike. Although the trail is usually muddy, it is a fairly easy stroll for the family and offers fruits, picnicking and swimming.

On the Trail: From the trailhead it is 1.2 miles on a cane road to the valley trail. Ahead, you can see the narrow canyon that contains the falls. The road terminates at a large, flat, grassy area that once served as a parking lot. On the left side of this open place, the road becomes a trail, which then crosses a dry stream bed and ascends gently into the canyon. Shortly, the trail reaches Kaluanua Stream, where it is necessary to rock-hop or wade.

In addition to the legends mentioned above, this enchanting lush island paradise is said to be the home of Kamapuaa (lit., "child of a hog"), who is half human and half swine. Near the end of the valley to the left of the trail, you will cross at the base of a dry fall. This is the site, legend recounts, where Kamapuaa turned himself into a giant hog so that his followers could escape a pursuing army by climbing up his back to safety on the ledge above. The deep impression where water only occasionally falls is said to have been made by the weight and size of his body. Mountain apple trees abound here and when ripe, this succulent, red, pear-shaped fruit is a treat.

The falls can be heard crashing to the valley floor and can be seen around the next turn in the trail after a stream crossing. The valley walls rise to 1600 feet, but the falls drop only 87 feet. The generous pool at the base is usually muddy and very cold. You might wish to swim or splash in the stream just below the pool. In any event, there is plenty of room for a picnic on the large rocks in this cool, shaded canyon.

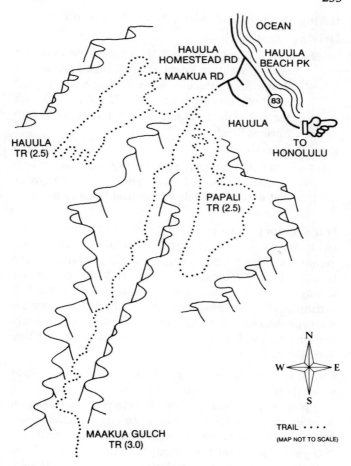

HAUULA

(Hiking Area No. 38)

Rating: See individual hikes.

Features: Views of valley and coastal area, swimming, waterfall, fruits, native and introduced flora.

Permission: None.

Hiking Distance and Time: See individual hikes.

Driving Instructions:

> *From Honolulu* (30 miles, 1 1/4 hours) drive northwest on H-1, right on Route 61 (Pali Highway), left on Route 83 to Hauula, left on Hauula Homestead Road opposite the north end of Hauula Beach Park for 0.2 mile and park at the intersection with Maakua Road.

Bus Instructions:

> *From Ala Moana Center* take bus #52 (Kaneohe / Circle Island) to Hauula Beach Park. Cross the highway and walk up Hauula Homestead Road to the trail-head.

Introductory Notes: Three good hikes, camping and swimming await the outdoorsperson in this Hawaiian community. In Hauula (lit., "abundant hau") you will find old Hawaii mixed with the new. You will find local people surf fishing, throwing a net, "talking stories" and having 3–4 generation ohana ("family") picnics on the beach. There are not many tourists who hike these trails, but you are likely to encounter local school children with their teacher or Boy Scouts with their leader.

Hauula, 2.5 miles loop, 1 1/2 hours, 600-foot gain (trail rating: hardy family).

Walk straight into the woods between the houses on Maakua Road, which becomes a dirt road after the last house. In 200 yards this dirt road becomes mere trail, and 100 yards farther, at a junction, the Maakua Gulch Trail veers left while the less-trod Hauula Trail goes straight ahead. A jeep road turns off to the right shortly before the junction. You pass through some heavy brush, ford a small stream and then switchback up a ridge to where Norfolk Island pines dominate. The fallen needles provide a soft underfooting and make the air aromatic. At midpoint along the ridge, do not take the trail entering on the right but bear left up the ridge. The trail switchbacks up the ridge, traverses

Waipilopilo (lit., "smelly water") Gulch, and then ascends along another ridge overlooking Kaipapau (lit., "shallow sea") Valley, from which you have good views of the Koolau Mountain Range and of the east-side coastline and of Hauula. The route then gently slopes and descends to join the initial portion of the trail, on which you retrace your steps.

Maakua Gulch, 3 miles one-way, 3 hours 1,100-foot gain (trail rating: strenuous).

Walk straight into the woods between the houses on Maakua Road, which becomes a dirt road after the last house. In 200 yards this road becomes mere trail, and 100 yards farther, at a junction, the Maakua Gulch Trail veers left while the less-trod Hauula Trail goes straight ahead. Just 140 yards farther, you pass the start of the Papali Trail on the left.

Maakua Gulch becomes narrower and narrower, and the trail twists and turns along a route which crisscrosses the stream countless times. Be prepared to get wet and to rock-hop throughout the last half of the hike, since the trail is in the stream bed there. The narrow canyon and its high, steep walls make this an enchanting hike. Another compensation is the frequent clusters of red mountain apple trees and a good supply of guava trees. The beautiful kukui (*Aleurites moluccana*) tree is common in the gulch. Nicknamed the "candlenut tree," the kukui tree was a valuable resource until the 20th century. Kukui-nut oil was burned for light, the trunk was used to make canoes if the more durable koa tree was not available, and beautiful and popular leis were made of the nuts. To make a lei, each nut must be sanded, filed and polished to a brilliant luster that is acquired from its own oil. Kukui is also the Hawaii State tree. The hike ends at the base of a small cascade — or, if you're an expert scrambler, the base of a small waterfall just above. At the bottom of the waterfall and the bottom of the cascade are pools large enough for a cooling dip.

Papali, 2.5 mile loop, 2 hours, 800-foot gain (trail rating: hardy family).

Walk straight into the woods between the houses on Maakua Road, which becomes a dirt road after the last house. In 200 yards this dirt road becomes mere trail, and 100 yards farther, at a junction, the less-trod Hauula Trail goes straight ahead but your trail veers left. Just 140 yards past the junction, on the left, is the overgrown start of the Papali (lit., "small cliff or slope") Trail. You have to duck and bend to get through the hau (Hibiscus tiliaceus) trees at the trailhead. In the wild, this yellow-flowered hibiscus grows twisting and branching along the ground, forming an impenetrable mass of tangled branches. The lightweight hau wood was used for canoe outriggers, fish floats, adze handles and fence posts. Maakua Stream slowly trickles through the hau grove and must be crossed. The trail then climbs sharply along switchbacks, passing concrete slabs that once supported water tanks. The trail heads toward the mountains for about a mile and then turns east and descends into Papali Gulch and crosses tiny Papali Stream. Although you'll share the scenic stream crossing with mosquitoes, pause in this serene place. Civilization seems a long way off. From here, the trail ascends along the ridge, until it rejoins the earlier trail segment near the concrete slabs. In the last mile of the hike you have outstanding views of Hauula town and north to Laie Point.

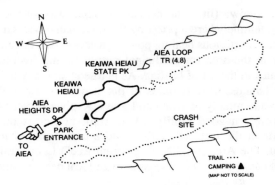

AIEA LOOP
(Hiking Area No. 39)

Rating: Hardy family.

Features: Views of Pearl Harbor, fruits, camping, Keaiwa Heiau.

Permission: Camping permits from Division of State Park (see Appendix).

Hiking Distance and Time: 4.8 miles loop, 3 hours.

Driving Instructions:

From Honolulu (12 miles, 1/2 hour) drive northwest on H-1, bear left at sign "Aiea #78," go right at "Aiea" turnoff and follow Moanalua Road downhill to a right turn on Aiea Heights Drive, and go to its end. After entering the park, follow the one-way road to the northeast end of the park and a sign marking the upper Aiea Loop trailhead.

Bus Instructions:

From Ala Moana Center take bus #11 (Honolulu\Aiea Heights) to Aiea and to the Kaamilo/Aiea Heights Drive junction. Walk up Aiea Heights Drive to Keaiwa Heiau State Park and to the trailhead.

Introductory Notes: Take time to visit the remains of the heiau (a pre-Christian place of worship) by the park entrance. Keaiwa (lit., "the mystery") Heiau was an ancient healing temple where a priest by the same name was said to have had mysterious healing powers. Keaiwa used the plants grown in the area for medicinal purposes, and instructed novitiates in the art of healing. As is true at so many heiaus in the Islands, little remains of the structures, since they were made mainly of wood and grass. Keaiwa Heiau State Park offers a good family hiking trail, first-class picnic grounds in the forested setting, and a comfortable campground. The Aiea (lit., "Nothocestrum tree") Loop Trail is likely to be crowded on weekends when local people come to enjoy the park and to hike.

On the Trail: The first part of the trail snakes along the ridge on a wide and well-maintained path where you can identify thin-barked eucalyptus, symmetrical Norfolk Island pine and ironwood (*Casuarina equisetifolia*), with its long, thin, drooping, dull green needles. Many of these trees are the result of a reforestation program begun by Thomas McGuire in 1928. The shade from the big trees and the trade winds make this part of the hike both cool and pleasurable.

The trail makes a sharp right turn at 1.6 miles, where a trail to Koolau Ridge departs eastward, and then follows the ridge above North Halawa (lit., "curve") Stream, from which views of the Koolau Mountains and North Halawa Valley are good. The trail descends through a forest of trees where you will find some native trees, including koa and ohia lehua. At the 3-mile point, look to the right of the trail for the remains of a C-47 cargo plane that crashed in 1943. Just beyond the crash site, a bridle path leads off to the left to Camp Smith and then the loop trail swings to the right and downhill to cross Aiea Stream. Before crossing the stream, you may choose to stroll along a trail to the left which follows the stream. The Aiea Loop trail crosses the stream and then climbs up to the campground and the lower Aiea Loop trailhead, which is just across the grass below the only toilet building in the camping area.

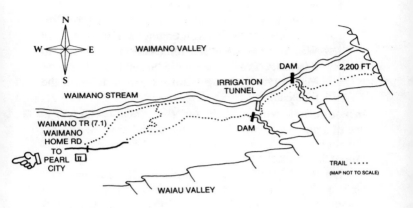

WAIMANO

(Hiking Area No. 40)

Rating: Difficult.

Features: Views from the Koolau Mountain Range, swimming, native and introduced flora.

Permission: None.

Hiking Distance and Time: 7.1 miles one-way, 4 hours, 1600-foot gain.

Driving Instructions:

From Honolulu (14 miles, 1/2 hour) drive northwest on H-1 to Pearl City (Exit 10) bear right on Moanalua Road to its end, then right on Waimano Home Road (1.7 miles) to the end at a guard shelter. The trailhead is on the left side of the fence at a trail register.

Bus Instructions:

> *From Ala Moana Center* take bus #53 (Honolulu/Pacific Palisades) to Pearl City Shopping Center (Kamehameha Highway and Waimano Home Road intersection). Transfer to Pearlridge-Pearl City shuttle bus and take to Komo Mai Drive. Walk up Waimano Home Road to the trailhead).

Introductory Notes: Waimano (lit., "many waters") is one of a number of hikes which take the hiker to viewpoints overlooking the east side of the island from the Koolau Mountain Range.

On the Trail: The trail parallels the fence a short distance and then an abandoned irrigation ditch above the stream. About 1/2 mile from the trailhead, a trail goes left to join the stream. Some ample swimming holes in the stream provide some relief from the heat and places to clean up, particularly on the return hike. Your trail continues to parallel the irrigation ditch until it reaches a dam and an irrigation tunnel after 2 miles. At the tunnel, which is no longer used, the trail switchbacks up to the crest of a ridge overlooking Waimano Stream. For the next mile, the trail follows the ridge above the stream. You can expect to find some generous pools to swim in, if you wish to scramble down the hillside to them. A dam just before the confluence of Waimano Stream and a smaller stream entering from the right mark the point where you start to ascend the ridge which leads to the Koolau crest.

The lower valley contains two of the most noble trees on the island. The kukui (*Aleurites moluccana*), or candlenut tree, a massive tree with maplelike leaves and black, walnut-sized nuts, was one of the most important trees to the island's economy. Kukui-nut oil was burned in stone lamps, the nuts were made into leis and a variety of costume jewelry, and the trunk was used to make canoes. The monkey-pod tree (Samanea saman) will commonly grow to 80 feet. It is a symmetrical tree with tiny, delicate, pink tufts when in bloom, and tiny, fernlike leaflets. From the handsome wood, beautiful and highly prized bowls and trays are made. Both trees as well as the familiar hau tree are conspicuous in the valley.

From the last dam, the trail climbs 1600 feet to summit. This is the most difficult part of the trail. Since the path here is overgrown in places, it is a good idea to wear long pants and a shirt. Periodically, you will have good views of Waimano Valley to the north (left) and of Waiau (lit., "swirling water") Valley to the south (right). However, the highlight of the hike, and the primary reason for making it, is to stand at the summit high above Waihee (lit., "squid liquid") Valley to the east. You will encounter strong winds at the summit. If rain or clouds obstruct your view, be patient, for the winds usually blow the obstruction away quickly.

Diamond Head — Honolulu — People

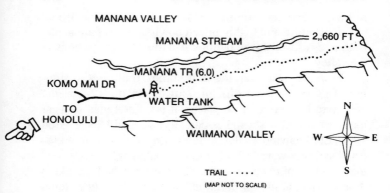

TRAIL · · · · ·
(MAP NOT TO SCALE)

MANANA
(Hiking Area No. 41)

Rating: Difficult.

Features: Views from the Koolau Mountain Range, native and introduced flora.

Permission: None.

Hiking Distance and Time: 6 miles one-way, 4 hours, 1700-foot gain.

Driving Instructions:

From Honolulu (15 miles, 1/2 hour) drive northwest on H-1 to Pearl City (Exit 10), bear right on Moanalua Road to its end, then right on Waimano Home Road (0.7 mile), and finally left on Komo Mai Drive to the end.

Bus Instructions:

From Ala Moana Center take bus #53 (Honolulu/Pacific Palisades) to Pearl City Shopping Center (Kamehameha Highway and Waimano Home Road intersection). Transfer to Pearlridge-Pearl City Shuttle bus and take to Komo Mai Drive. Walk up Komo Mai Drive to trailhead.

Introductory Notes: The Manana Trail is one of a number of trails which take you to peaks atop the Koolau

Mountain Range. This trail is little traveled and is overgrown in places, and should be attempted only by skilled hikers. (It is possible to connect with the Waimano Trail by following the cliffs to the south, but the connecting route is very dangerous and not advised). Rain and mud are frequently encountered in this relatively pristine place. If you are looking for solitude and for the joys as well as the trials present in a rain forest, then Manana will satisfy you.

On the Trail: A paved pedestrian passageway leads 0.4 mile to a water tank. Strawberry guava is abundant along this portion of the trail. From the tank, the Manana Trail climbs 1700 feet to a peak atop the Koolau Range. Eucalyptus, guava and koa trees are abundant along the lower part of the trail, where they are struggling to overcome the ravages of a severe fire in 1972. For your protection, stay on the ridgeline and avoid the side trails, most of which lead to Manana Stream to the north (left) or Waimano Stream to the south. Time permitting, you may wish to hike to Manana Stream for a swim. If so, it would be a good idea to mark your route down so you can follow it back.

In addition to the trees previously noted, look for the sandalwood tree (*Santalum freycinetianum*), with narrow, pointed, shiny leaves. Once an important source of income for the islands, the wood was exported for use in furniture and for its oil and perfume. In fact, China imported so much sandalwood that the Chinese once called Hawaii the "Sandalwood Islands."

A variety of ferns and low scrub dominate the upper part of the trail and seem to reach out to scratch and cut the legs and arms, so protective clothing is well-advised. Strong winds greet the hiker at the summit, but with any luck the air is clear, so that the views into Kaalaea (lit., "the ocherous earth") Valley can be enjoyed. A return via the Waimano Trail is possible for the daring and skilled hiker. The 1-mile hike south to it along the cliffs is extremely dangerous, and a miscalculation could drop the hiker 1500 feet or more to the valley below. Caution is well-advised.

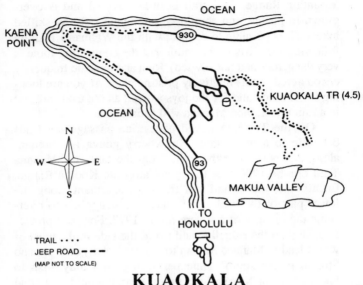

KUAOKALA
(Hiking Area No. 42)

Rating: Strenuous. Elevation gain 500 feet.

Features: Views of mountain and coastal area, fruits, camping.

Permission: Permit to hike and camp from the Division of Forestry (see Appendix).

Hiking Distance and Time: 4.5 mile loop, 3 hours, 500 foot elevation gain/loss.

Driving Instructions:

From Honolulu (41 miles, 2 hours) drive northwest on H-1, which becomes Route 93 when the freeway ends. Drive past Makua town to a military road and a guard shack on the right just before the end of the paved road. Go right on the military road and check in at the guard shack. Drive 2.6 miles on the military road to the designated parking area.

Bus Instructions:

From Ala Moana Center take bus #51 (Honolulu-
Makaha) to the end of the line near the surfing
beach north of Makaha. Walk or hitchhike to the
military road and guard shack.

Introductory Notes: A good hike, solitude and
magnificent views are what you will find in the Kuaokala
(lit., "back of the sun") Forest Reserve. The access road is
under military jurisdiction, so permits are a must.

On the Trail: The trailhead and the designated parking place are one and the same. If you look back about 100
yards along the road you drove on and then to the left to a
water tank, you will see the point at which you will emerge
from the loop hike. The route descends on the paved road
next to the parking area and continues on a dirt jeep road for
2.8 miles. The paved part of the road is lined with guava
trees whose fruit is some of the sweetest I have ever eaten.
These lemon-sized fruits are yellow and soft when ripe. The
trail makes a number of dips and turns in and out of small
gulches which are heavily shaded by eucalyptus, pine, and
cypress trees. After about one mile the trail ascends a ridge
over open country and then reaches a number of points from
which panoramas are possible of the saddle area between the
two mountain ranges of Oahu, of the Koolau Mountains to
the east and of the north shore. These viewpoints are pleasant places to pause. From the second vista point, at a gate
and cattle guard, look to the front across a gulch to the ridge
at the head of the gulch. You will be hiking along that ridge
overlooking Makua Valley. From the second vista point, the
trail makes a steep descent and snakes over the gulch's floor
before ascending to the ridgeline. Just before the ridge, at the
2.6-mile point at a turnout on the left, the remains of the
Kuaokala shack are partly visible through the tall grass.
From here, the foot trail is just 0.2 mile. A short distance
from the abandoned shack, you reach a four-road junction.
Follow the road to the front-right a short distance to a
turnout which was once the start of a jeep road and which

leads uphill to a group of eucalyptus trees. At this point you have your first view of Makua (lit., "parents") Valley.

The footpath part of the Kuaokala Trail begins to the right from the viewpoint overlooking Makua Valley and descends west along the north ridge above Makua Valley. After a descent, the trail ascends to a perch 1800 feet above the Makua Valley floor, where views of the valley and the west coast of Oahu are outstanding. Then the trail makes another descent and begins to turn north through open forest. The "golf ball" at the Kaena Point Satellite Tracking Station at the trailhead is now visible. The trail continues a circuitous path through the forest until it reaches a trail junction at the 4.0-mile point. The spur trail straight ahead ascends a short distance to a viewpoint, and the main trail turns to the right. Take the spur trail and enjoy the views. It is a good lunch spot. Return to the main trail and follow it to the water tank. Then walk down the paved road from the tank to the main road and turn right to reach the trailhead.

This is Hawaii too!

APPENDIX

For Maui, Lanai, and Molokai

(Write to)

Superintendent Haleakala National Park P.O. Box 369 Makawao, Maui 96768	• park informationl • crater cabin reservations

(In person)

Haleakala National Park HQ
Crater Road
☎ 572-9306

• park information
• crater camping permits
• crater cabin keys and
  information

Maui Land & Pineapple
Co.
Kahului, Maui 96732
☎ 877-3351

• camping at Windmill
  Beach
• permission to hike Puu
  Kukui

Division of State Parks
54 So. High Street
State Office Building
Wailuku, Maui 96793
☎ 243-5354

• camping permits for state
  parks
• cabin rental reservations
• camping permits for
  Molokai

Department of Parks &
Recreation
War Memorial Gym
Kaahumanu Avenue
Wailuku, Maui 96793
☎ 243-7389

• camping permits for Maui
  and Molokai county
  campgrounds

Division of Forestry
P.O. Box 1015
State Office Building
Wailuku, Maui 96793
☎ 243-5352

• hiking permits for
  Kahana Bird Sanctuary

Department of Parks and
Recreation
P.O. Box 526
Kaunakakai, Molokai
96748

• camping permits for One
  Alii (Molokai)

Koele Company
Lanai City, Hawaii 96763
☎ 565-6661

• camping permits for
  Hulopoe Bay

Camp Pecusa
800 Olowalu Village
Lahaina, Maui 96761
☎ 661-4303

• camping and cabin
  permits

For Oahu

Division of State Parks
1151 Punchbowl Street
Room 310
Honolulu, Oahu 96813
☎ 548-7455

• camping permits for state
  parks

Division of Forestry
1151 Punchbowl Street
Room 325
Honolulu, Oahu 96813
☎ 548-8850

• hiking permits
• camping and shelter use
  permits

Department of Parks &   • camping permits
Recreation
Honolulu Municipal
Building
650 So. King Street
Honolulu, Oahu 96813
☎ 523-4525 or 27

Network Enterprises, Inc.   • cabins and camping at
P.O. Box 503   Malaekahana State Park
Kahuku, HI 96731   (concession operated)
☎ 293-1736

For Hawaii

Superintendent   • park information
Hawaii Volcanoes National   • hiking permits
Park   • camping permits
Hawaii 96718
☎ (808) 967-7311

Volcano House   • rental camper cabins at
Hawaii Volcanoes National   Namakani Palo
Park   • hotel rooms at Volcano
Hawaii 96718   House
☎ (808) 967-7321

Department of Parks &   • camping permits for
Recreation   county parks
County of Hawaii
25 Aupuni Street
Hilo, HI 96720
☎ (808) 961-8311

Division of State Parks   • camping permits for state
State of Hawaii   parks
P.O. Box 936   • rental cabin information
75 Aupuni Street   and permits
Hilo, HI 96720   • hunting and fishing
☎ (808) 933-4200   requirements

Hawaii County Transit
System
25 Aupuni Street
Hilo, HI 96720
☎ (808) 961-8343

- bus information and
  schedules

For Kauai

Division of State Parks
State Building, Room 306
3060 Eiwa Street
P.O. Box 1671
Lihue, Hawaii 96766
☎ (808) 245-4444

- camping permits for state
  parks and for Kalalau
  Trail
- hiking information

Division of Forestry
State Building, Room 306
3060 Eiwa Street
P.O. Box 1671
Lihue, Hawaii 96766
☎ (808) 245-4433

- hiking information

Kokee Lodge
P.O. Box 819
Waimea, Hawaii 96796
☎ (808) 335-6061

- Kokee cabin information
  and reservations

Department of Parks &
Recreation
County of Kauai
4193A Hardy St. Bldg. 5
Lihue, Hawaii 96766
☎ (808) 245-1881

- camping permits for
  county parks (reservations
  by mail, but permit must
  be picked up in person)

Hanalei Camping &
Backpacking Inc.
Ching Young Village
P.O. Box 1245
Hanalei, Hawaii 96714
☎ (808) 826-6664

- complete line of camping
  & backpacking
  equipment; sales and
  rentals. (New store in
  Kekaha to serve
  Kokee/Waimea area)

INDEX

ORDER FORM

HIKING KAUAI $8.95

HIKING MAUI $8.95

HIKING HAWAII $8.95

HAWAII'S BEST
HIKING TRAILS $12.95

FORWARD TO:

NAME: _____

ADDRESS: _____

CITY: _____ STATE: _____ ZIP: _____

QUANTITY		PRICE	TOTAL
____	HIKING KAUAI	@ $8.95	=
____	HIKING MAUI	@ $8.95	=
____	HIKING HAWAII	@ $8.95	=
____	HAWAII'S BEST HIKING TRAILS	@ $12.95	=

CA residents add 7%
sales tax per book =

Postage/Handling
(Book rate) = $1.50
(Free postage/handling for
order of 2 or more books) _____

TOTAL ENCLOSED = ____

MAIL TO:

Hawaiian Outdoor Adventures
P.O. Box 869
Huntington Beach, CA 92648